DATE DUE

DEC 1 5 1999	
MAY 1 0 2003	

GAYLORD   PRINTED IN U.S.A.

RACE, ETHNICITY, AND SOCIOECONOMIC STATUS

RACE, ETHNICITY, AND SOCIOECONOMIC STATUS:
A Theoretical Analysis of Their Interrelationship

GENERAL HALL, INC.
23–45 Corporal Kennedy Street
Bayside, New York 11360

Publisher: Ravi Mehra
Editor: Eileen Ostermann
Associate Editor: Joanne Eckett
Composition: *Graphics Division,* General Hall, Inc.

LIBRARY OF CONGRESS CATALOG CARD NUMBER: 83–80157

ISBN: 0-930390-47-4 [paper]
      0-930390-48-2 [cloth]

Manufactured in the United States of America

RACE, ETHNICITY, AND SOCIOECONOMIC STATUS:

A THEORETICAL ANALYSIS OF THEIR INTERRELATIONSHIP

Charles Vert Willie
Harvard University

GENERAL HALL, INC.
Publishers
23–45 Corporal Kennedy Street
Bayside, New York 11360

This book is published with the assistance of a grant from the Maurice
Falk Medical Fund and is dedicated to my teachers and mentors:

J. I. Farrar
J. W. Towns
Mabel Jackson Chandler
A. Stephen Jackson
Walter R. Chivers
Benjamin E. Mays
G. Lewis Chandler
Mozell C. Hill
Earl H. Bell
William C. Lehmann
Douglas G. Haring
Eric Faigel
Robert Straus
Ernest M. Gruenberg
C. P. Johnson
Julius B. Richmond
William Willard
Peggy Wood
Margaret Daly

"The work of improving intergroup relations in America is carried out by dedicated professional agencies and individuals who deal as best they can with day-to-day problems of discriminatory behavior, but who for the most part are unable to relate their efforts to an adequate conceptual apparatus."

Milton M. Gordon (1961)

Acknowledgements

The chapters on theoretical implications were prepared originally for this book. Also "Ethnic Areas of Syracuse, New York, 1950," "Corpus Christi: A Triethnic Nonviolent Experience in School Desegregation," "Conflict, Withdrawal, Cooperation: Three Approaches to Social Action," "Demographic Basis for Social Action for Urban Educational Reform," "New Learnings for Sociology from the Civil Rights Movement," and "Social Theory for a Science of Humanity" are published for the first time in this volume.

Other material reprinted with permission of the publisher who holds the copyright and acknowledged with appreciation are articles from: Irwin Deutscher and Elizabeth J. Thompson (eds.), *Among the People: Encounters with the Urban Poor,* New York: Basic Books, 1968, pp. 53-66; *The Professional Geographer,* Volume XIII, Number 3, May, 1961, pp. 1-5; *Black/Brown/White Relations,* New Brunswick: Transaction Books, 1977, pp. 151-158; *The Ivory and Ebony Towers,* Lexington: Lexington Books of D. C. Heath Co., 1981, pp. 79-90; *The Sociology of Urban Education,* Lexington: Lexington Books of D. C. Heath Co., 1978, pp. 77-87; *The Journal of Black Psychology,* Volume 14, Number 3 (Winter, 1967), pp. 326-335; *Phylon,* Volume 26 (Fall, 1965), pp. 240-246; *American Sociological Review,* Volume 27, Number 4 (August, 1962), pp. 522-525; *American Sociological Review,* Volume 25, Number 2 (April, 1960), pp. 260-264; *New England Sociologist,* Volume 1 (Fall, 1978), pp. 13-22; *A New Look at Black Families,* Bayside, N.Y.: General Hall, 1981, pp. 193-206; *Oreo -- A Perspective on Race and Marginal Men and Women,* Wakefield, MA: Parameter Press, 1975.

This project was initiated during the author's sabbatical leave from the Harvard Graduate School of Education and was supported by a grant from the Maurice Falk Medical Fund. The contributions of Harvard and the advice of Philip Hallen, President of the Fund, are acknowledged with thanks.

Also, the expert editorial consultation rendered by Katharine Parker, clerical assistance provided by Elizabeth Blake, and the constant companionship given by Mary Sue, my wife, Sarah, Martin and James, our children, are acknowledged with appreciation.

Contents

PART I

INTRODUCTION

CHAPTER 1

Race, Ethnicity, and Socioeconomic Status
As Manifestations of the Human Condition

The Race and Social Class Controversy

During the closing years of the 1970s a major controversy erupted among sociologists in the United States. It had to do with the significance of race in the determination of life chances for blacks. William Wilson's book, *The Declining Significance of Race,* declared that race had less effect than other characteristics on their life chances, particularly in the area of employment. Wilson contended that economic class now is a more important factor than race in determining job placement for blacks, and that poverty among inner-city blacks is largely a function of their relatively poor training and inferior schooling [Wilson 1978:110, 120].

I have been a party to this controversy and have debated Wilson in forums at a university and at annual meetings of several professional associations. Also I have edited a book, *The Caste and Class Controversy,* that includes rebuttal arguments by several social scientists. In this book, I introduced a counterhypothesis that "the significance of race is increasing and that it is increasing especially for middle-class blacks who, because of school desegregation and affirmative action and other integration programs, are coming into contact with whites for the first time for extended interaction" [Willie 1979:157].

Wilson also referred to "equal employment legislation" in his discussion of the declining significance of race; in his words, this legislation had "virtually eliminated the tendency of employers to create a split labor market in which black labor is deemed cheaper than white labor regardless of the work performed" [Wilson 1978:110].

Both of us mentioned public law that prohibits discrimination in our arguments. Wilson claimed that such law had created new opportunities

2

for blacks who were sufficiently educated to take advantage of them. Even though disagreeing that the law has been fully effective and that limited education is the prevailing basis for employment discrimination, I nevertheless acknowledged that the law had created new desegregated opportunities for blacks and, at the same time, had exposed some who experienced these new opportunities to prejudices that were not present under conditions of segregation. Wilson's hypothesis attempted to explain why the black poor have been left behind. My hypothesis attempted to explain why the black affluent have not yet arrived. When analyzing the effects of antidiscrimination legislation, I emphasized occupation and income disparities between blacks and whites, and Wilson emphasized occupation and education disparities within the black population. My analysis was concerned largely with the range of income and occupational opportunities in the present economy. Wilson mainly was concerned with past industrial practices, labor-force trends, and associated behavior [Wilson 1979:159–176; Willie 1979:149–158].

When scholars use different data in their investigations and emphasize different aspects of the same data, there is bound to be disagreement in their conclusions. These differences probably represent different theoretical conceptions of society too. Unfortunately, race-relations research is highly descriptive and tends to proceed without theoretical guidelines explicitly stated. The absence of such is, in part, responsible for the severe controversy that surrounds studies of race, ethnicity, and socioeconomic status. The theoretical concepts that separate the parties to the contemporary controversy on the significance of race for life chances of blacks have been inadequately articulated. Conceptual differences, I believe, are at the root of the controversy.

Wilson's investigation proceeds by defining "three stages of American race relations (the preindustrial, industrial and modern industrial)." In each of these stages he describes "the role of both the system of production and the state in the development of race and class relations." Wilson contends that, although his book devotes considerable attention to the preindustrial and industrial periods of American race relations, it is his description of the modern industrial period that has generated controversy. He maintains that "in the modern industrial period the economy and the state have, in relatively independent ways, shifted the basis of racial antagonism away from black/white economic contact to social, political, and community issues." The net effect, according to his findings, is that "economic class has been elevated to a position of greater importance than race in determining individual black opportunities for living conditions and personal life experiences" [Wilson 1979:160–161]. Why economic class becomes most important as black–white contact becomes largely social and political is never clearly stated. Wilson concluded that "patterns of racial subjugation in the past created a vast black underclass as the accumulations of disadvantages were passed on from generation to generation, and the economic and technological revolution of modern industrial society threatens to insure it a permanent status." No evidence is provided of the extent of intergenerational poverty that is assumed to exist among blacks.

Wilson states that a growing number of black teenagers in ghettoes and in the inner city "do not have the same access to higher paying jobs for which they are qualified as do young whites with similar levels of formal education." He attributes inaccessibility of higher paying jobs for blacks not to racial or social discrimination (despite the fact that the blacks are said to be as qualified as the whites who get the jobs) but to "structural barriers to decent jobs created by chance in our system of production" [Wilson 1979:171, 170]. He does not identify discrimination as a contemporary structural barrier in employment.

Wilson does not disagree with the counterhypothesis that I offered about the increasing significance of race, largely because my hypothesis is an attempt to explain the discomfort of some affluent blacks. In Wilson's judgment, however, this is not the real problem in the black community [Wilson 1979:175]. The real problem, as he states it, is "the abominable and deleterious physical conditions of the isolated black poor" [Wilson 1979:175].

Wilson's analysis, which emphasizes historical structural barriers as impediments to human fulfillment, eliminates psychological discomfort and denies social discrimination as a real problem. Wilson's analysis of the human condition of poor blacks ignores some of their fundamental human experiences such as discomfort and discrimination and focuses on physical circumstances as if these were better explanations of their circumstances. Wilson's sociology places humanity at the disposal of history, which, according to Becker, has been a common practice of such scholars as Giddings, Sumner, and even Marx [Becker 1968:78].

Humanity and the Law of History

Of Marx's analysis, Becker said that Marx had to "shock his age out of its complacency." In his single-minded effort to show that human nature was social and historical and should not be approached psychologically (from within), Marx "threw the whole burden of perfectibility and progress into an automatic law of history." Humanity, in Marx's view, "turned out to be an objective thing, offered up passively to the forces of society and history." Marx was a humanist, said Becker; but he let his humanistic ideas drift to a social and historical determinism. In effect, he sacrificed thinking, feeling, and acting humanity to an ideology [Becker 1968:67, 66].

This is precisely what Wilson also has done in his analysis of the association between race and black life chances. He has sacrificed thinking, feeling, and acting poor blacks to an ideology of historical determinism. Blacks are pictured as passive individuals caught in the tentacles of a process that is beyond their control. Wilson's ultimate goal, of course, is to help poor blacks, even as Marx wished to help the proletariat. But Wilson's world view in the end denies the humanity of those whom he would help.

The Fallacy of Economic Determinism

The ultimate fallacy in Wilson's analysis is similar to the fallacy in Hegel's analysis: "[Hegel] attempts to systematize and to reduce things to monistic principles" [Becker 1968:66]. Although Wilson recognizes such factors as "differential power, racism, [and a] strong sense of group position" as significantly contributing to racial conflict, he believes that such conflict is most aggravated by "intergroup competition for scarce resources" [Wilson 1973:151]. His monistic principle is that "racial intolerance tends to be greatest in periods of economic decline, particularly for whites unable to advance themselves and forced by economic strains to compete more heavily with minority groups" [Wilson 1973:150]. Under these conditions, Wilson asserts, "the deteriorating circumstances of many lower-class blacks could worsen" [Wilson 1973:150–151].

Wilson, in his world view of economic determinism in history, discounts the self-initiated efforts of blacks for their own liberation. His assessment is that the nonviolent resistance strategy of blacks proved to be highly effective for only "a brief period of time" [Wilson 1973:131]. He portrays blacks as passive minority participants in a macrosocial process that is determined by the white majority. His orientation is illustrated well by this statement: "the moment the dominant group perceives particular minority gains as constituting a *distinct* threat to its sense of superior position, racial tensions intensify" [Wilson 1973:128]. Essentially, Wilson describes the historical process of group relations as managed by the actions of the dominant people of power, particularly their actions associated with fears and perceptions of threats from others.

I too am interested in understanding historical regularities in social relations, particularly in racial and ethnic relations. But I confess that my primary interest is in understanding urgent social problems that affect these populations. I focus less on the past because I know that "whatever regularities one might find ... will be modified by [ongoing] history and by human purpose" [Becker 1968:77]. Ernest Becker said that a sociology that is interested in making the world a better place in which to live "has to observe and analyze the continuing natural social experiments of group living." Thus, he pleaded for "an activist sociology, in addition to an analytic one" [Becker 1968:76–77].

An activist sociology is cognizant of daily happenings. A criticism I made against Wilson's theory of the declining significance of race was its inconsistency with race-relations reports in the daily newspaper. Indeed, I claimed that "a careful and critical reading of what is currently happening to black and brown populations in this country might have caused William Wilson to be more cautious in his conclusions" [Willie 1981a:28].

Sociology as the Study of Human Events

My effort has been to study human beings and what they do, by way of sociological analysis. I view sociology as a science of humanity rather than just a science of historical trends. In analyzing the continuing natural experiments of group living, one considers contemporary situations as well as historical trends. Moreover, one studies the psychological and social as well as the physical circumstances of life.

My analysis of contemporary race-relations experiences — those that are antagonistic and those that are harmonious — reveals a range of behaviors and events that contradict the monistic theory of economic determinism advanced by Wilson. In Corpus Christi, Texas, I discovered that the school desegregation court case that aroused much antagonism was financed by a labor union that consisted of black, white, and Mexican-American working-class people. These individuals cooperated with each other in a joint effort against discrimination, despite the scarce resources over which they allegedly competed and the segregated neighborhoods in which some lived. But in Indiana, Thomas Pettigrew found that some white workers opposed school desegregation and yet never thought of the interracial neighborhood in which they lived as strange or unusual [Pettigrew 1971:264].

The Boston mayor said that pairing two working-class communities such as Roxbury, predominantly black, and South Boston, predominantly white of Irish ancestry, would be unacceptable in a school desegregation plan, presumably because of the possibility of violent confrontation between these racial groups that are said to be a threat to each other's economic survival. Yet in Concord, Massachusetts, an affluent predominantly white suburb of Boston, there have been fights between Boston-based black students from Roxbury bused to that community daily and local white student residents of the town. These communities and their respective families are not in competition with each other over housing or occupational resources; nevertheless, their students have acted violently against each other.

In some communities, blacks and whites have experienced greater integration in the labor force than they have experienced in residential living. Albert Simkus reports that only recently has the residential integration of affluent blacks with affluent whites begun to catch up with that which has characterized low-income blacks and low-income whites in the past [Simkus 1978:81–93]. The United States Department of Housing and Urban Development reported that housing discrimination is widespread in the contemporary United States. Specifically, the national audit that the National Committee Against Discrimination in Housing was authorized to conduct discovered that between 20 and 30 percent of all rental or real estate agents contacted discriminated against blacks: agents tended to suggest twice as many apartments or houses for whites who contacted them, as for blacks [Eggers 1978:6–8].

With reference to income and occupation discrimination, I obtained these findings in a pilot evaluation study of a leadership development program for minorities sponsored by the Rockefeller Foundation. My study of black and brown professional and managerial individuals revealed that they received a median annual income that was 15 percentage points less than the median annual income for whites, and that educated blacks often had to obtain doctoral degrees to get jobs that were similar to those that some whites obtained with only an undergraduate college education or a master's degree [Willie 1980].

These findings, which come from an examination of contemporary events or "the continuing natural social experiments of group living" (to use Becker's words), are at variance with any monistic theory of interracial antagonism and interracial harmony. As stated by Pettigrew, "the American racial scene has always been highly complex, varied, and inconsistent, defying facile generalizations" [Pettigrew 1971:264]. Based on this analysis, I conclude that Wilson's conception of interracial antagonism as basically a function of economic determinism is in error. Such a view must be classified as a narrow "detached scientific ... opportunistic inductivism" [Becker 1968:77] that eliminates humanity from the science of human society.

Knowlege Developed through Action and Analysis

Presented now is a brief statement of my own world view that has guided and given direction to my studies of race, ethnicity, and socioeconomic status. I identify the historical precursors to my ideas as those of the eighteenth-century period of Enlightenment as manifested in Rousseau.

My concept of knowledge is that it emerges through action and analysis [Willie 1981b:107–108]. I am distrustful of critical reason that is divorced from programs of action. I believe that action and analysis inform and correct each other in the growth and development of knowledge. Although I respect analysis and reason, like Rousseau I do not place exaggerated trust in them; and I am more comfortable with reason that is tempered by action and action that is tempered by reason.

Among my ideal-types of the twentieth century is Martin Luther King, Jr., whose life was a manifestation of action and analysis, with each informing the other for the purpose of making this a better world. "Hugh Gloster of Morehouse College called him the archtype of an educated person — one who combined academic achievement and professional success with personal integrity and social concern. He said the life of Martin Luther King, Jr., was worthy of emulation by all" [Willie 1981b:13].

In 1966, I lectured at Morehouse, the college that nurtured Martin Luther King, Jr., before his manhood. It is both his and my alma mater. In the Founders Day address, I stated the expectation that our school would move into the second century of its existence supporting all its students, including those who think and those who act. Specifically, I said, "Morehouse will strive to impart to the activists the benefits of reasoned thought; and to the thinkers, the methods and techniques of effective action" [Willie 1966:9]. From my Morehouse College background, I obtained activist and analytical orientations that have been incorporated into my theory of knowledge and my system of sociology.

Also there was a strong moral influence in my college education that has affected my world view. Benjamin E. Mays, the college president when King and I matriculated at Morehouse, said that it would not be sufficient if the college produced only clever graduates who are fluent in speech. He said that a school should cultivate honest people who can be trusted, who are sensitive to that which is wrong in society, and who are willing to assume responsibility for correcting it [Willie 1978:13]. This influence certainly has contributed to the brand of moral sociology that I have developed. It is a sociology that is humanity-centered rather than one that is history-centered or system-centered.

To say that one's sociology is humanity-centered is more than to offer a slogan. It is a radical point of view that probably is best illustrated by contrasting it with a science that is object-centered. Genetics is an object-centered science — more precisely, a trait-centered science. Theodosius Dobzhansky explained that many who studied hybridization before Mendel did not discover the genetic laws of hereditability that were found by him because "they treated as units the complexes of characteristics of individuals, races, and species and attempted to find rules governing inheritance of such complexes." Dobzhansky said that this approach was in error, that Mendel was successful because he understood that "the inheritance of separate traits [and] not [the inheritance] of complexes of traits had to be studied" [Dobzhansky 1951:117].

In the methodological chapter of a comparative study of school desegregation in 10 communities throughout the United States, Susan Greenblatt and I said that understanding human society may require a method that is the opposite of object-analysis or trait-analysis useful in understanding nature. Maybe "we can understand the principles that govern various forms of [social] organization . . . only by using a method that analyzes complexes of characteristics rather than single traits" [Willie and Greenblatt 1981:19]. In this respect, our idea links up with that expressed by Pettigrew, who characterized race relations in human society as highly complex and even inconsistent. For these reasons, I have steered clear of monistic theories of human society that are deterministic.

Nature and Human Nature

The context within which behavior associated with race, ethnicity, and socioeconomic status is manifested is important to analyze, to know, and to understand. The context of humanity, which consists of people and their complex characteristics — including some that are contradictory — should be recognized as differing fundamentally from the context of nature, which is characterized by events of discrete and interrelated traits. The reality of nature is that of covariation in relationships among things. The reality of humanity is that of choice and of purpose among people. The assumptions about and methods for investigating nature and humanity may not be the same, because nature and humanity are different realities.

Alfred North Whitehead recognizes that there are assumptions about the unity of nature and even advocates the principle of unity [Whitehead 1957:30–31]. Nonetheless, he argues against attempts to conceptualize nature as bifurcated into two systems of reality such as nature apprehended in awareness, and nature that is the cause of awareness [Whitehead 1957: 30–31]. "What is asked for in the philosophy of science," he said, "is some account of the coherence of things perceptually known." To do this, Whitehead believes that one must refuse to countenance any theory of psychic additions to the object known in perception: "The problem of natural philosophy is to discuss the relations *inter se* of things known, abstracted from the bare fact that they are known." According to Whitehead, natural philosophy should never attempt to explain why there is knowledge. In nature, "There can be no explanation of the 'why' of knowledge. We can only describe the 'what' of knowledge" [Whitehead 1957:29–32]. Whitehead thus reduces determination of the meaning of nature principally to the discussion of the character of time and that of space. These, he said, are abstractions from events, the more concrete elements of nature [Whitehead 1957:33].

Given this conception of nature as events related in irrevocable time and space devoid of purpose, Whitehead asserts that a metaphysical science is needed that transcends the limitations of nature and that deals with purpose. Such a metaphysics, according to Whitehead, "exhibit[s] in its utmost completeness our concept of reality" [Whitehead 1957:32]. Sociology should be such a metaphysical science. It should consider the transcendent character of people. All sociological analysis should assume that people have the capacity to transcend their contemporary roles and statuses in life. Sociological analysis should never assume that people are in essence passive and unable to affect their social circumstances. I assert that the real problem of poor people, affluent people, any people, is their psychic and social circumstances. These have to do with the "why" of existence rather than the "what" of existence and point toward the transcendency of humanity, which is flexible and changeable because humanity is affected but is not bound by time and space.

Thus, in my world view, humanity is fundamentally different from the rest of nature. In nature, the parts are the foundation of the whole; each part is significant only as it contributes to the whole; defective parts are eliminated as useless. In humanity, the whole is the reason for being of each part; the whole is of value only as it benefits each part; less adequate parts of the whole are assisted through generous gifts and magnanimous sacrifices offered by its more adequate parts. Unlike nature, humanity is free, consisting of people who choose to feel, think, and act with purpose. Transcending time and space, humanity results in a bifurcated or dualistic relationship of the individual alone and the individual in association with others.

Examples of the absence of determinism in humanity and the ever-present possibility of transcending what would appear to be situational constraints may be found in the research by Robin Williams and Margaret Ryan. Regarding race mixing in education, these two researchers discovered that "public school desegregation or integration is only loosely correlated with the attitudes or prejudices of the population. Successful public school desegregation has been carried out in places where supposedly the prevailing attitudes favored segregation and where other institutions continued to be segregated." Williams and Ryan also found that "Segregation has persisted for years in other instances where attitudes were *relatively* favorable for integration." In some instances, they found that "school desegregation was successful in a completely segregated environment." Based on these findings, Williams and Ryan assert that "Without a careful local diagnosis it is impossible to predict whether the school or some other local institution will move first toward integration" [Williams and Ryan 1954:240–241]. The implication of their findings is that school desegregation is not a function of historical determinism. I assume that this principle is applicable in the analysis of other social problems as well.

Humanity as Free, Active, and Purposeful

My world view of humanity is at variance not only with that expressed by William Wilson but also with the two most popular contemporary theoretical explanations of race relations in the United States — the Marxist and the colonialist theories. The Marxists claim that capitalists are responsible for racial discrimination and the segregation of blacks into a restricted semislave caste system of limited opportunity so that their labor can be exploited without resistance for the economic benefit of the affluent.

The colonialists classify black ghettoes as contained communities that are exploited for the benefit of the dominant people of power and left in an undeveloped condition as a way of maintaining dependency and guaranteeing free access by those who wish to usurp the resources of the oppressed.

A common error in both theoretical explanations of race relations is the assumption of passivity on the part of blacks, the people of subdominant power. The Marxists deny that blacks are feeling, thinking, and acting people who have the privilege of choosing to cooperate or not to cooperate in their own oppression. The historical economic forces that enslave are described by the Marxists as beyond the control of the oppressed. The colonialists ignore the mutuality that is necessary for the continuation of any community, including one that is contained. The colonialists do not recognize that reciprocal relationships between people of dominant and subdominant power are necessary and essential for the survival of all. The power to veto repugnant social arrangements is a privilege of subdominants that cannot be curtailed by dominants. But even though veto action may contribute to the destruction of that which is oppressive, it can also get out of control because seldom are there normative guidelines for its use in an oppressive society. Thus, veto action can result in the destruction not only of that which is oppressive but of the total community as well. Consequently, subdominant people only reluctantly exercise their veto power because the consequences can be awesome for them as well as for others. But this power is an ever-present possibility and should be part of all theoretical explanations of race relations.

This discussion leads to the conclusion that freedom and power are common characteristics of the way of life of all racial, ethnic, and socioeconomic groups in human society. Any theory that denies their existence is erroneous. Freedom and constraint, choice and commitment are characteristics that are uniquely human.

Dominant and Subdominant Populations

Error in our knowledge of race, ethnicity, and socioeconomic status groups, therefore, emerges from two sources: the incorrect assumption that subdominant populations are passive and without any freedom of choice, and the inappropriate tendency to ascribe all power to members of the dominant populations and to analyze their actions only. Studies with such limited perspectives have contributed to our knowledge of intergroup relations. But the body of knowledge that they have generated is partial and sometimes distorted.

This discussion also has implications for the methodology of studying race, ethnicity, socioeconomic status, and their interrelations. Studies of these phenomena at this time in the United States should include analyzing differential adaptations as a function of the differential distribution of power. Power is the capacity to influence or force others to behave in prescribed ways. If all racial, ethnic, and socioeconomic status groups have power, our studies of social organization for these populations should be comparative studies that observe, analyze, and interpret the adaptations of the dominants and the subdominants within various populations. We should never assume that the way of life of the dominants is normative for all. Too often in the past, social scientists have followed this practice, erroneously projecting the adaptations of the dominants upon the subdominants. As Howard Taylor has said, the fallacy of "studying whites and then generalizing to blacks without studying blacks directly is consistently made in 'important' social science research documents" [Taylor 1977:245–246].

Our comparative investigations should analyze similarity and disparity in goals of dominant and subdominant groups of various racial, ethnic, and socioeconomic populations, their complementary and contraindicated functional relationships, and their experiences, if any, of achieving mutuality.

Another kind of comparative study is that of people in various racial, ethnic, and socioeconomic status populations acting as individuals and acting in association with others as a group. Paul Tillich has reminded us that "the courage to be as a part" is related to but different from "the courage to be as oneself." Specifically, Tillich states that "the courage to be as oneself is the courage to follow reason and to defy irrational authority." However, Tillich informs those who would glorify individualization that "self and world are correlated," that "only in the continuous encounter with other persons does the person become and remain a person." Tillich asserts that "the self cut off from participation in its world is an empty shell, a mere possibility." Yet, everyone should realize "that the courage to be as oneself is the necessary corrective to the courage to be as a part" [Tillich 1952:116, 88, 91, 157, 141].

Herbert Hyman has commented on the possible errors in interpretation that can result from failure to distinguish between data that have to do with the individual and data that are manifestations of the individual in association with others or the collectivity. He said that we should be careful about attempting to explain social change on the basis of psychological facts. If, for example, it is assumed that the proper measure of social change is the net change in individuals, half of the individuals could experience positive change and half negative change — thus canceling each other out and leading the investigator who relies only on data about individuals to conclude that there has been no change in a specific social system. Hyman stated that methods should be used that will measure not only changes in individuals but changes in the total population if some statement is to be made about social change [Hyman 1962:66–86].

As mentioned by Tillich earlier, Hyman also affirms that the individual and society are interrelated, and that researchers also should employ data-collection methods and techniques that will enable them to understand social norms. The absence of information about norms, he said, often makes it difficult to interpret the responses of individuals [Hyman et al. 1955:129-131]. Hyman's statement should be amended to recognize two sets of norms — norms of the dominant people of power and norms of the subdominant people. The two norms may or may not be the same, and for good reasons.

Not only is the normative behavior of the majority frequently projected upon the minority, as mentioned by Taylor; but also some social scientists characterize normative behavior of subdominants that may differ from that of dominants as inappropriate and even contraindicated. In his report on *The Negro Family, A Case for National Action,* Daniel P. Moynihan said, "It is clearly a disadvantage for a minority group to be operating on one principle, while the great majority of the population, and the one with the most advantages to begin with, is operating on another.... Ours is a society which presumes male leadership in private and public affairs. The arrangements of society facilitate such leadership and reward it. A subculture, such as that of the Negro American, in which this is not the pattern, is placed at a distinct disadvantage" [United States Department of Labor 1965:29].

What Moynihan did not realize is that "the equalitarian pattern of household decision making is the prevailing pattern among whites as well as blacks. Among whites, however, this pattern is under attack by residual practices of matriarchal and patriarchal dominance" [Willie 1981c:95]. Since the equalitarian pattern of decision making appears to be the norm for American households, I have asserted that "the cultural lag, if any, is found not among blacks but among middle-class white households that now are struggling toward the equalitarian goal" [Willie 1981c:96].

Moreover, instead of being contraindicated, I assert that the subdominant normative experience such as that of the employment of black women outside the home as workers in the national labor force "was a pioneering ... activity over the years which eventually resulted in an increasing number of white women being employed outside the home; ... had blacks been made over in the image of whites as prescribed [by Moynihan], white women would not have been able to observe the creative effects of work for pay as they were able to do by observing the work experience of black women. Back in 1940 only 25% of the mature white women 35 to 44 years of age were in the labor force compared with 45% of the black women" [Willie 1975:43]. Today, the gap between the proportion of women in the labor force in the two racial populations is narrowing. Clearly, it is informative to examine the norms of both dominant and subdominant populations.

Comparative Analysis

The chapters in this book deal with the issues of race, ethnicity, and socioeconomic status. They represent more than a quarter century of research and analysis by an activist sociologist. Using the methodology of comparative analysis, I have studied variations in racial and ethnic populations by holding socioeconomic status constant, and variations in socioeconomic status groups by holding race and ethnicity constant. Characteristics of the total community have been analyzed for the purpose of identifying norms regarding such experiences as social mobility and age. Some studies have to do with variations in the adaptations of individuals in racial, ethnic, and socioeconomic status populations; others are concerned with group similarities and differences.

Although comparison is the prevailing method, I have used a variety of data-gathering techniques and analytical strategies, including demographic studies, ecological analyses, surveys, case studies of families and community issues, and policy studies. I have found the use of a range of data-gathering techniques rewarding as a way of discovering the psychic, social, spatial, and temporal aspects of humanity as manifested in the various racial, ethnic, and socioeconomic status groups. The comparative method has helped me to control my tendency both to stereotype outgroups and to project ingroup norms upon others. Actually, the comparative method has yielded a metaphysical benefit. It has revealed the interdependence of minority and majority individuals because of their uniqueness and the complementary function of dominant and subdominant groups, as one group is incomplete without the other. Finally, the comparative method has revealed that studies of intergroup relations essentially are investigations of variations in power and authority.

Theory and Applied Social Science

My self-designation as an activist sociologist suggests that I am profoundly respectful of applied social science. As mentioned earlier, I believe that action and analysis inform each other. Several of the studies included in this book were products of my work with others to discover ways of solving urgent social problems such as mental illness, infant mortality, juvenile delinquency, poverty, and discrimination in the delivery of education, health, and welfare services. Despite my moral commitment to finding ways to make the world a better place in which to live, I believe that action without analysis can be as harmful as analysis without action; moral outrage is no substitute for reflective study.

A reflective approach requires the development of theory. Ernest Becker observed that when theory separates from practice, and practice disdains theory, "there [is] nothing left but to work within the ongoing social ideology, gathering data and hoping to patch things here and there" [Becker 1968:78].To summarize, he said, "when we cut off an applied science from close intercourse with its theoretical base there is no longer anything to feed and shape theory" [Becker 1968:73]. Under this condition, there is danger that humanity may be sacrificed to ideology, even by well-intentioned social reformers. Thus, at the end of each part of this book, I have written a chapter that indicates the theoretical implications of the various investigations and their analysis. I have added such a discussion because, in my judgment, a deficiency in contemporary race-relations research is the absence of an accumulative body of social theory pertaining to this aspect of social organization.

The Plan of Analysis

The analysis of the interrelationship among race, ethnicity, and socioeconomic status begins with a series of demographic studies that analyze the social ecological structure of the community and several social problems. It continues with institutional and community studies that focus on the family and the school. Then, macrosocial studies are presented that have to do with the stages of a social movement, particularly the civil rights movement and its leadership.

Intergroup Relations Theory

The reader has a right to know why this book was prepared. Approaching the fifty-fifth anniversary of my birth as the project began, I had been a professional scholar for three decades, beginning with my initial appointment as instructor in the Syracuse University Department of Sociology and Anthropology in 1952. It seemed to be an appropriate time to take theoretical stock of what I had learned about race, ethnicity, and socioeconomic status from my various involvements as a student, teacher, researcher, administrator, policymaker, planner, consultant, and concerned citizen. Although I believe that knowledge is sounder and more complete when it emerges from observational and analytical experiences that are informed by information derived from theory, I believe that the premature formulation of theory by an individual scholar of the social sciences and other wisdom fields runs the risk of justifying existing ideology and engaging in mythmaking; these are distinct possibilities when personal experience is limited or inadequate. Thus I have hesitated to attempt any systematic development of theory in the field of intergroup relations until my perspective was tempered with numerous personal and professional experiences, including some that can be classified as tragic and others as transcendent.

Even though the studies presented in this book and the discussion of their theoretical implications reveal an understanding of race, ethnicity, and socioeconomic status that is only partial and far from being definitive, it is time that I link my ideas with those of others in the field for whatever limited contribution they may make and for the benefit they may derive from being clarified and corrected by others. Ultimately, as a professional social scientist, I am interested in enhancing our understanding of social relationships in humanity so that the world can become a better place. To do this, one must follow in the path of the iconoclasts and demythologizers. With reference to our understanding of race, ethnicity, socioeconomic status, and their interrelationships, I have tried to walk that way.

References

Becker, Ernest. 1968. *The Structure of Evil.* New York: Free Press.
Dobzhansky, Theodosius. 1951. *Genetics and the Origin of Species.* New York: Columbia University Press.

18   INTRODUCTION

Eggers, Frederick J., et al. 1978. *Background Information and Initial Findings of the Housing Market Practices Survey.* Washington, DC: Department of Housing and Urban Development.

Hyman, Herbert. 1962. *Application of Methods of Evaluation.* Berkeley: University of California Press.

_____, et al. 1955. *Survey Design and Analysis.* New York: Macmillian-Free Press.

Pettigrew, Thomas F. 1971. *Racially Separate or Together.* New York: McGraw-Hill.

Simkus, Albert. 1978. "Residential Segregation by Occupation and Race in Ten Urbanized Areas." *American Sociological Review* 43 (February).

Taylor, Howard F. 1977. "Playing the Dozens with Path Analysis." In R.L. Hall (ed.), *Black Separatism and Social Reality.* New York: Pergamon Press.

Tillich, Paul. 1952. *The Courage to Be.* New Haven: Yale University Press.

U.S. Department of Labor. 1965. *The Negro Family, A Case for National Action.* Washington, DC: Government Printing Office.

Whitehead, Alfred North. 1957. *The Concept of Nature.* Ann Arbor: University of Michigan Press. First published in 1920.

Williams, Robin M., Jr., and Margaret W. Ryan. 1954. *Schools in Transition.* Chapel Hill: University of North Carolina Press.

Willie, Charles V. 1966. "Into the Second Century: Problems of Higher Education of Particular Concern to Morehouse College." *Morehouse College Bulletin* 35 (Spring): 7–10.

_____. 1975. *Oreo, A Perspective on Race and Marginal Men and Women.* Wakefield, MA: Parameter Press.

_____. 1978. "Racism, Black Education, and the Sociology of Knowledge." In C. V. Willie and R. R. Edmonds (eds.), *Black Colleges in America.* New York: Teachers College Press, pp. 3–13.

_____(ed.). 1979. *The Caste and Class Controversy.* Bayside, NY: General Hall.

_____. 1979. "The Inclining Significance of Race." In C. V. Willie (ed.), *The Caste and Class Controversy.* Bayside, NY: General Hall, pp. 145–158.

_____. 1980. *Leadership Development for Minorities, An Evaluation of a Rockefeller Foundation Program.* New York: Rockefeller Foundation.

_____. 1981a. *A New Look at Black Families.* 2nd ed. Bayside, NY: General Hall.

_____. 1981b. *The Ivory and Ebony Towers.* Lexington, MA: Lexington Books of D. C. Heath.

_____. 1981c. "Dominance in the Family: The Black and White Experience." *Journal of Black Psychology* 7 (February): 91–97.

_____, and Susan L. Greenblatt. 1981. "School Desegregation: Racial Politics and Community Conflict Processes." In C. V. Willie and S. L. Greenblatt (eds.), *Community Politics and Educational Change.* New York: Longman, pp. 9–27.

Wilson, William J. 1973. *Power, Racism, and Privilege.* New York: Free Press.

_____. 1978. *The Declining Significance of Race.* Chicago: University of Chicago Press.

_____. 1979. "The Declining Significance of Race, Revisited but Not Revised." In Charles V. Willie (ed.), *The Caste and Class Controversy.* Bayside, NY: General Hall, pp. 159–176.

PART II

DEMOGRAPHIC STUDIES

Ecological Analysis:
Individuals, Groups, and Their Environments

Social Problems Analysis:
Disease, Mortality, Delinquency, Poverty

CHAPTER 2

Land Elevation, Age of Dwelling Structure, and Residential Stratification

The probable association between land elevation and residential stratification has been alluded to by social scientists [1], architects [2], and housing specialists [3]. In general, they have observed that expensive housing is often erected on hilly sites. However, this investigator has not seen a systematic analysis of the probable association between these two phenomena at varying levels of stratification and elevation, including low and high status neighborhoods and flat as well as hilly terrain. Are expensive dwelling units erected, also, on flat surface areas? The observation reported above does not answer this or other questions regarding the continuity of association, if any, between residential stratification and land elevation.

The purpose of this paper is to explore the association between land elevation and residential stratification in an urban community. Tested is the null hypothesis, namely, that there is no association between the two variables.

Of secondary consideration in this study is the association, if any, between age of dwelling structure and land elevation. This variable was brought into the study because of its documented association with residential stratification [4]. Were an association found between land elevation and residential stratification, responsibility would devolve upon the investigator to determine whether land elevation had an independent association with residential stratification or was, in fact, but another example of the known association between dwelling structure age and the socioeconomic status level of residential areas.

Reprinted from *The Professional Geographer,* Volume XIII, May 1961, Number 3, pp. 1–5. The author was on the faculty of Syracuse University at the time this article was published.

Data and Method

The study area was Syracuse, New York, an industrial city approximately 25 square miles in size with a population of 220,583 persons in 1950, the study year. Census tracts were used as basic geographic units of analysis. There are 61 such tracts in Syracuse, 59 of which were used in this study. One tract was omitted because of its special institutional population, and another because of its sparse settlement of less than 50 persons.

A contour map of the city, based on findings of a survey conducted by the United States Department of Interior, was used to determine the elevation of census tracts. Because each census tract in Syracuse is relatively homogeneous and small—the average tract being less than two-fifths of a square mile—the land elevation at its center was more or less representative of the total census tract area. Land elevation was estimated for the center of all 59 tracts. It varied from a low of 373 feet to a high of 605 feet above sea level. Average elevation above sea level for the total city was 467 feet.

Residential areas of varying socioeconomic status were delineated on the basis of an analysis of the frequency distribution of composite socioeconomic status scores, building permits, real estate advertisements, historical documents, interview data, and inspection of neighborhoods. The principal instrument in delineating residential areas of varying status levels was the composite socioeconomic index. It consisted of five variables: average home value; average monthly rental; percent of single-family dwelling units; median school year completed by the adult population over 25 years of age; and percent of workers in the combined occupational categories of operatives, service workers, and laborers. The latter component was inverted so that it would vary directly with the other four. Excepting the percentage of single-family dwelling units, all variables intercorrelated with each other at .80 and above. The excepted variable intercorrelated with the other four at .59 and above. Thus, a significant and high association existed between the socioeconomic variables. Distributions of each variable by census tracts were converted into standard scores and integrated into a composite socioeconomic index. An average index score was derived for each census tract. A frequency distribution of index scores by census tracts was made, and tracts with similar scores were combined into a socioeconomic residential area.

Six socioeconomic residential areas were delineated in Syracuse [5]. They varied from area 1 in which a majority of persons were professional, technical, or managerial workers, graduates from high school and college, and owners of expensive well-kept homes, to area VI in which a majority of the persons were operatives, service workers, or laborers, had received no more than an elementary school education, and rented dwelling units in old and dilapidated structures.

To explore the secondary consideration of dwelling structure age and residential stratification, the median year of dwelling unit construction in each census tract was computed. Dwelling units in multiple-family structures that were converted from single-family structures were assigned the age of the structure in which it was located in Census Bureau tabulations. About half of the dwelling units in Syracuse, which was founded in 1825, were erected before 1895. By census tracts, the median year of dwelling unit construction ranged from 1873 to 1934.

Land elevation, year of dwelling unit construction, and socioeconomic status data were statistically analyzed by census tracts and by residential areas to determine the presence or absence of significant associations.

Findings

There was a direct and significant association between land elevation and socioeconomic status. By census tracts, these two variables intercorrelated at .73. More than half of the variance in the composite socioeconomic score of census tract neighborhoods could be attributed to their elevation above sea level, as indicated by the Pearson correlation coefficient.

The significant correlational association between land elevation and residential stratification was further documented by analysis of data presented in Table 2.1. About 40 percent of the city's total area is less than 425 feet above sea level; another 40 percent is between 425 and 525 feet; and about 20 percent is 525 feet or more above sea level.

That portion of the city with an elevation of less than 425 feet is largely flat land found in and around the center of the city, along its lake shores, and in valley routes that funneled traffic from north-south and east-west directions into Syracuse during the nineteenth century. Nearly 90 percent of area VI, the lowest in socioeconomic status, was found in the old and flat section of the city. On the other hand, 75 percent of area I, the highest in socioeconomic status, was found on hilly terrain more than 525 feet above sea level. This section, incidentally, was settled largely during the twentieth century.

Another important fact revealed in the socioeconomic area analysis had to do with upper and lower limits in the land elevation of residential

Table 2.1.

Percentage Distribution of Socioeconomic Areas, by Elevation of Residential Area Above Sea Level, Syracuse, 1950

Socioeconomic Area	Square Miles	Percentage of Square Miles by Land Elevation		
		Below 425 ft.	425–524 ft.	Above 524 ft.
I	1.89	—	25	75
II	3.25	—	14	86
III	6.40	41	53	6
IV	3.41	33	60	7
V	3.36	33	67	—
VI	4.37	89	11	—
Total City	22.68[a]	39	40	21

a. The total city area indicated in the table is less than 25 square miles because two of the 61 census tracts were omitted.

Table 2.2.

Average Median Year of Dwelling Unit Construction, and Average Elevation of Residential Area Above Sea Level, Syracuse, 1950

Socioeconomic Area	Average Median Year of Dwelling Construction[a]	Average Elevation Above Sea Level, in Feet[b]
I	1930	572
II	1926	551
III	1923	450
IV	1899	464
V	1890	444
VI	1879	406
Total City	1907	467

a. The median age of dwelling units was computed for each census tract. Medians of all census tracts in an area were averaged to obtain the average median age of dwelling units. Each median was weighted by the number of square miles in area census tracts.

b. Each area average was weighted by the number of square miles in area census tracts.

neighborhoods of varying status. No sections of the two lower areas, V and VI, were located on sites above 525 feet; and no sections of the two higher areas, I and II, were located on sites below 425 feet. However, some portions of all socioeconomic areas occupied a common range of 100 feet. Between 425 and 525 feet above sea level, there were neighborhoods of varying socioeconomic status ranging from area I through area VI.

Thus, it was seen that a greater proportion of the highest socioeconomic area was located on sites of higher elevation, and a greater proportion of the lowest socioeconomic area was located on sites of lower elevation. Moreover, there was a definite limit of elevation below which the higher areas did not descend, and a definite limit of elevation above which the lower areas did not ascend. On the basis of these facts it would seem that an association between land elevation and residential stratification was demonstrated.

The conclusiveness of this analysis, however, was tempered by two facts: (a) a portion of all socioeconomic areas, including a majority of the square mileage in the middle areas, III, IV and V, contained land of similar elevation; and (b) 47 percent of the variance in the composite socioeconomic score of census tract neighborhoods could not be accounted for by variation in land elevation, according to the correlation coefficient. Apparently a factor, or factors, other than land elevation had an effect upon the socioeconomic status level of residential areas. It was noted earlier that the lowest socioeconomic area was located in an old section of the city, whereas the highest area was in a recently settled section. Thus, the analysis was extended to determine: (a) the association, if any, between age of dwelling structure and residential stratification in Syracuse; and (b) the multiple contribution, if any, of age of dwelling structure and elevation of land above sea level to the socioeconomic status level of residential areas.

Table 2.2 showed the expected association between year of dwelling unit construction and socioeconomic status of residential areas. The association was linear, with a difference of 51 years between the 1930 average median year of dwelling unit construction in area I and the 1879 average median year in area VI. Also seen in Table 2.2 was a difference of 166 feet between the average elevation of 572 feet above sea level in area I and the average elevation of 406 feet in area VI. There was a tendency toward linearity in this distribution, with the exceptions of areas III and IV. This distribution confirmed the earlier conclusion that an association existed between land elevation and residential stratification. At this point, however, the question to be answered was which variable made the greater contribution to residential stratification—the linear distribution of year of dwelling unit construction, or the partially linear distribution of land elevation above sea level?

A series of correlation coefficients, including a multiple correlation coefficient, was computed to solve the problem. The Pearson correlation coefficient, by census tracts, between socioeconomic status and land elevation was .73; that between socioeconomic status and year of dwelling unit construction was .83; and that between land elevation and year of dwelling unit construction was .62. The multiple correlation coefficient between the three variables was .87, indicating that 12 percent of the variance in socioeconomic status, by census tracts, could be attributed to land elevation, 38 percent to year of dwelling unit construction, and 26 percent to the joint action of these two variables. Thus, year of dwelling unit construction made the greater contribution to variation in socioeconomic status by residential areas. Nevertheless, it was demonstrated that land elevation also made a significant and independent contribution, and thereby qualified as a new and different dimension of residential stratification. Age of dwelling unit continues to be probably the most significant single indicator of residential stratification, as defined by the five variable composite index used in this study. When correlated singly, about one-third of the variance in residential stratification remained unexplained; but, when year of dwelling unit construction was multiply correlated with land elevation, unexplained variance was reduced to slightly less than one-fourth.

Conclusion and Discussion

The facts presented and analyzed in this study were sufficient to reject the null hypothesis that there is no association between land elevation and residential stratification. Land elevation had a significant and direct association with the socioeconomic status level of residential areas. Neighborhoods of higher socioeconomic status tended to be situated on sites of higher elevation; conversely, neighborhoods of lower status tended to be situated on sites of lower elevation.

However, the independent contribution of land elevation to residential stratification was far less than the contribution of year of dwelling unit construction. The age of dwelling units in a neighborhood was seen as one of the best single indicators of the socioeconomic status level of a residential area.

In an urban community of differential terrain, one may account for about half of the variance in socioeconomic status of residential areas if one has knowledge of neighborhood variations in elevation above sea level; about two-thirds of the variance may be accounted for if one has knowledge of the differential age of dwelling units by neighborhoods; and about three-fourths of the variance in socioeconomic status by residential areas may be explained if one has knowledge both of the age of dwelling units in neighborhoods throughout the city and their elevations above sea level.

Living on a site that has a "view" is valued highly in American culture, even though some elevated sites have become so congested that a view is no longer possible. Nevertheless, the fact that high status neighborhoods were originally associated with sites of higher elevation persists. It should be pointed out, however, that slums inhabit hilly sites in some countries. Thus, the association between land elevation and residential stratification must be interpreted as a cultural phenomenon. Also, there are economic factors associated with the tendency to erect expensive dwellings on sites of higher elevation. Site preparation is more expensive on hilly terrain. Hence, builders tend to erect higher priced property on such land.

The findings of this study strongly indicate that consideration should be given to the factor of differential land elevation in any comparative analysis of the ecology of an urban community organization. It is possible that discrepancies between competing theories of urban organization are, in part, a function of differential land elevation in the cities that were studied. This analysis further points toward the need to consider land elevation as a significant condition of urban organization, and to discover the various ways in which communities and societies have adapted themselves culturally to this universal condition of existence.

Notes

This article is a revision of a paper presented at the Eastern Sociological Society meeting in New York, April 1959. Data were derived from a study conducted by the investigator while serving as research sociologist with the New York State Mental Health Commission on assignment from the Department of Sociology and Anthropology, Syracuse University. The project was supported by a grant from the Milbank Memorial Fund which is acknowledged with appreciation.

1.   Homer Hoyt, *The Structure and Growth of Residential Neighborhoods* (Washington, DC: Federal Housing Administration, 1939).
2.   A. B. Gallion and Simon Eisner, *The Urban Pattern* (New York: Van Nostrand, 1950).

3.   G. H. Beyer, *Housing: A Factual Analysis* (New York: Macmillan, 1958).
4.   Hoyt, *The Structure and Growth of Residential Neighborhoods;* Eisner, *The Urban Pattern.*
5.   C. V. Willie, "Socioeconomic and Ethnic Areas in Syracuse, New York" (Ph.D. dissertation, Department of Sociology and Anthropology, Syracuse University, Syracuse, New York, 1957).

CHAPTER 3

Age Status and Residential Stratification

Recent studies by Rossi, Glick, Beyer, [1] and others have suggested an association between the age of persons and their socioeconomic status, particularly as it relates to the kinds of housing in which they live. Although Rossi found that space requirements were stressed most frequently as the reason for moving from one dwelling unit to another, he also observed that "the ages of the household members and the social needs accompanying age grades are...important life cycle aspects which have housing implications" [2]. More specifically, Glick has stated that significant changes occur not only in family composition, as it proceeds through the life cycle, but also in the social and economic status of the family [3].

Apparently, the improved economic status of families in time is associated with their movement in space to neighborhoods of higher social status. The purpose of this study is to determine the association, if any, between the distribution of an urban population by age and variations in the socioeconomic status of residential areas. A test was made of the null hypothesis — that there is no difference in the distribution of the population of a city by age within residential areas of varying socioeconomic status levels.

Data and Method

The age distribution of the total population in the city was analyzed. This fact distinguishes this research somewhat from that of Rossi, Beyer,

Reprinted from *American Sociological Review,* Vol. 25, No.2, April 1960, pp. 260–264. The author was affiliated with the Upstate Medical Center, State University of New York, at the time this article was written.

[4] and Glick, who studied family units only. In the design of the study reported here, it was assumed that housing is an indicator of standard of living for single as well as family household units.

The study site was Syracuse, New York, an industrial city of approximately 25 square miles, the location of more than 500 manufacturing plants and the hub city of a metropolitan area in central New York State. Populations of two different years, 1940 and 1950, were analyzed in an attempt to discover the persistence, if any, of patterns of variation by age. There were 205,967 persons in Syracuse in 1940 and 220,583 persons in 1950.

Census tracts were used as basic units of analysis. Syracuse has been divided into six socioeconomic areas. A socioeconomic area consists of several census tracts with populations relatively similar in occupation, education, and such characteristics as house-type and rental or market value of dwelling units.

Specifically, the components of the socioeconomic status composite index are (1) average home value, (2) average monthly rental, (3) percent of single-family dwelling units, (4) median school year completed, and (5) percent of workers in the combined occupational categories of operatives, service workers, and laborers. The latter component was inverted so that it would vary directly with the other four and, therefore, could be included in a composite index. The problem of an appropriate index of social stratification remains to be solved, although a combination of several components seems to be a useful index. Haer has pointed out that Warner's Index of Status Characteristics (which consists of several components similar to those used in this study results in higher coefficients of predictability of other variables related to stratification or class more frequently than any of the components of the index used singly [5]. All components of the Syracuse index, except one indicating house-type, intercorrelate with each other at .80 and above, based on 1940 and 1950 census data. The correlation coefficients between percent of single-family dwelling units and the other four components range from .59 to .70. Thus, a significant and high association exists between all variables in the socioeconomic status index.

Residential areas of varying socioeconomic status were delineated on the basis of an analysis of the frequency distribution of composite socioeconomic status scores, building permits, real estate advertisements, topographical and social base maps, official reports, interviews with long-term residents, historical documents, Census Bureau publications, and field observations. A majority of employed persons in area I were professional, technical, or managerial workers, had graduated from high school and college, and lived in expensive recently built homes which they owned. In area VI, a majority of the employed were operatives, service workers, or laborers, had received no more than an elementary school education, and lived in old dilapidated multiple-family dwelling structures. Other socioeconomic areas varied between these extremes in population traits and environmental characteristics. In general, areas I to IV were above and V and VI were below the total city average in the distributions of most variables related to socioeconomic status. The socioeconomic organization of the city by residential areas was similar in 1940 and 1950 [6].

Age data were analyzed by census tracts, by socioeconomic areas, and for the total city. The population for each study period was divided into 13 five-year age categories and another category including all persons 65 years of age and over. Persons in each age category were treated as a single ecological variable — as a percentage of the total population in a census tract, a socioeconomic area, or the city.

Some of the 61 census tracts in Syracuse were eliminated from the study area because of the presence of special populations associated with educational institutions and public housing developments. The heavy concentration of students and residents of public housing in certain neighborhoods tended to distort their usual age distribution pattern. After making these and a few other adjustments, the final study area and population consisted of 59 census tracts with a population of 204,684 in 1940 and 55 census tracts with a population of 201,641 in 1950. Six socioeconomic areas were used in the 1940 analysis, but it was necessary to consolidate these six into three areas for the 1950 analysis because of the fewer numbers of census tracts included in the study area. In 1950, area A was a combination of I and II, B a combination of III and IV, and C a combination of V and VI.

The data were analyzed for both study periods to determine the presence or absence of statistically significant associations. Chi-squares and Pearson correlation coefficients were the principal statistical techniques used. Unless otherwise stated, the 5 percent level of confidence was considered to be the limit of statistical significance.

Findings

There was a definite association between the socioeconomic status level of residential areas and the age distribution of their populations. By census tracts, median age of the population intercorrelated with socio-economic status scores at .57 in 1940 and at .44 in 1950, indicating that about one-third of the variance in socioeconomic status of residential areas could be attributed to the median age of the population in 1940, and about one-fifth in 1950. In each instance, the correlation coefficient is statistically significant and there is a direct association; census tracts with populations of higher median age tend to have high socioeconomic status scores.

As shown in Table 3.1, however, only 6 of the 14 age categories are significantly associated with socioeconomic status. They include the categories spanning the years 15 to 29 and 35 to 54 in 1940, and 20 to 34 and 40 to 59 in 1950. For 1940, there is a negative or indirect association between the socioeconomic status level of census tracts and the proportion of persons 15 to 29 years of age living within them; for 1950, there is a negative association between socioeconomic status and the proportion of persons 20 to 34 years of age. The negative associations between age and socioeconomic status are similar for 1940 and 1950 in that they cover a 15-year period. However, the period of significant negative association with socioeconomic status, though similar in length of time, occurs five years later for 1950 than for 1940. The pattern observed among the younger age categories of adulthood for 1940 and 1950 is the opposite of that marking the older population of working age. There is a significant but positive association between socioeconomic status and the proportion of persons 35 to 54 years of age living in census tracts of the city in 1940. In 1950, the period of positive association also covers a 20-year span, but it includes persons 40 to 59 years of age. Here again is an association of similar length in time in each of the two study periods. The positive association between socioeconomic status and age, however, appears five years later in 1950 than in 1940. It would seem that age is significantly associated with variations in the socioeconomic status level of residential areas during the periods of reproduction and rearing of children and the principal working years. The period of significant correlation between age and socioeconomic status extends slightly more than the length of a single generation, a 40-year range.

Another important finding is that the period of significant association between age and socioeconomic status was not continuous. In 1940, as well as in 1950, there was a five-year span in adulthood after the years of negative association and before the years of positive association in which socioeconomic status and age show no association that is statistically significant. This holds for the categories 30 to 34 years of age in 1940, and 35 to 39 years of age in 1950 . A possible explanation of this discontinuity is that it represents a period of transition in residential mobility of the population. This is the "gear shifting age" in adulthood. During this five-year span most residentially mobile persons probably moved to neighborhoods of relatively higher social status. Some may have moved at the beginning of the period, others toward its close. Thus, persons 30 to 34 years of age in 1940 and 35 to 39 years of age in 1950 lived in neighborhoods of varying socioeconomic status, both high and low, depending on whether they moved at the beginning, toward the middle, or near the end of the transition period. Evidence for this supposition was found in a series of coefficients of variation computed by census tracts for populations in each of the five-year age categories. The lowest coefficients were found in the age categories 30 to 34 years in 1940 and 35 to 39 in 1950. A coefficient of .11 for these two age categories during both of the study periods indicates that persons 30 to 34 years and 35 to 39 years in 1940 and 1950, respectively, were fairly evenly distributed throughout the city with little variation in their proportion of the total population in each census tract. This fact helps to explain the low correlation coefficient and thus the discontinuity in significance between age and socioeconomic status by residential area during this unique five-year period in adulthood.

Table 3.1

**Age Status Intercorrelated With Socioeconomic
Status, by Census Tracts, Syracuse, 1940 and 1950**

| | Correlation Coefficient | |
Age	1940	1950
0-4	−.23	−.25
5-9	−.11	.06
10-14	−.19	.14
15-19	−.39[a]	−.03
20-24	−.49[a]	−.30[a]
25-29	−.62[a]	−.69[a]
30-34	.18	−.70[a]
35-39	.63[a]	−.07
40-44	.81[a]	.61[a]
45-49	.55[a]	.73[a]
50-54	.30[a]	.65[a]
55-59	.18	.39[a]
60-64	.03	−.06
65 and over	.10	.03

a. Correlation coefficient is significant at the 5 percent level of confidence.

As seen in Table 3.2, the age distribution of the population differs by socioeconomic areas. To illustrate, in 1940 the mode of the population distribution for adults was in the 40 to 44-year age category in area I and in the 20 to 24-year age category in area VI. In 1950, the mode advanced to the 45 to 49-year age category in area A and the 25 to 29-year age category in area C. Hence, the largest proportion of the population by five-year age categories was in the middle-adult years in the higher socioeconomic areas and in the young-adult years in the lower socioeconomic areas. Chi-squares, which were computed for the total population as distributed by age among the socioeconomic areas during the two study periods, indicate that the age status of the population varied with the socioeconomic status level of residential areas and that the association between these two variables is significant at the 1 percent level of confidence.

To identify specific age categories in each area that contributed to the significant chi-squares, observed-expected ratios were computed. Had the total population in the study area been equally distributed throughout the city, its percentage distribution by age in each socioeconomic area would have been similar to its distribution by age within the total city. Therefore, the population distribution by age in the total city is the *expected* ratio, and the actual distribution by age within each socioeconomic area, the *observed*. Ratios greater than one indicate that more persons than expected populated a specific age category while smaller ratios indicate the presence of fewer persons than expected in a specific age category of the socioeconomic area. This part of the analysis was restricted to adult years within the total 40-year age range of significant association revealed earlier by the coefficients of correlation reported in Table 3.1.

Table 3.3 shows that observed-expected ratios for the adult years — ages 20 to 54 in 1940 — form a series of stair-steps in appearance between the six socioeconomic residential areas. The observed population is not greater than the expected among adults until age 35 in the two higher areas, I and II, age 30 in area III and age 25 in area IV; in the two lower socioeconomic areas V and VI, the observed was greater than the expected population at age 20 — the beginning of adulthood. This regular stair-step pattern also describes the specific ages at which the expanded adult population in a socioeconomic area tapers off to fewer than the expected up to age 55. For example, in 1940, there were fewer adults than expected after age 50 in area III, after age 45 in area IV, after age 40 in area V, and after age 30 in area VI. Table 3.3 indicates a similar pattern for the 1950 data, although different age categories are involved. It is not until age 40 that more adults than expected appear in the highest socioeconomic area,

Table 3.2.
Percentage Distribution of Total Population by Socioeconomic Areas, Syracuse, 1940 and 1950

Age	1940 Socioeconomic Area I	II	III	IV	V	VI	Total	1950[a] Socioeconomic Area A	B	C	Total
0– 4	5.65	5.06	5.88	5.84	6.01	7.06	6.13	7.32	8.89	9.31	8.96
5– 9	7.02	5.77	6.70	5.91	5.97	7.55	6.48	7.55	6.66	6.88	6.86
10–14	7.83	7.24	7.57	6.88	6.97	8.68	7.52	6.07	5.20	5.60	5.50
15–19	8.45	8.42	7.84	7.73	8.36	10.34	8.66	6.23	6.02	6.12	6.09
20–24	7.24	7.81	7.61	8.73	9.00	10.10	8.84	6.89	8.06	8.40	8.14
25–29	5.35	6.34	7.27	8.71	8.45	8.78	8.11	6.40	8.14	9.38	8.65
30–34	7.46	7.67	8.37	8.39	8.02	7.14	7.88	5.93	7.55	8.30	7.81
35–39	8.58	7.91	8.48	7.70	7.45	6.19	7.42	6.69	7.30	7.17	7.18
40–44	10.07	8.57	8.57	7.62	7.02	6.13	7.38	7.72	7.10	6.44	6.80
45–49	9.19	8.24	8.06	7.39	7.21	6.98	7.47	8.02	6.80	5.83	6.39
50–54	7.07	7.80	6.48	6.41	6.67	6.23	6.59	7.97	6.88	6.03	6.52
55–59	4.94	5.93	5.04	5.41	5.41	4.64	5.19	7.24	6.21	5.82	6.09
60–64	4.00	4.56	4.08	4.42	4.61	3.71	4.25	5.64	5.00	5.04	5.08
65–69	2.91	3.85	3.18	3.66	3.66	2.96	3.40	4.14	3.94	4.00	3.99
70–74	1.95	2.34	2.26	2.46	2.61	1.87	2.31	2.87	2.84	2.77	2.80
75 and over	2.29	2.49	2.61	2.74	2.58	1.64	2.37	3.32	3.41	2.91	3.14
Total	100.00	100.00	100.00	100.00	100.00	100.00	100.00	100.00	100.00	100.00	100.00

a. For 1950, area A includes socioeconomic areas I and II minus tracts 36, 44, and 56, which were eliminated because of the presence of public housing and student populations not tabulated as residents of these tracts in 1940; area B includes socioeconomic areas III and IV minus tract 43, eliminated because of its student population; area C includes socioeconomic areas V and VI.

Table 3.3.
Observed-Expected Ratio of Population by
Socioeconomic Areas, Syracuse, 1940 and 1950

	1940						1950[a]		
	Socioeconomic Area						Socioeconomic Area		
Age	I	II	III	IV	V	VI	A	B	C
0–4	.92	.83	.96	.95	.98	1.15	.82	.99	1.04
5–9	1.08	.89	1.03	.91	.92	1.16	1.10	.97	1.00
10–14	1.04	.96	1.01	.91	.93	1.15	1.10	.95	1.02
15–19	.98	.97	.91	.89	.96	1.19	1.02	.99	1.00
20–24	.82	.88	.86	.99	1.02	1.14	.85	.99	1.03
25–29	.66	.78	.90	1.07	1.04	1.08	.74	.94	1.08
30–34	.95	.97	1.06	1.06	1.02	.91	.76	.97	1.06
35–39	1.16	1.07	1.14	1.04	1.00	.83	.93	1.02	1.00
40–44	1.36	1.16	1.16	1.03	.95	.83	1.14	1.04	.95
45–49	1.23	1.10	1.08	.99	.96	.93	1.26	1.06	.91
50–54	1.07	1.18	.98	.97	1.01	.94	1.22	1.06	.92
55–59	.95	1.14	.97	1.04	1.04	.89	1.19	1.02	.96
60–64	.94	1.07	.96	1.04	1.08	.87	1.11	.98	.99
65–69	.86	1.13	.94	1.08	1.08	.87	1.04	.99	1.00
70–74	.83	1.01	.98	1.06	1.13	.81	1.02	1.01	.99
75 and over	.97	1.05	1.10	1.16	1.09	.69	1.06	1.09	.93

Note: Horizontal lines enclose adult age categories significantly associated with socioeconomic status, according to a census tract correlational analysis, and with an excessive number of persons. The percentage distribution of the total city population is the expected. Were the population equally distributed throughout the city, the percentage distribution in each socioeconomic area would be the same as that in the total city and the ratio for each age category would be 1.00; ratios greater than 1.00 indicate an overrepresentation of observed in relation to the expected population.

a. In 1950, area A combined I and II, area B combined III and IV, area C combined V and VI.

A, age 35 in area B, and age 20 in area C. A decisive stair-step pattern describing the age periods at which the excessive adult population tapers off is not visible in the consolidated three areas of 1950. However, area C — the lowest in socioeconomic status — has fewer persons than expected after age 40. The overall pattern revealed by the observed-expected ratios supports the conclusion that an association between age and socioeconomic status characterizes *all* socioeconomic areas.

It was noted that fewer young adults, ages 25 to 29, than expected are found in the higher socioeconomic areas. This finding probably reflects a tendency for offspring of families in high status neighborhoods to find housing in residential areas of less high status when separate and independent households are first established. A finding which tends to corroborate this supposition is that more young adults, ages 20 to 24, than expected are in populations of the lower socioeconomic areas. Apparently, such neighborhoods have served as a residential point of entry for the young as they first seek independence from their families of orientation, notwithstanding the social status of their parental families.

The analysis of observed-expected ratios suggests a principle concerning social mobility. Table 3.3 shows that the excessive adult population in most socioeconomic areas extends over a period of roughly 20 years, although the specific ages involved in this period vary by socioeconomic area. By inference, it would appear that a significant number of adults in all socioeconomic areas moved at least once in 20 years to a neighborhood of higher status. These findings suggest the principle that a tendency toward upward social mobility in residential status with increase in age status exists within *all* segments of the population.

Summary and Conclusions

This study provides sufficient evidence to reject the null hypothesis that there is no difference in the distribution of the population by age in varying socioeconomic areas. The proportion of young adults living in residential areas of lower status and the proportion of middle-aged adults living in the higher-status areas are greater than might occur by chance. A significant and direct association exists between variations in the population of an urban community by age status, and between variations in its residential areas by socioeconomic status. This principle does not apply, however, to all parts of the age continuum: it would appear to be restricted to a 40-year age span representing the principal productive years of adulthood.

Because of the kinds of data analyzed in this study, only inferential conclusions may be made about age status and social mobility by residential area. These conclusions are (1) that there is a tendency toward upward social mobility by residential area as age increases; and (2) that this tendency characterizes populations in lower as well as higher socioeconomic areas in an urban community. Again, the application of these conclusions is restricted to the 40-year span of principal productive years.

Notes

Paper read at the annual meeting of the American Sociological Association, Chicago, September 1959. Acknowledged with appreciation is the assistance of the Milbank Memorial Fund in the form of a grant to the Department of Sociology and Anthropology of Syracuse University, for support of research by the author, who worked on assignment from the University with the New York State Mental Health Commission during the course of the investigation.

1.   Peter H. Rossi, *Why Families Move* (Glencoe, Ill.: Free Press, 1955); Paul C. Glick, *American Families* (New York: Wiley, 1957); and Glenn H. Beyer, *Housing: A Factual Analysis* (New York: Macmillan, 1958), p. 33.
2.   Rossi, *Why Families Move,* p. 178.
3.   Glick, *American Families,* p. 88.
4.   See Beyer, *Housing: A Factual Analysis;* and Glenn H. Beyer, Thomas W. Mackesey, and James E. Montgomery, *Houses Are for People* (Ithaca: Cornell University Housing Research Center, 1954).
5.   John L. Haer, "Predictive Utility for Five Indices of Social Stratification," *American Sociological Review* 22 (October 1957): 541–546.
6.   Charles V. Willie, "Socioeconomic Analysis of Syracuse, New York, 1940," in New York State Department of Mental Hygiene, ed., *Technical Report of the Mental Health Research Unit* (Syracuse: Syracuse University Press, 1955), pp. 27–48; and Willie, "Socioeconomic and Ethnic Areas in Syracuse, New York, 1950" (Ph.D. dissertation, Syracuse University, Syracuse, New York, 1957).

CHAPTER 4

The Ethnic Areas of Syracuse, New York

An analysis of the population, housing, and geographic characteristics of ethnic areas in Syracuse is presented in this chapter. The Census Bureau publishes a total population count of Negroes by census tracts. But for other ethnic groups, only the number of foreign-born is reported. Because the foreign-born population of any specific group is never the majority of a total census tract population, one must exercise caution in concluding a cause and effect relationship between the presence or absence of some specific form of behavior among the people of a tract and the ethnic heritage of its population. No information about second and third generations is available for nationality ethnic groups. To delineate ethnic neighborhoods is a valuable procedure, however, if it may be assumed that where foreign-born of a specific ethnicity live there also may live some of their progeny. Ethnic neighborhoods for nationality groups outlined in this study, therefore, are based on data pertaining to foreign-born only.

Foreign-born white persons constitute about 11 percent of the 220,583 persons in Syracuse in 1950. Of the total population, 2 percent is Negro and less than 1 percent is of other nonwhite ethnic groups. Syracuse, then, has a population predominantly born in the United States; 87 percent of its residents are native-born and white. Of the 23,000 to 24,000 persons in this city born in other lands, the continent of Europe is represented by four out of every five foreign-born. The second highest number — 13 percent of all foreign-born — comes from Canada, mostly the English-speaking provinces of the Dominion. Asia is the continent of birth for only 2 percent of the foreign-born; and less than 2 percent come from the rest of the world, including Central and South America, Africa, and Australia.

From Charles V. Willie, *Socioeconomic and Ethnic Areas in Syracuse, New York,* unpublished doctoral dissertation, Department of Sociology and Anthropology, University of Syracuse, 1957, pp. 223–269.

38

One may identify those groups that enter into the conscience of the community by determining the numbers in ethnic populations and patterns of residential segregation. There are 4,586 Negroes in Syracuse. Of the foreign-born populations, those that surpass the one thousand mark in numbers of persons living in this city are the Italian, Polish, German, Russian, Irish, Canadian, and English. Most of the Russian foreign-born in this community are Jewish. The Irish included in this study are persons born in Erie and exclude individuals from Northern Ireland. The Canadian are mostly non-French-speaking nationals of Canada. Although persons from England and Wales and from Canada constitute foreign-born populations each of more than 1,000, they are not included in the following analysis of ethnic areas because they tend to disperse themselves throughout the city, unlike the populations from Ireland, Germany, Russia, Poland, and Italy as well as the Negro population. The latter six groups, therefore, are the subjects of this analysis.

A census tract is classified as part of an ethnic neighborhood if there are three or more times the number of a specific ethnic group within it than expected, were members of that ethnic group equally distributed throughout the city. Were members of each ethnic group dispersed in a nonsegregated manner, the proportion expected in each census tract population would be equal to the proportion of that ethnic group within the total city. For example, 2 percent of the total city population is Negro. If there were no concentration of this population in a certain area of Syracuse, Negroes would constitute not more than 2 percent of the total population of any one census tract. According to this criterion, ethnic neighborhoods have been delineated for all six of the populations mentioned above. There are two Russian foreign-born neighborhoods in two different sections of the city. Likewise, two different Polish neighborhoods are identified. For the other four ethnic groups, however, all census tracts comprising each ethnic neighborhood are contiguous and form a composite unit. Ethnic neighborhoods for the six groups cover 35 percent of the area of the   city in square miles.

In Table 4.1 are presented the numbers in each ethnic group and the extent of its residential segregation. The least segregated in terms of the concentration of foreign-born is the Irish ethnic group and the most segregated is the Negro ethnic group. The four to five thousand Negroes in Syracuse are so concentrated that it is probable the next person any one Negro meets will be another Negro 25 times out of 100. A similar interpretation of interethnic group interaction may be expressed for the other five groups according to probability measures presented in Table 4.1. It is

Table 4.1.

**Ethnic Group Population and Probable Intragroup
Contact, Syracuse, 1950**

Ethnic Group[a]	Total Population	Probable Intra-Group Contact P*[b]
Irish foreign-born	1,482	.01
German foreign-born	2,333	.02
Russian foreign-born	1,604	.03
Polish foreign-born	2,871	.06
Italian foreign-born	6,853	.09
Negro	4,586	.26

a. Ethnic group populations for Irish, German, Russian, Polish, and Italian refer to foreign-born only. Data on second and third generation of foreign-born are not available.

b. P* The probable intragroup contact usually represented by the symbol P* is based on two assumptions: (l) that meetings occur only between persons of the same census tract, and (2) that every person in the tract has an equal chance of meeting every other person in the tract. Assumption 2 allows the interpretation of P* as the minimum probable interaction among members of the same group. Assumption 1 is necessary if the probable within-group interaction due to differential concentration by census tracts is to be measured. The probability that the next person a random individual from a specific group will meet is also from the same group is the sum of the products of two probabilities: (a) the probability of the individual from a specific ethnic group next meeting a person from that group in his census tract, and (b) the probability that a random individual from a specific ethnic group is in a particular census tract. If a specific ethnic group were homogeneously mixed throughout the city, then the proportions of that group in every census tract would equal the proportion of that group in the city.

Note: This table presents data regarding the measurement of ecological segregation, using techniques developed by Shevsky and Williams and later refined by Wendell Bell, "A Probability Model for Measurement of Ecological Segregation," *Social Forces* 32 (May 1954), 357–364.

seen that the second most segregated group is Italian. And in the following order of increasingly less residential segregation are Polish, Russian, and German foreign-born ethnic groups ending with the Irish mentioned before.

Of the less segregated ethnic groups, one might suppose that the majority of their foreign-born live outside the ethnic neighborhood. This is true of the Irish and German. More than 75 percent of all foreign-born in these two groups live outside their respective ethnic neighborhoods. On the other hand, more than 90 percent of all Negroes (the most segregated group) live within the ethnic neighborhood. But the Russian foreign-born who are mostly Jewish show an exception to this pattern. While they are less segregated than the Polish and Italian, more of the Russian foreign-born than of the former two groups live within the ethnic neighborhood and fewer Russian foreign-born than any other group, excepting Negroes, live outside the ethnic neighborhood. The explanation is that while Russian foreign-born are dispersed in the community, the movement out of one ethnic neighborhood has been accompanied with the formation of another neighborhood—and hence, the two different Russian neighborhoods today when formerly there was only one. The data supporting the above discussion are presented in Table 4.2. When the two Russian foreign-born neighborhoods are combined, they become the largest of any ethnic neighborhood in the city. A combination of two processes—one of dispersion and the other of concentration—appear to be at work simultaneously and, therefore, account for this unique circumstance of Russian foreign-born who are mostly of the Jewish community.

Figures 4.1 through 4.6 show the location of ethnic areas within the city. Areas of heavy ethnic concentration are referred to in this text as ethnic neighborhoods. Here are found specific ethnic groups in proportions three or more times greater than the percentages these specific groups represent in the total city population. The geographic directional sector in which each neighborhood is located is given now. Detailed description of the neighborhood will be found in another section of this chapter.

The Irish neighborhood covers about 3 percent of the total city and is located on the West Side, some portions of it touching the right of way of the New York Central Railroad, while other sections border or surround Erie Boulevard and West Genesee Street industrial arterial routes. The census tracts of this neighborhood are, on the average, 1.81 miles removed from the central business district. About one-third of the Irish neighborhood is devoted to mixed residential and business usage, the remainder being of residential property only. The German neighborhood is

Figure 4.1.

Irish Foreign – Born Population
Syracuse by Census Tracts
1950

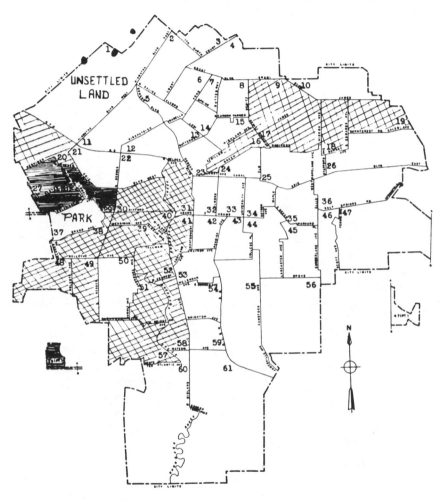

■ Heavy Irish Concentration
⊠ Medium Irish Concentration
☐ Light Irish Concentration

The ratio of observed to expected percentage of Irish foreign-born is 3.0 or greater in tracts of heavy concentration, between 1.0 and 3.0 in tracts of medium concentration, and less than 1.0 in tracts of light concentration.

Figure 4.2.

German Foreign – Born Population
Syracuse by Census Tracts
1950

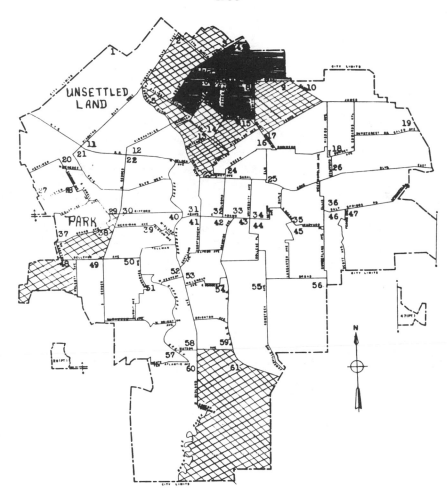

■ Heavy German Concentration
⊠ Medium German Concentration
☐ Light German Concentration

The ratio of observed to expected percentage of German foreign-born is 3.0 or greater in tracts of heavy concentration, between 1.0 and 3.0 in tracts of medium concentration, and less than 1.0 in tracts of light concentration.

Figure 4.3.

Russian Foreign–Born Population
Syracuse by Census Tracts
1950

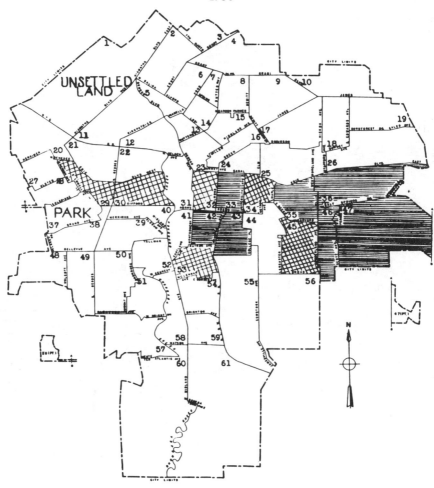

Many Russian-born are Jewish
■ Heavy Russian Concentration
⬚ Medium Russian Concentration
☐ Light Russian Concentration

The ratio of observed to expected percentage of Russian foreign-born is 3.0 or greater in tracts of heavy concentration, between 1.0 and 3.0 in tracts of medium concentration, and less than 1.0 in tracts of light concentration.

Figure 4.4.

Polish Foreign – Born Population
Syracuse by Census Tracts
1950

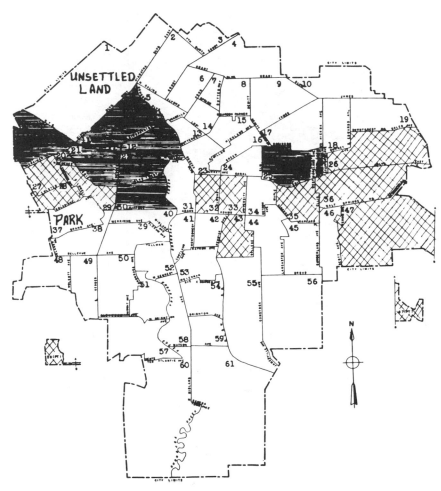

■ Heavy Polish Concentration	The ratio of observed to expected percentage of Polish foreign-born is 3.0 or greater in tracts of heavy concentration, between 1.0 and 3.0 in tracts of medium concentration, and less than 1.0 in tracts of light concentration.
⊠ Medium Polish Concentration	
□ Light Polish Concentration	

Figure 4.5.

Italian Foreign – Born Population
Syracuse by Census Tracts
1950

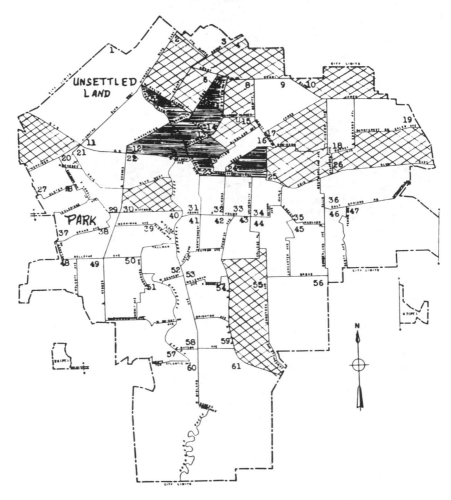

■ Heavy Italian Concentration
⊠ Medium Italian Concentration
☐ Light Italian Concentration

The ratio of observed to expected percentage of Italian foreign-born is 3.0 or greater in tracts of heavy concentration, between 1.0 and 3.0 in tracts of medium concentration, and less than 1.0 in tracts of light concentration.

Figure 4.6.

**Negro Population
Syracuse by Census Tracts
1950**

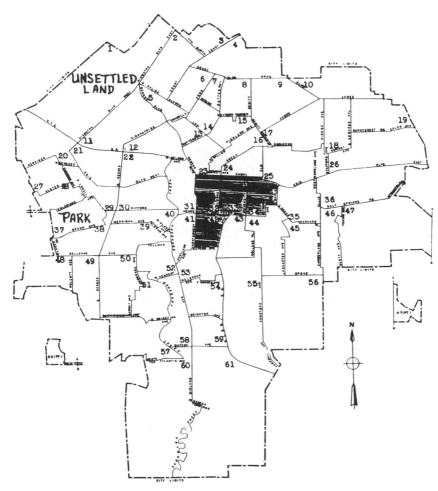

■ Heavy Negro Concentration
⊠ Medium Negro Concentration
☐ Light Negro Concentration

The ratio of observed to expected percentage of Negroes is 3.0 or greater in tracts of heavy concentration, between 1.0 and 3.0 in tracts of medium concentration, and less than 1.0 in tracts of light concentration.

located on the North Side of Syracuse, an average of 1.51 miles from the city center. It covers about 5 percent of the city's total area and is a section reserved for residential properties only. The two Russian neighborhoods combined represent about 12 percent of the total city square mileage. They are located on the East Side, the smaller of the two being less than a mile away from the downtown section on the Lower East Side; the second Russian foreign-born neighborhood is the most distance from the central business district of any of the ethnic groups. It is an average of 2.60 miles out from the city center. About 40 percent of the Lower East Side Russian neighborhood is of mixed residential and business land use. Its sister neighborhood toward the periphery of the city, however, is exclusively residential. On the North Side are located the two Polish neighborhoods, one northeast of the central business district and the other northwest of it. These two neighborhoods cover about 10 percent of the total city. Nearest the downtown section is the larger Polish neighborhood only 1.23 miles away to the northwest. It is located on the flat lands surrounding industrial sites in that portion of the city which was once swamp land of Onondaga Lake backwash. The New York Central Railroad and the industrial arterial routes of Erie Boulevard and West Genesee Street also pass through this neighborhood, all of which is an admixture of residential and business properties. The smaller Polish neighborhood northeast of the center is also a site of mixed property usage. It borders Erie Boulevard and surrounds the New York Central Railroad too, although it extends in a northerly direction beyond these travel routes. This smaller Polish neighborhood consists of only one census tract which is 1.58 miles removed from the city center. Fused between the Polish and German neighborhoods on the North Side is the Italian section consisting of 7 census tracts which average approximately four-fifths of a mile beyond the city center. This neighborhood covers a little better than 5 percent of the total city. Through it passes United States Route 11 over North State and North Salina streets. Three-quarters of its land are devoted to mixed residential and business properties. The Negro neighborhood is located on the near-in Lower East Side of Syracuse, less than a mile away from the downtown section. It extends over portions of four census tracts representing around 3.5 percent of the total city area. Nearly 75 percent of the land in this area which borders Erie Boulevard at some points as well as the South State Street portion of Route 11 is of mixed residential and business usage.

While each of the ethnic neighborhoods is positioned in a distinct locality, all are not completely autonomous. The German and Italian sections meet and overlap in census tract 7 on the North Side. The Italian section

Table 4.2.

**Distribution of Ethnic Populations Within Total City
by Type of Neighborhood, Syracuse, 1950**

Ethnic Population	Type of Ethnic Area (In Percentages)			Total City Ethnic Population	
	Heavy Ethnic Concen- tration[a]	Medium Ethnic Concen- tration[b]	Light Ethnic Concen- tration[c]	Number	Percent
Irish	17.89	49.86	32.25	1,482	100
German	25.38	35.75	38.87	2,333	100
Russian	59.42	22.69	17.89	1,604	100
Polish	54.41	22.29	23.30	2,871	100
Italian	42.96	35.15	21.89	6,853	100
Negro	92.78	—	7.22	4,586	100

a. Areas of heavy ethnic concentration consist of census tracts in which are found three or more times the expected number of persons in each ethnic group.

b. Areas of medium ethnic concentration consist of census tracts in which are found the expected and upwards to three times as many of the ethnic group as expected.

c. Areas of light ethnic concentration consist of census tracts in which are found fewer persons of specific ethnicities than expected.

Note: The expected distribution of ethnic numbers in any census tract is based on the percent of each ethnic group in the total city population.

also is overlapped by the larger Polish neighborhood in tract 12 on the North Side. And two census tracts—33 and 42—comprise sections of the Russian (Jewish) and Negro neighborhoods on the Lower East Side of the city. In fact, more than half of the Negro neighborhood is jointly populated by Russian foreign-born and Negroes, each group in proportions three times greater than the expected concentration.

In the second part of this chapter the distribution of housing and population characteristics will be analyzed. Specifically, it will be determined if the dwellings of the city are equally distributed throughout all ethnic neighborhoods by construction year of dwelling unit structure, by type of dwelling structure, and by condition of dwelling as reflected in home value. Also measured will be the distribution of home owners and tenants within the ethnic areas as well as their occupational pursuits. These characteristics will be measured to determine if they are equally distributed throughout all ethnic neighborhoods as a further test of the null hypothesis. Here, as previously, the technique of analysis involves the computation of a ratio—a ratio of the observed distribution of a phenomenon in relation to its expected distribution. The expected, of course, is the percentage distribution or average of a particular population or housing characteristic for the total city.

The first factor analyzed has to do with the average construction year of dwelling units. In a way, this feature of housing gives some indication of the kind of section in which ethnic neighborhoods are located. It was stated that Syracuse may be divided into the old and the new—the old largely settled before the twentieth century and the new developed principally during the 1920s and afterwards. Were dwelling units equally distributed throughout the city by year of structure erection, one might expect within each ethnic area 5 percent of the units to be of recent construction within the past 10 years, another 6 percent to have been built during the depression period and following from 1930 through 1939, 21 percent to have been erected during the 1920s and the majority—68 percent—to have been established before 1920. This is the percentage distribution of dwelling units by year of structure erection expected for each ethnic neighborhood. Actually, 40 percent more dwelling units than expected are older structures built before 1920 in four of the six ethnic neighborhoods. This fact, revealed in Tables 4.3 and 4.4, indicates that most of the ethnic sections in Syracuse are located in the older portion of the city. The only two groups for which this is not true are the German and one of the Russian foreign-born neighborhoods—the Russian area designated as neighborhood A that extends to the city periphery on the East Side. The German

Table 4.3.

Distribution of Dwelling Units in Ethnic Areas
by Year of Construction, Syracuse, 1950

Ethnic Neighborhood	Before 1920 Units	%	1920–1929 Units	%	1930–1939 Units	%	1940–1950 Units	%	Total Dwellings Reporting Units	%
Irish	1,985	83.4	340	14.3	40	1.7	15	0.6	2,380	100
German	2,605	62.0	1,255	29.8	255	6.1	90	2.1	4,205	100
Russian A[a]	925	33.0	1,120	39.9	540[e]	19.2	222	7.9	2,807	100
Russian B[b]	2,685	69.5	465	12.0	715	18.5	—	—	3,865	100
Polish A[c]	4,600	95.4	180	3.7	40	0.8	5	0.1	4,825	100
Polish B[d]	650	82.2	120	15.0	20	2.5	10	1.3	800	100
Italian	5,450	87.6	680	10.9	95	1.5	—	—	6,225	100
Negro	4,135	73.7	705	12.6	760[e]	13.5	10	0.2	5,610	100

Year of Structure Construction

a.   Bradford Hills, Scottholm, and Salt Springs sections extending to the city periphery.

b.   Lower East Side section.

c.   West End, Park Avenue, and industrial sections northwest of city center and near Onondaga Lake.

d.   Lincoln Park section near Teall and Burnet avenues northeast of city center.

e.   This number includes the units in Pioneer Homes low-rent housing project.

Table 4.4.

**Ratio of Observed to Expected Percentage of Dwelling Units
in Ethnic Area by Year of Construction, Syracuse, 1950**

Ethnic Neighborhood	Year of Structure Construction (In Ratio)			
	Before 1920	1920–1929	1930–1939	1940–1950
Irish	1.23	.70	.26	.13
German	.92	1.39	.94	.46
Russian A[a]	.49	1.87	2.97	1.72
Russian B[b]	1.03	.56	2.86[e]	.00
Polish A[c]	1.41	.17	.12	.02
Polish B[d]	1.22	.70	.39	.28
Italian	1.30	.51	.23	.00
Negro	1.09	.60	2.09[e]	.04

a. Bradford Hills, Scottholm, and Salt Springs sections extending to the city periphery.

b. Lower East Side section.

c. West End, Park Avenue, and industrial sections northwest of city center and near Onondaga Lake.

d. Lincoln Park section near Teall and Burnet avenues northeast of city center.

e. These high ratios reflect the presence of low-rent public housing units in Pioneer Homes Development in tract 42.

Table 4.5.

Dwelling Units in Ethnic Areas by Type of Structure, Syracuse, 1950

Ethnic Neighborhood	Single-Family Units		Multiple-Family Units		Total Dwellings Reporting	
	Units	%	Units	%	Units	%
Irish	897	38.2	1,452	61.8	2,349	100
German	2,200	52.1	2,024	47.9	4,224	100
Russian A[a]	1,753	60.0	1,170	40.0	2,923	100
Russian B[b]	422	10.5	3,584[e]	89.5	4,006	100
Polish A[c]	1,082	22.3	3,773	77.7	4,855	100
Polish B[d]	298	37.8	491	62.2	789	100
Italian	1,371	21.5	4,995	78.5	6,366	100
Negro	785	13.5	5,050[e]	86.5	5,835	100

a.   Bradford Hills, Scottholm, and Salt Springs sections extending to the city periphery.

b.   Lower East Side section.

c.   West End, Park Avenue, and industrial sections northwest of city center and near Onondaga Lake.

d.   Lincoln Park section near Teall and Burnet avenues northeast of city center.

e.   This number of multiple dwellings includes more than 200 units in the Pioneer Homes low-rent public housing development.

Table 4.6.

**Ratio of Observed to Expected Percentage of Dwelling Units
in Ethnic Areas by Type of Dwelling Structure, Syracuse, 1950**

	Type of Dwelling Structure	
Ethnic Neighborhood	Single-Family Units	Multiple-Family Units
	Ratio	Ratio
Irish	1.10	.95
German	1.50	.73
Russian A[a]	1.73	.61
Russian B[b]	.30	1.37
Polish A[c]	.64	1.19
Polish B[d]	1.09	.95
Italian	.62	1.20
Negro	.39	1.33

a. Bradford Hills, Scottholm, and Salt Springs sections, extending to the city periphery.

b. Lower East Side section.

c. West End, Park Avenue, and industrial sections northwest of city and near Onondaga Lake.

d. Lincoln Park section near Teall and Burnet avenues northwest of city center.

Table 4.7.

**Dwelling Units in Ethnic Areas by Occupancy Status
of Dweller, Syracuse, 1950**

Ethnic Neighborhood	Owner		Tenant		Total Dwellings Reporting	
	Units	%	Units	%	Units	%
Irish	1,361	58.8	954	41.2	2,315	100
German	2,747	66.0	1,414	34.0	4,161	100
Russian A[a]	2,074	72.1	802	27.9	2,876	100
Russian B[b]	668	17.1	3,234	82.9	3,902	100
Polish A[c]	1,827	38.3	2,939	61.7	4,766	100
Polish B[d]	443	57.3	330	42.7	773	100
Italian	2,213	35.5	4,029	64.5	6,242	100
Negro	924	16.2	4,777	83.8	5,701	100

a. Bradford Hills, Scottholm, and Salt Springs sections, extending to the city periphery.

b. Lower East Side section.

c. West End, Park Avenue, and industrial sections northwest of city center and near Onondaga Lake.

d. Lincoln Park section near Teall and Burnet avenues northeast of city center.

Table 4.8.

Average Home Value by Ethnic Area, Syracuse, 1950

Ethnic Neighborhood	Dwellings Reporting	Average Home Value
Irish	740	$ 8,666
German	1,929	8,866
Russian A[a]	1,502	16,330
Russian B[b]	165	7,943
Polish A[c]	722	6,727
Polish B[d]	244	7,151
Italian	928	7,098
Negro	257	8,563

a.   Bradford Hills, Scottholm, and Salt Springs sections, extending to the city periphery.
b.   Lower East Side section.
c.   West End, Park Avenue, and industrial sections northwest of city center and near Onondaga Lake.
d.   Lincoln Park section near Teall and Burnet avenues northeast of city center.

Table 4.9.

Ratio of Observed to Expected Percentage of Owned Homes in Ethnic Areas by Average Home Value, Syracuse, 1950

Ethnic Neighborhood	Average Home Value Ratio
Irish	.76
German	.77
Russian A[a]	1.43
Russian B[b]	.69
Polish A[c]	.59
Polish B[d]	.62
Italian	.62
Negro	.75

a.   Bradford Hills, Scottholm, and Salt Springs sections, extending to the city periphery.
b.   Lower East Side section.
c.   West End, Park Avenue, and industrial sections northwest of city center and near Onondaga Lake.
d.   Lincoln Park section near Teall and Burnet avenues northeast of city center.

section is old, however, most of it having been settled before 1920; but a goodly number of dwellings — about 3 out of every 10 — were constructed during the building boom of the 1920s. Neighborhood A of the Russian foreign-born is totally different from the German neighborhood or any of the other four ethnic groups, including neighborhood B of Russian foreign-born on the Lower East Side. Only a third of the dwellings in neighborhood A of Russian foreign-born were constructed before 1920, and 70 percent more units than expected were erected within the past ten years. Of the six ethnic group neighborhoods, this is the only one in which the observed number of dwellings is greater than the expected for the most recent 1940 to 1950 decade. While these data suggest that housing by age of dwelling structure are not equally distributed throughout the city, they also indicate that the neighborhoods settled by Negroes, Italian, Polish, Irish, and a portion of the Russian foreign-born populations are similar in that they occupy first settled sections of the city. Excepting neighborhood A of Russian foreign-born, all other ethnic neighborhoods carry medians pertaining to year of dwelling structure construction that fall at some year in the nineteenth century.

Although most of the ethnic groups populate older sections of the city, there are some differences in the characteristics of each neighborhood by house type and occupancy status of dweller, as shown in Tables 4.5, 4.6, and 4.7. Approximately 35 percent of all dwelling units in Syracuse are of the single-family type; the remainder are housed in multiple-family structures. One might guess that a higher proportion of single-family units make up the housing supply in Russian neighborhood A located near the city periphery. This is so. In addition, 50 percent more dwellings than expected are of the single-family variety in the German foreign-born neighborhood. The smaller Polish neighborhood B northeast of the business district and the Irish section each show a slight overrepresentation of single-family structures in relation to the expected, although single-family homes comprise less than a majority of available and occupied units in the latter two ethnic neighborhoods. The larger Polish neighborhood A near Onondaga Lake, the Italian section, and the Lower East Side smaller Russian neighborhood B as well as the Negro district are definitely tenement areas in which more than three-quarters of the dwellings are in multiple-family structures. The distribution of dwellings in multiple-family buildings exceeds by 20 percent or more the expected in the four ethnic areas. There are differences, then, in the house type composition of ethnic neighborhoods. In general, the Russian, German, and Irish neighborhoods show more single-family homes than expected. The majority of dwellers are home owners in major neighborhoods of the first three ethnic groups while tenant occupancy predominates in the major neighborhood populated by Negroes and Italian and Polish foreign-born.

Since a majority of the residents in the major Russian neighborhood A and also in the German and Irish neighborhoods own their homes, it may be of interest to investigate the value of these dwellings in relation to the city average, which is $11,459 for 1950. Data on average home value of ethnic neighborhoods are presented in Tables 4.8 and 4.9. In only one ethnic neighborhood, Russian foreign-born neighborhood A, the average value of homes exceeds the city average. The other neighborhoods are quite similar in that the average value of owned homes for all is below the city average, from one to two-fifths below the city average. The German neighborhood comes closer than any of the remaining groups, and the German neighborhood falls short of the city average home value better than $2,500. Hence, it may be stated that owned homes of varying value are not equally distributed throughout the city. Eliminating the Russian neighborhood A from the analysis, it is found that the value of owned homes in all other ethnic residential areas lay within a range of approximately $2,000. This fact leads to the additional conclusion that little difference exists in the average value of owned homes by ethnic neighborhoods, excepting the larger Russian neighborhood. A conclusion of this nature was anticipated in the analysis of dwelling structure median year of construction. Lower values usually are associated with older homes, particularly homes located in areas settled before the turn of the century. It was further indicated in an earlier part of this chapter that portions of many of the ethnic sections are devoted to mixed residential and business land usage. They also spread predominantly over sites of lower elevation. These environmental conditions frequently are associated with property of lower value.

According to the analysis thus far, ethnic neighborhoods (excepting the Russian foreign-born A) appear to be similar in median year of dwelling structure erection and in value of owned homes. They differ most in house type and in occupancy status of dwellers. More home owners are found among the Irish, German, and Russian foreign-born than among the Polish and Italian foreign-born and Negroes. More single-family dwellings appear in neighborhoods of the former three groups, too. Essentially, differences between the six ethnic groups being analyzed seem to be associated with behavior rather than condition of existence. Of the housing factors considered in this study, the tendency toward home ownership is the most differentiating between the Irish, German, and Russian on the one hand and the Polish, Italian, and Negroes on the other. This difference is believed to be one of behavior possibly associated with subcultural values, employment opportunities, income, or community customs that limit or make possible the fulfillment of personal aspirations pertaining to home ownership. The data at hand do not lend themselves to an investigation of the suppositions advanced above. It is possible, however, to consider the distribution of persons by occupation in relation to ethnic neighborhoods. This analysis will follow.

For the total city population, professional and technical workers are 12 percent of the employed and proprietors or persons in official and managerial capacities represent one out of every 10 employed. About 18 percent are clerical workers and approximately half of this percentage follow sales occupations. Among the manual workers, craftsmen, foremen, and persons in kindred jobs account for 15 percent of the employed and 21 percent are engaged in semiskilled work as operatives; less than 5 percent are laborers. One out of every 10 persons employed is engaged in some sort of service work; but private household work of the domestic service kind is pursued for a livelihood by less than 2 percent of the employed population. In the following analysis private household workers are eliminated because they sometimes live at the place of employment. The distribution of persons by occupation for the total city is the expected distribution for each ethnic neighborhood, were the employed of all occupational pursuits equally distributed throughout the city.

It is readily apparent from an analysis of Tables 4.10 and 4.11 that persons in various occupation groups are not equally distributed throughout the community. It is further evident that great differences appear in the occupational characteristics of each ethnic neighborhood. The occupational pursuits of persons in Russian foreign-born neighborhoods are quite different from the jobs of persons populating the other ethnic neighborhoods, especially the persons in Russian neighborhood A. Here are found fewer laborers, service workers, operatives, skilled workmen, and persons in the clerical occupations. An overrepresentation from one-half to more than twice the number expected is found among professional and sales workers, proprietors and persons in managerial and official positions. The other Russian foreign-born neighborhood on the Lower East Side is similar in many respects to the rest of the ethnic neighborhoods except that a higher proportion of professional and technical workers than expected live within it.

The two Russian neighborhoods are omitted in the remainder of this analysis. Attention is focused on variations by occupation between the

Table 4.10.

Occupation by Ethnic Area, Syracuse, 1950

Ethnic Neighborhood	Laborers		Service Workers		Private Household Workers		Operatives		Craftsmen and Foremen		Sales Workers		Clerical Workers		Proprietors Managers Officials		Professional Technical Workers		Total Employed Reporting Occupation	
	N	%	N	%	N	%	N	%	N	%	N	%	N	%	N	%	N	%	N	%
Irish	133	3.6	376	10.3	43	1.2	789	21.6	618	16.9	258	7.1	831	22.7	229	6.3	378	10.3	3,655	100
German	230	3.7	513	8.2	50	.8	1,575	25.1	1,174	18.8	486	7.8	1,196	19.2	530	8.5	491	7.9	6,245	100
Russian A[a]	69	1.5	245	5.5	203	4.6	396	8.9	415	9.3	646	14.5	607	13.6	1,050	23.6	824	18.5	4,455	100
Russian B[b]	464	8.1	869	15.2	155	2.7	1,199	20.9	668	11.7	452	7.9	680	11.9	394	6.9	842	14.7	5,723	100
Polish A[c]	493	6.9	890	12.5	50	.7	2,339	33.0	1,199	16.8	337	4.7	1,135	15.9	372	5.2	305	4.3	7,120	100
Polish B[d]	117	8.6	168	12.4	12	.9	397	29.2	230	16.9	70	5.2	207	15.3	83	6.1	73	5.4	1,357	100
Italian	613	6.7	982	10.8	76	.8	2,836	31.4	1,439	15.8	621	6.8	1,390	15.3	571	6.3	557	6.1	9,085	100
Negro	718	8.6	1,305	15.6	260	3.1	1,899	22.7	1,006	12.1	675	8.1	1,041	12.5	589	7.1	851	10.2	8,344	100

a. Bradford Hills, Scottholm, and Salt Springs sections, extending to the city periphery.

b. Lower East Side section.

c. West End, Park Avenue, and industrial sections northwest of city center and near Onondaga Lake.

d. Lincoln Park section near Teall and Burnet avenues northeast of city center.

Table 4.11.

Ratio of Observed to Expected Percentage of Employed Persons in Ethnic Areas by Type of Occupation, Syracuse, 1950

Ethnic Neighborhood	Laborers	Service Workers	Private Household Workers	Operatives	Craftsmen and Foremen	Sales Workers	Clerical Workers	Proprietors Managers, Officials	Professional and Technical Workers
Irish	.86	1.04	.75	1.05	1.14	.77	1.28	.65	.84
German	.88	.82	.50	1.22	1.27	.84	1.08	.88	.65
Russian A[a]	.36	.55	2.89	.43	.63	1.56	.77	2.44	1.51
Russian B[b]	1.92	1.53	1.70	1.02	.79	.85	.67	.71	1.20
Polish A[c]	1.64	1.26	.44	1.61	1.14	.51	.90	.54	.35
Polish B[d]	2.04	1.25	.57	1.42	1.14	.56	.86	.63	.44
Italian	1.60	1.09	.50	1.53	1.07	.73	.86	.65	.50
Negro	2.04	1.57	1.95	1.10	.82	.87	.70	.73	.83

Type of Occupation (In Ratio)

a.   Bradford Hills, Scottholm, and Salt Springs sections, extending to the city periphery.

b.   Lower East Side section.

c.   West End, Park Avenue, and industrial sections northwest of city center and near Onondaga Lake.

d.   Lincoln Park section near Teall and Burnet avenues northeast of city center.

Irish, German, Polish, Italian, and Negro neighborhoods. Neighborhoods for these five ethnic groups are quite similar in that white-collar workers are grossly underrepresented in most of them. Of these five groups, the Irish and German neighborhoods are the only two in which there are more white-collar workers of any sort than expected. About a fifth of the employed in these two ethnic neighborhoods are clerical workers; this proportion, being greater than the expected, is one factor which differentiates the Irish and German neighborhoods from the Polish, Italian, and Negro neighborhoods. Also within the Irish and German sections there are fewer laborers than expected. Otherwise, these two neighborhoods are similar in occupation composition to the Polish, Italian, and Negro areas. A great similarity between neighborhoods of all five ethnic groups is seen in the distribution of semiskilled workmen or operatives. From one-fifth to one-third of all employed are semiskilled. This proportion is greater than the expected in Irish, German, Polish, and Italian foreign-born as well as in Negro neighborhoods. Classified as semiskilled are such jobs as railway breakman or switchman, bus driver, taxicab driver or chauffeur, truck driver, delivery man, and factory workers including metal filers, grinders, polishers, and the like. Even more similar than the distribution of operatives among the ethnic areas is the distribution of craftsmen, foremen, and other skilled workers. In this instance, however, the similarity is limited to only four of the five ethnic groups considered here. For the Negro neighborhood, craftsmen are underrepresented in relation to the expected, as are all other categories above skilled workmen in the occupational hierarchy. Similarities in the distribution of skilled workmen is limited to neighborhoods of the Irish, German, Polish, and Italian foreign-born. Another occupation category which shows a similar distribution among most of the ethnic neighborhoods is service workers. Included in this category are such persons as charwomen, janitors, porters, guards, watchmen, waiters, bartenders, barbers, and beauticians. In four out of the five ethnic neighborhoods under analysis more service workers than expected reside. The exception this time is the German area, in which service workers are underrepresented. In fact, the last two occupation categories below the semiskilled, including service workers and laborers, are underrepresented in the German neighborhood.

One might summarize this discussion on the distribution of occupations by major ethnic neighborhoods in the following manner. By and large, the ethnic residential areas provide the semiskilled and skilled workmen for the factories. This observation is true of all ethnic neighborhoods except two — the Negro in which skilled workmen are underrepresented and the major Russian neighborhood wherein both skilled and semiskilled workmen are fewer than expected. Another summary statement is that few ethnic neighborhoods are the residential home sites for white-collar workers. Only the major Russian foreign-born neighborhood shows an overrepresentation in as many as three white-collar occupational categories. The Irish and German neighborhoods show a slight excess in one white-collar occupational category, that of clerical workers. For the most part, the breakthrough into white-collar jobs has been experienced in proportions greater than expected by only three of the six ethnic groups, and by two of these three in only a limited way. Finally, it may be said that one-half to twice as many laborers as expected are located in the Polish, Italian, and Negro neighborhoods.

The analysis of housing characteristics reveals that the Irish, German, Polish, Italian, and Negro sections of the city are similar in many respects but that a greater proportion of home owners live in the Irish and German sections than is true of the other neighborhoods mentioned. It may be recalled that of these same five ethnic groups, the Irish and German neighborhoods are the only two in which there is an overrepresentation of white-collar workers. Highest family income in the city is found in the major Russian neighborhood located toward the city periphery. Median family income in the Irish and German neighborhoods is similar and also lower than median income in the larger Russian neighborhood. The family income in the Irish and German neighborhoods is almost 15 percent higher than the median income of families in the major Polish and Italian neighborhoods and upwards to 45 percent higher than median family income in the Negro neighborhood. It is suggested (since these data do not warrant a conclusive judgment) that increase in home ownership among residents of Russian, Irish, and German neighborhoods is a function of values associated with level of employment or job prestige and higher family income rather than due to unique subcultural customs of each ethnic group. The behavior of home ownership, existing in association with higher family income and greater employment in the white-collar occupations, is found among three populations of different religious ethnicity — Russian foreign-born predominantly Jewish, Irish foreign-born predominantly Roman Catholic, and German foreign-born predominantly Protestant. Also, it is evident that these three ethnic groups have different national heritages. Notwithstanding these differences in religious as well as national ethnicity, similar behavior with reference to home buying occurs when there tends to be similar circumstances of income and employment.

In the final portion of this chapter the conditions and characteristics of each ethnic neighborhood are described. The Irish settlement is on the West Side of the city. It is a small neighborhood of seven-tenths of a square mile located in census tracts 27, 28, and 29, an average of 1.81 miles from the city center. Most of it is located on land of lower elevation, from 415 to 460 feet above sea level. However, one section of the Irish neighborhood known as Tipperary Hill rises as high as approximately 565 feet above sea level. This is an extremely old section of the city. Its settlement dates back before the days of Syracuse incorporation in 1825. In fact, James Geddes had salt boiling works in this section near Onondaga Lake when the nineteenth century began. The lower portions of the Irish neighborhood lie along the glacial cross-channel in the western division of Syracuse. Through this neighborhood was laid West Genesee Turnpike. It also bordered the Erie Canal and now touches West Erie Boulevard (Route 5) and the New York Central Railway. Mixed residential and business land use comprise the lower portion of the Irish neighborhood, parts of which extend to the city limits on the West Side. In general, the neighborhood is of below average socioeconomic status according to the composite socioeconomic index, although some sections of the neighborhood such as the Tipperary Hill area are above the city average. The total neighborhood spreads into socioeconomic areas IV and V. It is heavily populated, there being close to 12,000 persons per square mile. Of all Irish foreign-born in Syracuse, 18 percent live in the Irish neighborhood. However, Irish-foreign-born represent only 3 percent of the neighborhood's total population.

The German neighborhood is found on the North Side of Syracuse in census tracts 4, 6, 7, and 8, east of Onondaga Lake. A portion of it extends to the city periphery. This neighborhood is 4.77 square miles in size and is located about 1.51 miles from the central business district. Land elevation varies from approximately 495 feet in the early settled sections of this neighborhood to 520 feet above sea level toward the city periphery. A portion of this neighborhood is the site of one of the earliest communities, the village of Salina later annexed to Syracuse. Salina Village existed on an economy of salt production and had a street plan long before the swamp area (later to become the center of Syracuse) was drained. Because of the hilly nature of this neighborhood there are few business establishments and thus it is designated as a section of residential properties only. One major thoroughfare — Grant Boulevard running east and west, enabling traffic to by-pass the downtown section — dissects the neighborhood. However, it is not an industrial arterial route. Schiller Park is another major landmark of the area. The socioeconomic status level of the neighborhood is below average, although some sections — particularly the sites of higher elevation near the city periphery — carry a socioeconomic status score that is above the city average. Included in the German neighborhood are sections of socioeconomic areas IV and V. The neighborhood is populated in a rather dense way; there are 12,467 individuals per square mile. Actually the density is even greater because a good portion of the liveable space is decreased by the presence of Schiller Park and Woodlawn Cemetery, which were included in the square mileage count for the total neighborhood. Of all German foreign-born in Syracuse, 25 percent live within the ethnic neighborhood. They constitute 4 percent of the neighborhood's total population.

The Polish community is distributed in two separate neighborhoods. The major Polish neighborhood is northwest of the city center on the North Side near Onondaga Lake and spills over into the adjacent West End section on the city's West Side. This neighborhood consists of six census tracts, 11, 12, 20, 21, 22, and 30, approximately two square miles in area and is around one and one-quarter miles from the city center. The second Polish area is a small neighborhood of four-tenths of a square mile encompassed in one census tract — number 25. It, too, is on the North Side, but it is not adjacent to the larger Polish section. This smaller neighborhood is approximately 1.58 miles from the downtown section, northeast. Both neighborhoods are in older sections of the city, the larger one covering the flat lands at the mouth of Onondaga Lake into which the Barge Canal terminal extends. The land in this section is less than 400 feet above sea level; it accommodates industries, warehouses, and arterial routes such as West Erie Boulevard, West Genesee Street, and the New York Central Railroad. This same railroad passes through the smaller Polish neighborhood to the east. Also East Erie Boulevard borders this second Polish neighborhood northeast of the downtown section. Burnet Avenue going east and Teall Avenue running north are other major routes to and through the smaller Polish neighborhood, which has as its most outstanding landmark Lincoln Park, the summit of which is more than 600 feet above sea level. There are some residential properties on the slope ascending to this park. Hence the smaller Polish neighborhood to the northeast consists of great variations in land elevation. Down near the canal it formerly bordered, 400 to 420 feet elevations are common along this glacial cross-channel. As one moves in a northerly direction toward Lincoln Park, homes are built on higher sites. Most of tract 25, however, is along the older settled section near Burnet Avenue and Erie Boulevard, a section quite similar to the larger Polish neighborhood northwest of the city center. In fact, the major portions of both neighborhoods of the Polish community are so similar that each of them is classified as an area of mixed residential and business land usage. Both neighborhoods are old; at least half of the dwellings in their census tracts were erected before the 1880s and 1870s. The lowest socioeconomic scores for any ethnic neighborhoods are found in these two. This is largely because of the 100 percent existence of mixed residential and industrial land use in these areas. The Polish neighborhoods are located exclusively in socioeconomic area VI. The presence of many nonresidential properties in these two sections is indicated by their sparce populations. Only seven to eight thousand persons per square mile live herein. But dwelling units are largely multiple-family structures and each structure, therefore, presents a higher population density per liveable space than is represented by the measure given above. When the two Polish sections are combined it is seen that 54 percent of all Polish foreign-born in Syracuse live in the ethnic nationality neighborhoods. This number of Polish foreign-born represents 8 percent of the total population in the Polish areas.

A third neighborhood on the North Side of the city is that of the Italian foreign-born. It is completely enclosed and does not extend to the city limits at any point. Seven census tracts — 5, 7, 12, 13, 14, 23, and 24 — are situated between the Polish and German neighborhoods covering an area of 1.23 square miles at an average distance of eight-tenths of a mile from the central business district. The land is mostly flat and ranges from 373 feet upwards to 495 feet in some residential sections but never exceeding a height of 500 feet above sea level. The flat lands are used extensively for industrial works and commercial travel. Less than a quarter of the Italian neighborhood is devoted exclusively to residential land use. U. S. Highway 11 passing along North Salina Street is a major north-south travel route that passes through the Italian neighborhood. It is a modern version of the Onondaga Valley land route traversed by the Iroquoi Indians into the Allegheny Plateau scores of years ago. The Oswego Canal, dug during the first half of the nineteenth century, wound its way through the Italian section to connect up with the Erie Canal. Today Oswego Boulevard fills in the bed of the old canal. Other principal travel routes through this area are Lodi, Court, and Park Streets. With mention of such old landmarks, one might deduce that the Italian neighborhood covers a very old section of the city. This deduction is correct. While some portions border Erie Boulevard through which the completed canal passed in 1825, other sections extend over the territory formerly a part of the village of Salina, the salt town to the north that was settled before Syracuse. Actually, Division Street in the Italian neighborhood was a border between Syracuse and Salina during the years of great competition between these two settlements as they grew against each other. Hence, 1866 is the median year of dwelling unit construction in the Italian neighborhood. In terms of status level, the socioeconomic index score is low, almost one standard deviation below the city average. The neighborhood extends into socioeconomic areas V and VI only. Even with a good portion of this section devoted to industrial and commercial usage, the population density is high. There are 17,265 persons to every square mile in the Italian neighborhood. Of all Italian foreign-born in the city, 43 percent reside in the ethnic neighborhood. They constitute 14 percent of the total population in the Italian section.

On the East Side of the city are neighborhoods of two ethnic groups — Negroes and Jews. Like the Italian section, the Negro neighborhood is completely enclosed with no outlet to the city periphery. It is located on the Lower East Side in four census tracts — 32, 33, 34, and 42 — that encompass an area of 3.41 square miles that is eight-tenths of a mile from the center of the city. This is an old section of the city just east of the downtown Walton Tract, in which were erected some of the first homes in the community known today as Syracuse. The median year of dwelling construction for the area is 1855. It was settled largely after the swamp drainage project of the 1820s. Most of the land is flat, ranging between 400 and 415 feet above sea level. In the yesterdays, this section extended to the bank of the Erie Canal; and through this neighborhood passed East Genesee Turnpike, too. The New York Central Railroad was once routed through this section over Washington Street. So the Negro neighborhood at one time existed beside the railroad tracts. Since South Salina is the major downtown street, heavy truck traffic over the north-south Route 11 is diverted to South State Street through the Negro neighborhood when Route 11 approaches the theatre and retail district on South Salina Street. Almost three-quarters of the Negro section, then, are an admixture of business and residential properties. The City Hall, County Court House, and one of the first public low-rent housing developments in Syracuse are located here. The socioeconomic status index score is low for the total neighborhood; it is below the city average, although not the lowest in the city. The Negro neighborhood primarily of socioeconomic areas V and VI extends into one census tract in area IV. In this Lower East Side neighborhood is found the highest population density in the city. There are 25,215 persons per square mile. And one might guess that an even greater density would be measured were the space devoted to nonresidential properties subtracted from the area's total square mileage. In this ethnic area live 95 percent of all Negroes in Syracuse. They constitute one-fifth of the area's total population.

The Jewish community is identified in this study by the presence of Russian foreign-born. This community exists in two separate and different East Side neighborhoods. The older neighborhood on the Lower East Side overlaps portions of the section heavily populated by Negroes. The lower East Side Jewish neighborhood is found in census tracts 33, 42, and 43. This area is seven-tenths of a square mile in size and is an average of nine-tenths of a mile from the central business district. Much of the land in this neighborhood is flat, averaging 400 to 415 feet above sea level. However, in the most distant section of this neighborhood (in relation to the city center) it rises to an estimated height of 490 feet above sea level. About 60 percent of this ethnic area is of mixed residential and business usage, with only 40 percent devoted exclusively to residential properties. Like the adjacent Negro neighborhood, this is an old section of old properties, most of which were erected before the turn of the century. It is also densely settled with 22,048 persons per square mile and has a below average rating on the socio-economic status index, extending into areas IV, V, and VI only. In contrast with this older Jewish neighborhood on the Lower East Side is the more recently settled Jewish neighborhood on the periphery of the city's East Side. It spreads through Scottholm, Salt Springs, and Bradford Hills sections in census tracts 35, 36, 46, and 47, covering an area of 2.35 square miles and located at an average distance of 2.60 miles from the center of the city. This section of the city is relatively new in comparison with the Lower East Side Jewish neighborhood. The median year of dwelling construction is 1924. Most of the dwellings are single-family type homes erected on sites of varying elevation most of which are higher than 500 feet, while some points in the Bradford Hills section rise above a level of 600 feet. The socio-economic status level of this neighborhood is high. Its status index score is about one and one-half standard deviations above the city average and there are less than 5,000 persons per square mile in this neighborhood. Nearly one-third of all Russian foreign-born persons in Syracuse live in the old lower East Side Jewish neighborhood, and approximately 28 percent of all Russian foreign-born live in this more recently settled Jewish neighborhood. When totals for the two neighborhoods are combined, it is observed that roughly 60 percent of all Russian foreign-born in the city live in Jewish neighborhoods. They represent about 4 percent of the total population in these neighborhoods. It is clear from this analysis that the larger Jewish neighborhood on the far East Side is not only unlike its companion neighborhood on the Lower East Side but is very much unlike any of the other ethnic neighborhoods considered in this analysis.

Summary

In Syracuse, there are seven ethnic groups in which are found more than 1,000 persons of foreign birth. Negroes constitute the eighth major ethnic group. Of the total city population, 10 percent is foreign-born, 2 percent is Negro, and less than 1 percent is of nonwhite persons other than Negro. A large majority of foreign-born come from Europe, and the second highest percentage come from non-French-speaking sections of Canada. Very few foreign-born come from Central or South America, Asia, Africa, or Australia. Persons born in England and in non-French-speaking Canada tend not to settle and live in distinct subcultural neighborhoods in Syracuse. Hence, only six of the larger ethnic groups are considered in this study. They are, in order of increasing degree of segregation by neighborhoods, the Irish, German, Russian, Polish, and Italian foreign-born, and Negroes. Most of the Russian foreign-born in Syracuse are Jewish. They populate two different neighborhoods, as do the Polish foreign-born. One of the Jewish neighborhoods is of more recent formation than the other. Both Polish neighborhoods are similar. Most ethnic neighborhoods are located in older sections of the city, excepting one of the Jewish areas. Another common characteristic among the ethnic neighborhoods is that a majority of their dwellings are in multiple-family structures. This is true of all ethnic neighborhoods except the recently settled Jewish neighborhood and the German neighborhood, where there is no mixed residential and business land use as occurs in neighborhoods of the other four ethnic groups. Home ownership is higher in Irish and German neighborhoods and in the newer Jewish neighborhood. There are also more white-collar employees in these three neighborhoods and fewer laborers than expected. This is a fundamental difference between the Irish, German, and larger Jewish neighborhoods and neighborhoods of the other three ethnic groups. Excluding the two Jewish neighborhoods, the greater similarities in occupation occur among the skilled and semiskilled workmen, all of whom are represented in proportions greater than expected in Irish, German, Polish, and Italian neighborhoods. Semiskilled workers are overrepresented in the Negro neighborhood, too, but not so for craftsmen, foremen, and other skilled employees. An overrepresentation of laborers is seen in the Negro, Italian, and Polish sections.

The Jewish community is distributed in a unique manner. It is distributed in two separate and different neighborhoods. In general, the less segregated an ethnic group the more of its foreign-born lived outside the ethnic neighborhood. However, the Jewish community is less segregated than Italian and Polish communities. Nevertheless, more Russian foreign-born live within the Jewish neighborhood than is true of the proportion of Italian and Polish foreign-born who live within their respective ethnic neighborhoods. An explanation lies in the fact that there are two Jewish neighborhoods of differential socioeconomic status. And while the process of dispersion was taking place another process of concentration appears to have been in operation. For the other ethnic groups such as the Polish, Italian, Irish, and German, dispersion of foreign-born has not been accompanied by a concentrating process for the same group elsewhere. Another significant fact, ecologically, is that more than 90 percent of all Negroes in this community live within the ethnic neighborhood on the Lower East Side.

The six ethnic groups form distinct neighborhoods. On the North Side are three — Polish, Italian, and German sections. The Italian neighborhood is positioned between the Polish and German neighborhoods and partially overlaps the two. The Irish neighborhood is located on the West Side of the city. And the Negro section as well as the two Jewish neighborhoods share the East Side. The Lower East Side accommodates the overlapping older Jewish and Negro neighborhoods while the more recently settled Jewish neighborhood near the periphery and along the city limits of the East Side stands alone, unlike any other ethnic neighborhood in the city.

It has been suggested in this analysis that the effects of ethnic culture may be secondary to other divisions of social organization in relation to some forms of learned behavior. For example, among three ethnic groups of different nationality, heritage and religious persuasion, the behavior of home ownership is similar for Irish, German, and Russian foreign-born in which a higher proportion than expected are employed in white-collar jobs and have family income from medium to high. The extent to which occupational status and family income are more importantly related to forms of behavior other than home buying is not determined.

The delineation of ethnic neighborhoods is thought to be useful for purposes of ecological analysis. The investigation, however, is limited in that data available on ethnicity, excepting race, are restricted to foreign-born persons only. Specific foreign-born or racial ethnic groups never represent a majority of the population in an ethnic neighborhood. Nevertheless, ethnic neighborhoods are delineated on the assumption that many second and third generations of foreign-born groups live in the same neighborhood in varying numbers and, therefore, perpetuate the unique ethnic culture. This unproved assumption places some limitation on the utility of ethnic neighborhoods as presently identified.

CHAPTER 5

Theoretical Implications:
Individuals, Groups, and Their Environments

It is appropriate to begin the theoretical assessment of the association among race, ethnicity, and socioeconomic status with a discussion based on ecological studies. These are studies of the community context — both physical and social.

Several scientists have emphasized the value of contextual analysis. We know that individual behavior and group behavior are influenced by settings and circumstances. Whitehead states that events happen in space and time; thus, the two are interconnected [Whitehead 1957:124].

Beyond these aspects of nature, norms of social organization condition behavior. George Peter Murdock states that "most people show in marked degree an awareness of their ... cultural norms, ... including the circumstances ... considered appropriate and the sanctions ... for nonconformity" [Murdock 1951:95]. This finding led to the conclusion that culture is integrative, that "the elements of a given culture tend to form a consistent and integrative whole" [Murdock 1951:96]. Robert Nisbet calls norms "the common stock of those living within a given culture," the "vital core of culture." He asserts that "all human behavior is normatively directed." Culture is defined as "the total of designs, themes, or ideal types that is to be found in any social aggregate ... that has continuing identity" [Nisbet 1970:222-224]. The structure and process of social organization and its cultural norms are conditioned by their spatial and temporal context.

It is important to examine not only the central tendencies of individual behavior and group behavior, but also their dispersion. Thus, comparison should be not only among norms but also among variations of events around the norm, with neither normative events nor those that vary from the norm classified as more or less important in social organization. Ruth Benedict observed that "the possible human institutions and motives

71

are legion" and that "wisdom consists in a greatly increased tolerance toward their divergencies" [Benedict 1951:101].

A deficiency in sociological analysis especially with reference to the study of race, ethnicity, and socioeconomic status is the tendency to assess the behavior of various groups in relation to a single norm rather than to multiple norms. Usually the norm of the dominant people is used as the ideal type for the total society. While ideal types are helpful ways of summarizing our observations of society, one should recognize that the use of several group-specific ideal types may be required for a proper understanding of a society. In all societies, there are at least two ideal types — that of the dominant people of power and that of the subdominants. Since culture as defined by Nisbet is a composite of ideal types, both dominants and subdominants contribute to the structure and process of social organization. The norms of neither one nor the other may be ignored.

Moreover, one should recognize that specific sectors of a range may be normatively organized in ways that differ from the norms of other sectors of the same range. Anglo norms constitute one ideal type in American society; also there are ideal-type norms in other racial and ethnic groups. The other norms, in the words of Benedict, should be studied "with increased tolerance" and not ignored or classified as deviant because of their variation from the requirements of "Anglo conformity" [Gordon 1971:264–283]. Our ecological studies that revealed variations in the medians, means, or modes of age of the population, year of dwelling unit construction, and land elevation by socioeconomic status areas are evidence of the existence of multiple norms in social organization. Neither the norm of area I (highest in status) nor that of area VI (lowest in status) should be classified as deviant. Each socioeconomic area serves a unique function in the scheme of community organization. The various areas with different norms are interdependent.

Another major deficiency in the sociological studies of race, ethnicity, and socioeconomic status is the focus almost exclusively on social structure, ignoring social process. Contextual analysis emphasizes time and space as interconnected. In this respect the study of social process is as essential in understanding intergroup relations as the study of social structure. We tend to focus on social structure because Anglo conformity or conformity to any dominant-group ethos as an ideal type emphasizes order [Higham 1971]. However, T. Dunbar Moodie states that "human action is, ... characteristically, a response to exigencies in the context of one or more symbolic universes which are available to the consciousness of the individual as a result of socialization" [Moodie 1976:127]. Further, he states that "when ...

'habitual' action proves ineffective in meeting the exigency, a new process of articulation, goal-formation and action may take place." Finally, he believes that "the existence of 'established patterns of interaction' ... are obviously crucial to sociology. However, if we overlook ... the fact that reciprocity of expectation is often problematic, we attribute to 'institutions' an unchanging existence which they simply do not have" [Moodie 1976: 127]. Moodie reminds us that "events defined as action responses to articulated exigencies make up the substance of all human conduct. Hence any 'analytical' distinction between social status and social dynamics will lead to false deductions for sociological explanation" [Moodie 1976:135].

We may be inclined to focus on structure and ignore process or change because the latter demonstrates transiency and consequently our vulnerability, especially that of controlling dominants. Richard Korn claims that in the end "[the bigot] can be saved only by those who survived the worst he could do to them — his victims" [Korn 1968:196], which is another way of saying that dominants ultimately are dependent on subdominants. According to S. N. Eisenstadt, "the systemic nature of social life implies that all ... groups are to some extent interdependent and that the changes in any one of them may, at certain points, impinge on others," despite their relative autonomy [Eisenstadt 1968:xxiv]. The ecological studies of socioeconomic and ethnic populations in time and space, therefore, enable us to understand the interactive aspects of social structure and social process.

The clustering of a racial or ethnic group in a ghetto community that is physically delimited and relatively isolated from the dominant group is both a function of the unique characteristics and needs of the specific group and the way the group is perceived by others. George Bernard Shaw's character Eliza Doolittle discovered "the difference between a flower girl and a lady is not so much how she acts but how she is treated." My modified version of her statement is that "the difference between ... social classes and races in society is how they act as well as how they are treated" [Willie 1981a:220].

That racial and ethnic groups tend to inhabit central city neighborhoods initially is probably due to the characteristics of such groups and such neighborhoods. Such neighborhoods tend to be places of early settlement where the houses are older. There is a greater probability that the maintenance of such structures will be inadequate and therefore may be bought or rented at prices that are lower than elsewhere in the city. The age level of the adult members of ethnic groups that initially populate inner-city neighborhoods is in the younger range. Their occupational skills tend to be limited to blue-collar, clerical, or semiprofessional occupations that receive less pay than the professional and managerial white-collar occupations. The central city neighborhoods tend to be settings where housing is sought even by younger adult offspring of the dominant-group members when they first establish independent households. In this respect, the offspring of dominant families are not very different from households of racial and ethnic minority groups in terms of place of residence at the beginning of adulthood. Thus, it is fair to conclude that inner-city neighborhoods probably serve the needs of both immigrant and Anglo families when adults in these families are young.

However, the ecological studies revealed that, in time, most individuals are upwardly mobile, that their mobility is reflected by movement to a neighborhood characterized by a socioeconomic status level that is higher than the one in which the household lived initially. How the members of each group adapt to their changing needs and experiences probably depends, in large measure, on the way each group is perceived and reacted to by others.

Clearly, the group with an Anglo heritage perceived the Irish, German, Jewish, Italian, Polish, and Afro-American populations as having differing characteristics and reacted in accordance with these perceptions. Nathan Glazer and Daniel Moynihan claimed that the German immigrants were certainly much closer to the old Americans than were the Irish who arrived in the same period. Many Germans were Protestant, were skilled workers or even members of the professions. All of this greatly facilitated German assimilation [Glazer and Moynihan 1971:295]. Our ecological studies revealed that when German immigrants left the ethnic ghetto, they tended to distribute themselves throughout the community without further concentration.

The Irish and Jewish populations were perceived as differing significantly from the Anglo heritage in terms of religious tradition. Although the occupational skills that members of these two groups developed enabled them in time to become upwardly mobile in socioeconomic status, their social mobility was restricted largely to neighborhoods of higher status where other ethnic-group members resided. Thus, mobility of Irish and Jewish populations was facilitated by expanding their ghettoes to include higher status neighborhoods toward the city periphery and on sites of higher elevation adjacent to the old ethnic areas. Irish and Jewish people probably would have distributed themselves more or less randomly throughout the city if there had not been barriers to such movement.

Certainly blacks who are closer to Anglos in religious tradition and language would have distributed themselves more or less randomly throughout the city, as did German Protestants, if they had not been prevented from such action. The black experience, however, has differed from that of the Anglo and the other ethnic groups of European national heritage. Its members grew older but did not obtain better jobs at rates similar to those for individuals in German, Irish, and Jewish populations. Even when blacks eventually obtained better jobs, they were prohibited from moving to higher status neighborhoods as was customary for others in the total population. The black ghetto did not expand to higher status areas as did the Irish and Jewish ghettoes. These facts have resulted in Karl Taeuber and Alma Taeuber classifying blacks as the most segregated minority group in the United States [Taeuber and Taeuber 1969:68]. They state that "the net effect of economic factors in explaining residential segregation is slight" for blacks, compared with other groups. In other words, "improving the economic status of Negroes is unlikely by itself to alter prevailing patterns of racial residential segregation" [Taeuber and Taeuber 1969:94, 95].

Thus, the black experience in the United States has been remarkably different from that of the other groups studied. None has been contained as rigidly as blacks. While there is differentiation by socioeconomic status within the black community, all levels have been forced to live together. The black experience is fundamentally different from the experience of social stratification by residence for other groups. Different socioeconomic strata in other groups, including Anglos, have tended to separate from their group members, with each status level isolating itself geographically from other levels of unlike kind.

One consequence of the congregating of blacks of all socioeconomic status levels within the same neighborhood is this: Blacks have retained the welfare of the black community as the central concern of all blacks. Black leadership has not been able to fractionate into representatives of economic, political, or other institutional interests. Whether poor or affluent, learned or unlettered, the central concerns of black leaders are "those associated with problems of interracial relations and the effects of minority group status, and more specifically, with attempts to change the existing social structure of the community" [Barth and Abu-Laban 1970:386-387]. In summary, it is characteristic of black leaders to be deeply concerned with "race betterment" rather than individual enhancement. Most black leaders in the ecologically identifiable community have been involved in a range of activities toward this end including protest organizations [Barth and Abu-Laban 1970:388].

On the basis of this and other findings, I have developed a theory about the circumstances and conditions associated with the increasing power of subdominant populations to press for institutional reform: "A subdominant population is likely to intensify its press for ... action with reference to equal access and equitable distribution of community resources when it grows in numbers from a small minority to a large minority, and when it changes socioeconomically from a homogeneous to a heterogeneous population. Essentially, the size of a subdominant population and its socioeconomic differentiation are interrelated phenomena that determine the pattern of its press for social action." I further point out that "if blacks were dispersed throughout the nation without discrimination, they would constitute not more than 11 percent of the total population in any locality. Under these conditions their relative strength in numbers would be below the critical mass of approximately one-fifth that is necessary to mount effective campaigns for ... reform against community institutions practicing racial segregation and discrimination" [Willie 1981b:131]. In the days of slavery, blacks were about one-fifth of the nation, were clustered on plantations, but were not diversified economically. They, therefore, could not mount and sustain a rebellion.

Given these unique experiences, the black population in cities has developed different strategies of leadership and different community norms while continuing to participate in the normative system or the common core of values of the community at large [Willie 1981b:218]. Blacks in particular have an appreciation of diversity, are more inclined to be inclusive than other groups because of their ghetto existence that has lumped all sorts and conditions of people together. Blacks know from experience that there is strength in diversity [Willie 1981c:3–14]. Despite the continuing push toward Anglo conformity in the United States, blacks now are beginning to affirm their unique norms as something of value for the nation. Figuratively, they say the nation is better if it looks like a salad bowl rather than the product of a melting pot. They appear to be on firm ground in terms of the wisdom of the humanities and scientific theory. In 1856, Ralph Waldo Emerson wrote, "It need not puzzle us that Maldy and Papuan, Celt and Roman, Saxon and Tartar should mix. ... The best nations are those most widely related ..." [quoted in Higham 1971:220]. Theodosius Dobzhansky, a famous American geneticist, said that "a species [is] polymorphic if it contains a variety of genotypes, each of which is superior in adaptive value to the others in some habitats which occur regularly in the territory occupied by the species," and that a "polymorphic population [is] in general, more efficient in the exploitation of ecological opportunities of an environment than genetically uniform ones" [Dobzhansky 1951:132–133].

While acknowledging that our society has a common core of values, this discussion also identifies diversity as something of value. Moreover, it has pointed out the importance of recognizing multiple ideal types in a common culture, especially those of dominant and subdominant populations, and their unique norms that have emerged through interactive experiences of social structure and social process. The efforts of ethnic and racial minority groups to resist the push toward Anglo conformity have been endorsed as ultimately benefiting the total society in that a polymorphic population is more capable of exploiting environmental opportunities. Finally, the discussion indicates that subdominant populations probably have achieved a greater sense of community than dominant populations; and dominant populations probably have achieved a greater sense of personal success than individuals in subdominant groups. The subdominants of various status groups within the socioeconomic structure cooperate with each other for group survival while dominants tend to separate from others of dissimilar status groups for the purpose of achieving individual fulfillment. Dominants tend to sacrifice the benefits of collective support in their drive for upward social mobility. Subdominants limit their range of personal fulfillment by promoting the integrity of their group. Social advancement and personal enhancement are interrelated and so are dominant and subdominant populations. They have something to teach each other and, therefore, are complementary.

References

Barth, Ernest A. T., and Baha Abu-Laban. 1970. "Power Structure and the Negro Sub-Community." In *The Structure of Community Power*. New York: Random House, pp. 381–388. First published in 1959.

Benedict, Ruth. 1951. "The Diversity of Culture." In Robert W. O'Brien, Clarence C. Schrag, and Walter T. Martin (eds.), *Readings in Sociology*. Boston: Houghton Mifflin, pp. 96–101. First published in 1934.

Dobzhansky, Theodosius. 1951. *Genetics and the Origin of Species*. New York: Columbia University Press.

Eisenstadt, S. N. 1968. *Comparative Perspectives on Social Change*. Boston: Little, Brown.

Glazer, Nathan, and Daniel P. Moynihan. 1971. "Beyond the Melting Pot." In Norman R. Yetman and C. Hoy Steele (eds.), *Majority and Minority*. Boston: Allyn and Bacon, pp. 283–298. First published in 1963.

Gordon, Milton M. 1971. "Assimilation in America: Theory and Reality." In Norman R. Yetman and C. Hoy Steele (eds.), *Majority and Minority*. Boston: Allyn and Bacon, pp. 261–283. First published in 1961.

Higham, John. 1971. "Toward Racism: The History of an Idea." In Norman R. Yetman and C. Hoy Steele (eds.), *Majority and Minority*. Boston: Allyn and Bacon, pp. 230–252.

Korn, Richard R. 1968. *Juvenile Delinquency*. New York: Crowell.

Moodie, T. Dunbar. 1976. "Social Order as Social Change: Towards a Dynamic Conception of Social Order." In George K. Zollschan and Walter Hirsch (eds.), *Social Change*. Cambridge, MA: Schenkman, pp. 123–138.

Murdock, George Peter. 1951. "Uniformities in Culture." In Robert W. O'Brien, Clarence C. Schrag, and Walter T. Martin (eds.), *Readings in General Sociology*. Boston, Houghton Mifflin, pp. 93–96. First published in 1940.

Nisbet, Robert A. 1970. *The Social Bond*. New York: Knopf.

Taeuber, Karl E., and Alma F. Taeuber. *Negroes in Cities*. New York: Atheneum.

Whitehead, Alfred North. 1957. *The Concept of Nature*. Ann Arbor: University of Michigan Press.

Willie, Charles V. 1981a. *A New Look at Black Families*. 2nd ed. Bayside, NY: General Hall.

_____.1981b. "The Demographic Basis of Urban Educational Reform." In Adam Yamolinsky, Lance Liebman, and Corinne S. Schelling (eds.), *Race and Schooling in the City*. Cambridge, MA: Harvard University Press, pp. 126–135.

_____.1981c. *The Ivory and Ebony Towers*. Lexington, MA: Lexington Books of D. C. Heath.

CHAPTER 6

The President's Commission on Mental Health —
A Minority Report on Minorities

On February 17, 1977, President Jimmy Carter established the President's Commission on Mental Health that consisted of 20 persons. The Commission was asked to "identify the mental health needs of the Nation" and was authorized by Executive Order to conduct "public hearings, inquiries and studies" that may be necessary for the purpose of identifying these needs. To inform the Commission about ways of achieving these goals, public hearings were held in the Eastern and Western regions of this nation.

At our organizing meeting in the White House, Julius B. Richmond, a member of the Commission, later appointed Surgeon General and Assistant Secretary of the Department of Health, Education and Welfare, reflected the attitudes of other commissioners when he said, "We want the people to give testimony at our hearings and to know that what they say will be taken seriously." This is not an antiprofessional perspective. It is a recognition that health is a community affair and cannot be limited to the wisdom of professionals, although what they have to say is important and must be weighed and considered.

On the basis of several hearings throughout the nation and material presented to us by several task panels of the nation's foremost mental health authorities and volunteers interested in health, we arrived at these and other conclusions about mental health and minorities.

(1) Unemployment, inadequate education, poor housing, slum community environments, and various forms of institutionalized discrimination

Reprinted from *New England Sociologist,* Volume 1, (Fall, 1978), pp. 13–22. The author was Professor of Education and Urban Studies, Harvard Graduate School of Education, at the time this chapter was published. He served on the President's Commission on Mental Health by the appointment of President Jimmy Carter.

such as sexism, racism, and elitism are stress-producing circumstances and also are barriers to the provision of effective service. They are associated with variations in the incidence and prevalence of mental disorders by population groups, and therefore must be dealt with in any effective program of prevention.

(2)   Recent immigrants, poor people, older people, racial and ethnic minorities, and women are high-risk populations for the development of mental disorders because of their exposure to extraordinary stress, their lack of opportunity to participate in and gain a measure of control over their social environment, because of the absence of sufficient institutional and community supports that sustain them during periods of difficulty, and because of their experience of cross pressures due to contradictory role expectations.

(3)   Priorities for mental health programs vary by cultural groups and majority or minority status in society. For example, one group may emphasize intervention among individuals, while another may focus on institutions. One group may emphasize prevention over treatment, while another group may have the reverse set of priorities. It is important to recognize these different sets of priorities as valid and real. They are based on the varying existential histories of groups, their social locations in society, and the varying ways in which society has adapted to the groups. A common error in planning and in the making of policy for mental health and other public enterprises is to project the interests and needs of the dominant people of power upon those with less power. Thus, the interests and needs of men are projected upon women. The interests and needs of adults are projected upon children and adolescents. The interests and needs of the white majority are projected upon black and brown minorities. The interests and needs of professionals are projected upon the consuming public. When this is done, both plans and policies often are too limited to meet the requirements of all situations.

(4)   Various therapies are needed to reach people in varying social locations in society. Because specific populations have differentially developed capacities for verbal communication, a variety of approaches are needed to establish contact and a relationship, such as music, art, and dance therapies. Words are wonderful; but they are not the only means of communication.

(5)   Community support groups can help relieve anxiety and generate sufficient trust and confidence to face new problems and difficult experiences. Such groups enable people to cope with danger and should be recognized for their therapeutic effect in enabling people to do that which

they could not do alone. Alcoholics Anonymous, and Overeaters Anonymous are examples of such groups. There are these and many more that support and sustain individuals and give them the strength to deal with their personal difficulties. They sometimes enable people to accept the more formal therapies.

(6) Definition of the intervention unit for the purpose of rendering mental health care must be expanded to include collectivities as well as individuals, if prevention as well as treatment is to be accomplished. This conclusion is based on evidence that the family is a place of much strife and even some violence, that institutionalized discrimination fractionates society and contributes to group hostility and hate, and that premature mortality such as found in many minority groups and among the poor often results in severe stress for the survivors. Intervention, particularly for secondary and tertiary prevention, should focus on groups as well as individuals.

(7) Training programs for professional personnel at all levels of the mental health care-giving system must include people who are bilingual and people who have indigenous knowledge of the various racial, ethnic, and other special populations in the society. While professionals who are not members of a particular group may understand the way of life of its members, still such persons may be handicapped in rendering services because members of the special population do not trust the individual or the institution with which one is affiliated. Trust of the care-giving system is engendered when that system includes within it professionals who identify with the group members who are receiving treatment. The members of special populations tend to believe that a care-giving system that is diversified, that has some professionals who identify with the group whose members receive the service — special populations tend to believe that such a system will not place the interests of the institution above those of the patient. Trust is an important component in the mental health care-giving system. The presence of people like oneself contributes to trust.

(8) Institutional practices that some professional mental health personnel believe are necessary and essential for the protection of society as well as the care of mentally disordered patients are on a collision course with what many patients see as an invasion of their freedom and a denial of their constitutional and human rights. Assertions of the right to prescribe treatment deemed to be appropriate in terms of conventional professional standards is countered with assertions of the right to refuse treatment that is described as inappropriate and inhumane by the patient. A philosophical issue is involved in how to resolve institutional and individual rights when they are in contention with each other. In a democratic society, individual

rights take precedence over institutional rights. However, it should be recognized that this exposes the society to certain risks. A society may choose at any time to limit the risk to which its members are exposed. But it cannot do this and remain democratic and open unless the individual whose rights are limited for the sake of others is granted due process and other constitutional safeguards. Because this issue is unresolved and has not been given adequate attention, the President's Commission on Mental Health recommended the establishment of advocacy systems for the representation of mentally disabled individuals. The Commission also recommended that each state should have a "Bill of Rights" for all mentally disabled persons.

Of course, there were other conclusions such as those pertaining to making the service system more responsive. The Commission believed that mental health centers should be able to operate with more flexible catchment areas and a limited number of services that are in keeping with the needs of a local community and its capacity to support certain services.

The Commission strongly emphasized that any national health insurance program for the future should not discriminate against mental illness. To show that it meant business, the Commission recommended that we make an effort in this direction by eliminating the discrimination against mental illness that currently exists in Medicare and Medicaid legislation.

The Commission recommended that we stop the erosion of research that has been permitted to occur and immediately pump new money into mental health studies. Specifically, the Commission recommended that a total of $48 million be added to the research budget of the Alcohol, Drug Abuse, and Mental Health Administration so that by fiscal year 1980 $240.6 million would be available for research. The Commission said that "sufficient and stable funding of mental health research is a key element in generating and developing knowledge" [1978, p. 47]. To demonstrate its belief in the efficacy and necessity of research, the Commission in its 1977 *Preliminary Report* asked the President to propose increases in funding for fiscal year 1979 for research at the National Institute of Mental Health, the National Institute on Alcoholism, and the National Institute on Drug Abuse. "If Congress adopts these proposals, the first step will have been taken toward repairing the damage of the past decade," stated the Commission's *Report* [1978, p. 47]. We reminded the nation, however, that such would be only the first step and that the full amount recommended in the final *Report* is necessary and essential, since private sources provide only 4 percent and state governments only 8 percent of the funds for mental health and behavioral science research [p. 47].

The Commission also recommended that we pay attention to prevention and that we make it a high priority item on the mental health agenda.

So that the prevention of mental illness and promotion of mental health become a visible part of our national life, the Commission recommended the creation of a Center for Prevention to be established in the National Institute of Mental Health and that no less than 10 percent of the NIMH budget within 10 years should be spent on prevention [1978, p. 54]. We know that prevention is close to the heart of the President and that he will give this recommendation serious attention. Our *Preliminary Report* was forwarded to the President in September, 1977. Mrs. Rosalynn Carter, the First Lady, said, "When I gave Jimmy the report, we didn't have a recommendation about prevention, and that was the first thing he asked me" [National Institute of Mental Health, 1977]. Even in the final *Report,* it is clear that the Commission did not arrive at a policy regarding prevention but did set forth a strategy and a mechanism that are manifested in the proposed Center for Prevention.

Obviously the *Report to the President* from the President's Commission on Mental Health is incomplete. Nevertheless, the recommendations set forth, if implemented, can move this nation in a positive and forward direction so that high quality mental health care is available to all who need it [1978, p. 9].

We were able to reach the conclusions that were reached and formulate the proposals that were recommended because we stood on the shoulders of the Joint Commission on Mental Illness and Health and the findings of its 1961 report that recommended, among other things, out-patient community-based services as opposed to in-patient care in large state hospitals.

Perhaps the greatest influence upon the Commission's recommendations came not from the past but from the extraordinary diversity of the Commission itself and the range of people in terms of socioeconomic, racial, ethnic, sex, and patient status who talked to the commissioners about their hopes and fears, and their problems and possibilities.

We have such a great belief in rationality that most of us are inclined to think our way through. We tend to forget that all knowledge is partial. In the field of mental health, the knowledge that professionals have is incomplete unless coupled with the knowledge of consumers of services. It should go without saying that the majority cannot plan effectively without advice, assistance, and input from minorities.

In putting together the 1977–1978 President's Commission on Mental Health, the organizing group believed in the principles of diversity and complementarity and acted upon them in the kinds of persons recommended for membership. First of all, the Commission had persons on it who had experienced patient status in the mental health care-giving system. Their contribution was invaluable and protected all of us from the folly of conjecturing about how it feels to be a patient and then basing our plans and policies upon our conjectures and other fantasies.

The director of the Joint Commission on Mental Illness and Health said that some of its staff and Commission members in 1961 "were a little uncertain as to whether a person from the ghetto, who is depressed or paranoid, was reacting normally to his life situation, or abnormally as compared to the person who might be adjusted and happy in similar surroundings." Because of this "uncertainty," the Joint Commission, according to its director, adhered to "a medical base" model, and believed that "less success" would be experienced if attempts were made to attack broad social issues "such as racism, poverty, and education" [Ewalt 1977, pp. 17, 18, 19].

When the Joint Commission made its report, more than a decade and a half ago, the staff director said its members were aware that "people who are deprived by reason of race or poverty have a higher incidence of all kinds of illness," but it failed to make recommendations regarding these stress-producing circumstances, largely because many of the Commission members and staff "did not feel that improvement of socioeconomic and racial conditions were the domain of preventive psychiatry," although they admitted that the discipline could make a contribution in the area [Ewalt 1977, p. 18].

There was no hesitation on the part of the President's Commission on Mental Health in 1978 to emphatically state that "America's mental health problems cannot be defined only in terms of disabling mental illnesses and identified psychiatric disorders. They must include the damage to mental health associated with unrelenting poverty and unemployment and the institutionalized discrimination that occurs on the basis of race, sex, class, age, and mental or physical handicap" [1978, p. 9]. Moreover, the Commission said that mental health services and programs must focus attention on "the special status of the groups which account for the diversity" in our society [1978, p. 5], and serve these groups in terms of their special needs.

The President's Commission could speak forthrightly on the need to develop programs that counter the effects of institutional discrimination and to refer to these as bonafide preventive approaches in mental health because it had among its members blacks, Hispanics and a Native American. Some of these commissioners had experienced ghetto living at some period in their personal histories and could testify from first-hand experience. It is almost unbelievable that in the past (just a decade and a half ago) a national commission could express uncertainty whether paranoia and depression were abnormal when found among individuals who inhabit a ghetto. The President's Commission knew that paranoia and depression were negative effects among black and brown racial minorities as well as among the white majority. It knew this because one-third of its membership came from these racial minority groups and could tell other Commission members that no one ought to experience conditions that require these adaptations. And it knew this because Commission members listened to the people of all walks of life in four public hearings. Knowledge that isolation, alienation, discrimination, and other forms of arbitrary exclusion are harmful and tend to trouble the emotions and thoughts of individuals is not new. What is new is the acknowledgement by an authoritative commission that these must be seriously considered along with the development of a more responsive service-delivery system, if the goal is to treat as well as prevent mental disorders. This Commission had to say what it said because of what it heard in the public hearings and because of the kinds of people who were members and the kinds of experiences they had had.

It is significant that there was no minority report to the final *Report* of the President's Commission on Mental Health in 1978. This was largely because, in my judgment, the minority report became the majority report. This is as it should have been. Sociologist Robert Merton has said, "... it is not infrequently the case that the nonconforming minority in a society represents the interests and ultimate values of the group more effectively than the conforming majority" [Merton 1968, p. 421].

The President's Commission endorsed unequivocally the principle that services ought to be rendered on a population-specific basis. Each minority group ought to be helped to deal with those unique experiences that are troubling to the thoughts and emotions of its members. The members of the President's Commission came to the conclusion that population-specific services was the more appropriate strategy after hearing how different are the problems that specific groups encounter. For example:

A Chicano person said that the "traditional medical model has only a limited approach to mental health problems when unemployment, low income, and other social problems are involved." He said that "minorities need a measure of control over their lives rather than endless talk therapies."

An Asian-American said, "Recent immigrants appear to be a high-risk population." He said that "any treatment program for mental disorders among recent immigrants could not be effective without a major training program to increase the number of bilingual mental health personnel."

A black physician said that "a major problem for minorities has resulted from racism, sexism, and classism ... [that in some states there are] more black youths in institutions than [there are] in colleges and universities."

A person from Alaska said that "suicide and alcoholism are reaching epidemic proportions" there.

A West Coast woman said that "women are an endangered group" and that "in and out of the family they suffer sex-role stereotyping."

Because all at some period in life are members of one or more minorities, the minorities who addressed the Commission spoke not only for themselves but for the nation as a whole. To the minorities should go our eternal thanks for causing us to recognize that a population-specific approach is the only approach that will provide the greatest good for the greatest number. Thus, I conclude these remarks with this tribute:

Blessed are the minorities, for they shall fulfill the goals of the majority and thereby save our society.

References

Ewalt, Jack R. 1977. "The Birth of the Community Mental Health Movement." In Walter Barton (ed.), *An Assessment of the Mental Health Movement.* Lexington, MA: Lexington Books.

Joint Commission on Mental Illness and Health. 1961. *Action for Mental Health.* New York: Wiley.

Merton, Robert K. 1968. *Social Theory and Social Structure.* New York: Free Press.

National Institute of Mental Health. 1977. "An Interview with Rosalynn Carter." *Mental Health Matters,* a nationally broadcast radio program.

President's Commission on Mental Health. 1977. *Preliminary Report to the President.* Washington, DC: Public Committee for Mental Health.

President's Commission on Mental Health. 1978. *The Report to the President.* Washington, DC: Government Printing Office.

Washington, Jerome. 1977. "Prison: A Big Business Plays Con Game of Rehabilitation." *Core Magazine,* Winter/Spring.

CHAPTER 7

Racial, Ethnic, and Income Factors
in the Epidemiology of Neonatal Mortality

Charles V. Willie and William Rothney

Evidence on the difference in infant mortality rates between white and nonwhite populations is inconclusive. For example, a report of the National Office of Vital Statistics (from 1949 to 1951 which include the first two years of this study) indicates that the infant mortality rate of 45.5 per 1,000 live births in the nonwhite population is 65 percent greater than the infant mortality rate of 27.7 in the white population of the United States [1]. However, Alfred Yankauer in a 1947 study of the New York City population found that in neighborhoods where more than 75 percent of nonwhite parents reside the neonatal mortality rate of 52.7 per 1,000 live births among nonwhite persons is less than two points greater than the rate of 51.0 among white persons who reside in the same neighborhoods [2]. Clearly, discrepancy exists in the findings of these reports. This discrepancy has not been resolved because studies of variation in infant mortality rates between racial and ethnic populations seldom control adequately for socioeconomic status.

The purpose of this study is to determine whether infant mortality rates, particularly neonatal mortality rates, vary by racial and by ethnic neighborhoods when socioeconomic status is held constant.

Also, the distribution of neonatal mortality is studied in relationship to the distribution of families of varying income levels within racial and ethnic neighborhoods and within the total city. In a previous report, it was pointed out (1) that the distribution of median family income, by census tracts, had only a modest association, intercorrelating at .53, with the distribution of socioeconomic status (consisting of occupation, education, and housing items); and (2) that family income correlated significantly with the distribution of neonatal mortality rates, by census tracts, while the

Reprinted from *American Sociological Review,* Vol. 27, No. 4, August, 1962, pp. 522–525.

socioeconomic status index did not [3]. Thus, it would seem that socioeconomic status as subsequently defined in this study and family income are not interchangeable variables. This study is designed to hold socioeconomic status constant. However, it cannot be assumed that family income is also held constant. A secondary consideration in this investigation, then, is the three-way association, if any, among neonatal mortality, racial or ethnic neighborhood, and family income.

Data and Method

The study area is Syracuse, New York, an industrial city of approximately 25 square miles, with a population of 220,583 persons in 1950. Because of the small numbers of infant deaths that occur during a single year, it is necessary to combine several years. The study utilized data for the years 1950 through 1956 and is limited to the neonatal period, since 80 percent of all infant deaths (excluding stillbirths) occur during the first month of life.

The study includes four racial and ethnic populations in Syracuse — Negro, Native White, Italian, and Polish — that have neighborhoods in the lowest socioeconomic area of the city. The study is limited to these groups that have significant populations in area VI, lowest in the hierarchy of residential areas according to an ecological investigation [4], so that socioeconomic status and age of parents are held relatively constant.

Median age of women in the child-bearing years, 20 to 44, is computed for each racial and ethnic neighborhood. Medians for Negro, Native White, Italian, and Polish populations are 30, 31, 30, and 31 years, respectively. Thus, age of mothers appears to be constant for the four neighborhoods and cannot account for variations, if any, in neonatal mortality rates.

Census tracts are the basic units of analysis. A socioeconomic status score, derived for each census tract, is a composite of five factors representing occupation, education, and housing characteristics of the population. Specifically, the variables are (1) percentage of persons in the combined occupational categories of operatives, service workers, and laborers; (2) median school year completed by the adult population over 25 years of age; (3) average monthly rental; (4) average market value of own homes; and (5) percent of single-family dwelling units. (The first factor is inverted so that it will vary directly with the other four.) All factors in the socioeconomic index, except one indicating house-type, intercorrelate with each other at .80

and above. The Pearsonian correlation coefficients between percent of single-family dwelling units and the other four factors range from .59 to .70. Thus, a significant and high association exists between all variables in the socioeconomic status index. Distributions of all variables are converted into standard scores with assigned means of 100 and assigned standard deviations of 10. Standard scores for the five factors are averaged into a composite socioeconomic score for each census tract, and tracts with similar standard scores are combined into a single socioeconomic area. Six areas incorporating several neighborhoods are delineated; they range from area I, high in socioeconomic status, to area VI, low in socioeconomic status. Composite index scores, for individual census tracts, range from 85 to 123. The average socioeconomic status score for the four racial and ethnic neighborhoods is 92, well below the city assigned mean of 100. A difference of five between the highest and lowest average score of the four neighborhoods, is, of course, not statistically significant at the five percent level of confidence. Thus, socioeconomic status is held constant for all four neighborhoods.

Racial and ethnic neighborhoods are delineated by a method similar to one used by Shevky and Williams to measure ethnic segregation [5]. When the percentage of a racial or ethnic population in a census tract is three or more times greater than the percentage of that population in the total city, a census tract is designated as part of the racial or ethnic neighborhood. This is the method used to identify neighborhoods with high proportions of Italian and Polish foreign born. Data on foreign born only are available in census publications for determining the boundaries of the two ethnic neighborhoods. Because of the high degree of segregation of the Italian and Polish populations (40 to 50 percent of their foreign born are concentrated in identifiable neighborhoods), it is assumed that many second and third generations of these families also lived near their foreign-born kinsmen [6]. The same method is used to delineate the Negro neighborhood. However, the total Negro population is included. The Native White neighborhood consists of those census tracts in socioeconomic area VI, with few Negroes and few foreign born, in which the percentage of Native White is greater than that in the total city population; more than 90 percent of the residents in these census tracts are native born and white.

A few census tracts are eliminated from the study because they are neighborhoods that include two or more racial or ethnic populations in significant numbers. The final study area consists of 15 census tracts, two in the Negro neighborhood, three in the Native White neighborhood, and five each in the Italian and Polish neighborhoods. There are 52,497 persons in these tracts, about one-fourth of all persons in the city. The final study population consists of 8,626 live births and 197 neonatal deaths.

Unless otherwise stated, associations resulting from the statistical analysis are considered significant if they would occur by chance less than 5 times out of 100.

Findings

For the total city, principal causes of death during the neonatal period are congenital malformations, complications associated with prematurity, and injuries at birth [7]. There are 34,700 live births and 658 neonatal deaths in the total city for the seven-year study period, resulting in a neonatal mortality rate of 19 per 1,000 live births.

As seen in Table 7.1, socioeconomic status is fairly similar for all neighborhoods. The neonatal mortality rate for the four racial and ethnic neighborhoods combined is only slightly higher at 23 than the total city rate. By individual neighborhoods, however, there is great variation with the Negro and Native White rates of 32 and 30 respectively, being significantly higher than the rates of 20 and 15, and in that order, in the Italian and Polish neighborhoods. It should be noted that Negro and Native White neighborhoods consisting of two different racial populations have similar, almost identical, rates. At the same time, the neonatal mortality rate in the Native White neighborhood contrasts with and differs significantly from the mortality rates found in neighborhoods populated by white persons of Italian and Polish ancestry.

The analysis, thus far, demonstrates that Negro and Native White populations, though different racially, have similar neonatal mortality rates when socioeconomic status is held constant. Also, it demonstrates that the neonatal mortality rate of white native-born persons in a lower socioeconomic neighborhood differs from rates of other Caucasian populations in neighborhoods of similar socioeconomic status. Because the Native White and Negro neighborhoods with different racial populations have similar rates, and because the neighborhoods of white native born and white foreign born have different rates, though racially similar, doubt is cast upon any hypothesis that racial factors directly contribute to variations in the distribution of neonatal mortality by residential neighborhoods.

Since socioeconomic status as defined in this study and family income are not interchangeable variables, the family finance factor is introduced into the analysis at this point to see if it helps to explain the wide variations in neonatal mortality rates among different neighborhoods. Family income data are reported by census tracts and include the total earnings of all family members in one household for a single year. As seen in Table 7.2, income is unequally distributed among the racial and ethnic populations included in this study. Median family income varies from a low of $1,584 in the Negro neighborhood to a high of $3,121 in the Polish neighborhood. The Italian and Native White populations are second and third, respectively, following

Table 7.1.

Neonatal Mortality Rate Per 1,000 Live Births and Socioeconomic Status by Racial and Ethnic Neighborhoods, Syracuse, 1950–1956

Neighborhood	Live Births	Neonatal Deaths	Mortality Rate	Average Socio-Economic Score[a]
Negro	1,442	46	32	96
Native White[b]	1,749	52	30	91
Italian	3,226	66	20	90
Polish	2,208	33	15	91
Total	8,626	197	23	92

a.   The average socioeconomic status score for the total city is 100. Socioeconomic status is derived from a composite standard score of five variables reflecting occupation, education, and housing characteristics of the population. The composite score ranges from 85 in the census tract of lowest status to 123 in the tract of highest status.

b.   That portion of the neighborhood in the lowest socioeconomic area.

Table 7.2.

Annual Median Income of Family by Racial and Ethnic Neighborhood, Syracuse, 1950

Neighborhood	Median Family Income
Negro	$1,584
Native White[a]	2,101
Italian	2,676
Polish	3,121

a.   That portion of the neighborhood in the lowest socioeconomic area.

the Polish in the hierarchy of annual family income by racial and ethnic neighborhoods.

Using all 15 census tracts in the racial and ethnic neighborhoods, a Spearman rank correlation coefficient was computed because of the small numbers of units in the analysis. For the variables, median family income and neonatal mortality rates, a correlation coefficient of $-.75$ gave definite evidence of a significant negative association. As median family incomes decrease neonatal mortality rates increase. The Negro and Native White populations in the lowest socioeconomic area of the city have similar high neonatal mortality rates notwithstanding their racial difference. It would appear that the similarities in high neonatal mortality rates is explained by the low-income status of families that populate these two neighborhoods. More than half of the families in the combined census tracts of these two neighborhoods received less than $40 per week in 1950. As a contrast, the Polish neighborhood has a low infant mortality rate of 15 and a median family income of $3,121, indicating that half of its families received incomes of $60 per week or more in 1950.

The high association between family income and neonatal mortality found to exist in some neighborhoods of the lowest socioeconomic area is quite different from the association between these two variables throughout the entire city. When family income and neonatal mortality rates were intercorrelated for the remaining 42 census tracts not included in the racial and ethnic neighborhood analysis, the Pearsonian correlation coefficient of $-.06$ was small and obviously not statistically significant. This finding corresponds with a conclusion arrived at in an earlier investigation that the historical association between infant mortality and economic conditions of life is diminishing [8].

Nevertheless, a highly significant association exists between neonatal mortality and family income in part of the city, indicating that a critical income level must exist at some point along the continuum of family finances above which there is little, if any, association and below which there is significant association between neonatal mortality and this economic variable. To determine that critical level, a histogram was constructed, as seen in Figure 7.1 [p. 94]. By median family income, census tracts were grouped into 11 income intervals ranging from $1,500 to $4,500 and over. By inspection, it is seen that $2,700 is the critical level below which there is a regular increase in neonatal mortality rates as the median incomes of families decrease. Above $2,700, fluctuations in the distribution of family income and neonatal mortality rates by census tracts is irregular and insignificant. Illustrating the very definite association between low-income status and neonatal mortality, two census tracts in which half of the families earned less than $1,600 a year in 1950 have mortality rates of 40 or above; these are twice as great as the neonatal mortality rate for the total city.

Conclusions

Under the conditions of this analysis, it may be concluded: (1) that Negro and Native White populations have similar neonatal mortality rates when socioeconomic status is held constant; (2) that Native White populations in lower-income neighborhoods have neonatal mortality rates greater than the rates of white populations in higher income neighborhoods; (3) that neonatal mortality rates are intercorrelated with family income in neighborhoods where at least half of the households receive less than $2,700 per year; and (4) that no association exists between the distribution of neonatal mortality by neighborhoods and family financial status above the critical median income level of $2,700 per year.

The association between infant mortality and economic circumstances of life is diminishing. As with all generalizations, however, the conditions under which a phenomenon will or will not occur should be specified. Our data refine this generalization by indicating that the probability of death during the neonatal period is heightened in neighborhoods where at least half of the families have incomes of less than $2,700 per year. The specific income level, below which the occurrence of neonatal mortality is significantly increased, may vary in time and by region. But the principle of a *critical income level* should persist as long as poverty exists.

While better care of premature children and more skillful handling of mother and child in the delivery room might further reduce the neonatal death rate, the importance of medically attended pregnancies cannot be overemphasized. Although our data do not indicate this, it is quite possible that part of the increased incidence of neonatal mortality among families below the critical income level of $2,700 is due to inadequate prenatal care experienced by pregnant women in these families. A nationwide family survey sponsored by the Health Information Foundation in 1953 discovered that "medical skills were utilized less fully in families with annual incomes of less than $3,000. ... One out of seven mothers in this group did not see a physician during pregnancy, and approximately two thirds had fewer than seven prenatal physician visits [9]. In Rochester, New York in 1951, Alfred Yankauer and associates found that difference in the neonatal mortality rate between two populations of women in the lowest social class "was related to the amount of prenatal care sought" [10].

Figure 7.1.

**Median Annual Family Income and Neonatal Mortality Rate per 1,000
Live Births, By Census Tracts, Syracuse, N.Y., 1950–1956**

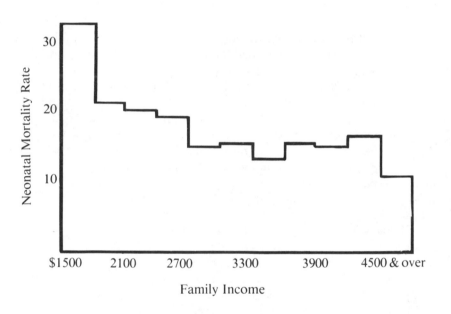

Why pregnant women in lower-income families do not seek prenatal care, even when it may be available without charge, is a sociological problem worthy of further research and study. One possibility is that lower-income people are constricted in their ability to reach out to community health and welfare services for help. Were this hypothesis confirmed it would indicate the importance of professional workers in health and welfare seeking out the poor rather than waiting for community services to be sought. A second possibility is that many lower-income women do not know what services are available. A third possibility is that variation in the use of medical services during pregnancy may be a function of variation in cultural values of different populations of people. As stated by Odin Anderson, "the next steps in research in infant mortality which may yield useful information ... should be directed toward relationships between infant mortality ... and *mothercraft,* specific infant care customs and practices ..." (Italics added) [11]. As the total rate decreases, the proportion of infant deaths attributable to different causes may increase. Thus, several hypotheses should be studied.

Notes

Revision of a paper read at the annual meeting of the American Sociological Association, St. Louis, Missouri, August 1961. Acknowledged with appreciation is the assistance of the Bureau of Vital Statistics of the Syracuse Health Department in making available data on infant births and deaths. Dr. David E. Bigwood, Jr., is commissioner of the Department and Mrs. Ada Carr is director of the Bureau. The authors were affiliated with the State University of New York College of Medicine in Syracuse when this study was conducted.

1. National Office of Vital Statistics, "Infant Mortality, United States, 1915–50," *Vital Statistics Special Reports* 45 (27 July 1956): 13.

2. Alfred Yankauer, Jr., "The Relationship of Fetal and Infant Mortality to Residential Segregation," *American Sociological Review* 15 (October 1950): 645.

3. Charles V. Willie, "A Research Note on the Changing Association Between Infant Mortality and Socioeconomic Status," *Social Forces* 37 (March 1959): 222–225.

4. Willie, "Socioeconomic and Ethnic Areas in Syracuse, New York." (Ph.D. dissertation, Syracuse University, Syracuse, New York, 1957), pp.167–222.

5. Eshref Shevky and Marilyn Williams, *The Social Areas in Los Angeles,* (Berkeley: University of California Press, 1949), pp. 47–57.

6. Willie, "Socioeconomic and Ethnic Areas in Syracuse," pp. 223–269.

7. Syracuse Department of Health, "Annual Report of the Bureau of Vital Statistics," (typewritten, 1956).

8. Willie, *"Research Note,"* pp. 225–227.

9.   Health Information Foundation, "Maternity Care and Its Costs in the United States." *Progress in Health Services* 6 (January 1957): 4.

10.   Alfred Yankauer, Jr., Kenneth G. Goss, and Salvator M. Romeo, "An Evaluation of Prenatal Care and Its Relationship to Social Class and Social Disorganization." *American Journal of Public Health* 43 (August 1953): 1003.

11.   Odin W. Anderson, "Infant Mortality and Social and Cultural Factors." in E. Gartly Jaco (ed.), *Patients, Physicians and Illness,* Glencoe: The Free Press, 1958, p. 23.

CHAPTER 8

Race and Delinquency

Charles V. Willie, with Anita Gershenovitz, Myrna Levine,
Sulochana Glazer, and Roy J. Jones

The task of this analysis is to determine (1) the extent to which deprivation and alienation are associated with juvenile delinquency and (2) variations in the experience of these two phenomena by Negro and white populations in Washington, D.C. It has been assumed that personal behavior is, in part, a response to stimuli of situations in which persons find themselves. To date, we have given much attention to the responding individual, but little concern to the stimulating situation. As stated by Leslie Wilkins, we tend to say of the criminal, "He did it — deal with him." This is because "crime has not been considered as a failure of social controls" [1]. But there is increasing evidence of the critical importance of social situations and environmental circumstances in juvenile delinquency.

Albert Reiss, Jr., and Albert Rhodes, studying more than nine thousand white boys twelve years of age and over in Tennessee, discovered that residential areas are "an independent source of variation in the rate of delinquency ..." [2]. Although boys from lower status families have a greater tendency to become delinquent, Reiss and Rhodes found that "a low status boy in a predominantly high status area with a low rate of delinquency has almost no chance of being classified a juvenile court delinquent" [3].

The deprivation theory of juvenile delinquency emphasizes the situations and circumstances surrounding youth. Richard Cloward and Lloyd

Reprinted from *Phylon*, vol. 26 (Fall 1965), pp. 240–246. The senior author was research director of Washington Action for Youth, a delinquency–prevention planning program, sponsored by the President's Committee on Juvenile Delinquency and Youth Crime, in Washington, D.C. when this article was written. The co-authors were members of the research staff of Washington Action for Youth.

97

Ohlin state that delinquency is essentially a response to being deprived of either the means or opportunity to attain the culturally valued symbols of success. In a society where certain core values of achievement and success are shared by all, Cloward and Ohlin believe that the probability of becoming a delinquent is increased among those classes of youth who come from a milieu of deprivation and, therefore, lack the means for achieving success [4]. Failing for numerous reasons to attain the level of skills that provides entry to the occupational system, some youth find their life-chances greatly circumscribed. Other youth who have sufficient skills may be rejected because of race, religion, or other factors which may be regarded as barriers.

Erik Erikson's theory of alienation is another explanation of juvenile delinquency[5]. While alienation may be associated with deprivation, the rejection of one class of persons by another is a possibility not restricted to any economic category. Erikson states that the adolescent stage of life is a period when youth are unsure of themselves. Their insecurity is aggravated by an adult society which ignores or is indifferent to their presence and is intolerant of their participation. Alienated youth often fail to adopt the goals and values of adult society because they are cut off from adult assistance in socialization. The rejection of youth by parents, often found in broken and disorganized families, is one example of alienation. At the community level, racial discrimination results in another kind of alienation.

These two theories do not provide a complete explanation of the causes of juvenile delinquency. Some deprived neighborhoods have low juvenile delinquency rates. Not all youth who experience family disintegration and racial discrimination are delinquent. It is necessary, therefore, to determine the extent to which variations in the geographic distribution of delinquency are associated with variations in conditions of deprivation and alienation.

Method

The 6,629 juveniles referred to Juvenile Court in Washington, D.C. during a thirty-three-month period from July 1959, through March 1962, were the basic population for this analysis. Although Juvenile Court has jurisdiction over youngsters seven through seventeen years of age, more than 90 percent of all offenses are committed by juveniles ten through seventeen. This age group was used for computing rates and the number of youth ten through seventeen years of age in 1960 (multiplied by 2.75 to correspond with the thirty-three-month period over which delinquency cases were collected) is the base population. All descriptive data of racial characteristics, socioeconomic and family circumstances of life were obtained from the 1960 Census.

Census tracts are the basic geographic units of analysis. There are 125 census tracts in the District of Columbia, 115 of which were used in this analysis. Ten were eliminated from the study because of either small or special populations.

Five highly correlated socioeconomic factors [6], indicating occupational and educational characteristics of the population and housing characteristics of the environment, were grouped in a composite index that was used to measure variations in deprivation. Census tracts with similar socioeconomic status scores were classified as a single socioeconomic area. Five socioeconomic areas were delineated, ranging from area I with high proportions of expensive homes, luxury apartments and dwelling units in good repair, to area V with high proportions of low-priced homes, shabby apartments and dilapidated dwellings, as shown in Table 8.1. Area I, the highest socioeconomic area, also had a large number of college graduates and white-collar workers in its population, contrasting with area V, the lowest, which had many persons without high school diplomas and a majority of semiskilled and unskilled among its workers. In general, areas I, II, and III were above average, and IV and V were below average in socioeconomic status.

A family composition variable — the proportion of children under eighteen years of age growing up in households where one or both parents were absent — was used to measure alienation. Alienation was defined as a condition of estrangement between youth and adults in which youth were cut off from necessary supports. Separation between parents and children may result in alienation. Moreover, it is difficult to fulfill essential parental roles when the father, mother or both parents are separated from their offspring. The city was dichotomized into areas of high and low rates of alienation by grouping those census tracts in which the proportion of children in broken families was above and below the city average of 30 percent.

In the following presentation, variations in the socioeconomic status level of residential areas will be analyzed. The association between juvenile delinquency and these areas will be determined. Then variations in the distribution of Negro and white populations by residential areas will be analyzed. A similar pattern is followed for analyzing alienation. A study of differential rates of juvenile delinquency in residential areas classified by family status will be followed by an analysis of racial characteristics of the population.

Table 8.1.

Distribution of Occupational, Educational, and Housing Variables and Delinquency Rates, by Socioeconomic Areas, Washington, D. C., 1960

Socio-economic Area	Percentage of Operatives, Service Workers and Laborers	Median School Year Completed	Median Value of Owner-Occupied Homes	Median Gross Monthly Rental for Tenant-Occupied Dwellings	Percentage of Sound Dwelling Units	Composite Socio-economic Score[a]	Delinquency Rate[b]
I.	10.3	13.8	$25,000 +	$119	97.8	63	4.3
II.	18.3	12.5	17,200	87	96.0	56	16.1
III.	35.1	11.7	13,600	78	93.9	51	26.9
IV.	53.5	9.9	13,000	74	85.7	46	33.9
V.	72.9	8.3	11,800	69	58.5	37	63.6
Total City	36.2	11.7	$15,400	$ 81	89.7	50	29.2

Note: These data were obtained from the 1960 Census.

a.   The composite score is a consolidation of standard scores for all five variables. (Standard scores for the occupational factor were mirrored so that its distribution varied directly with the other four factors which had assigned means of 50 and assigned standard deviations of 10).

b.   These rates are based on data obtained over a 33-month period, July 1959 to March 1962. The 1960 population 10–17 years was used in computing rates. This population was multiplied by 2.75 for purpose of computing annual rates. The rates refer to the number of youth per 1,000 referred to Juvenile Court and are based on 6,269 juveniles referred to Juvenile Court in the District of Columbia during the study period.

Findings

To see if the theory of deprivation accounts for differences in juvenile delinquency among white and Negro populations, we correlated juvenile delinquency rates and socioeconomic status scores for the 115 census tracts in the city used in this study. The correlation coefficient of .65 indicated that 44 percent of the variance in delinquency by neighborhoods could be attributed to socioeconomic circumstances of life of the population. As socioeconomic status decreased, juvenile delinquency tended to increase.

Next we looked at delinquency rates in the five socioeconomic areas and found a continuous increase from a rate of 4.3 in area I, highest in socioeconomic status, to a rate of 63.6 in area V, lowest in socioeconomic status. The juvenile delinquency rate in the lowest socioeconomic area was 15 times greater than the rate in the highest socioeconomic area. In a few census tracts in the poorest socioeconomic area, at least 100 out of every 1,000 youths between the ages of ten and seventeen years are referred to Juvenile Court each year. This experience may be contrasted with tracts in the highest socioeconomic area where less than five out of every 1,000 youth are referred to court during the course of a year.

The association between juvenile delinquency and deprivation was seen most clearly when the analysis was limited to the two below-average socioeconomic areas, IV and V. In these two areas were found one-third of the land area in Washington, one-half of the children ten to seventeen years of age, and more than two-thirds of the juvenile delinquents. It was clear that these below-average socioeconomic areas were contributing far more juvenile delinquency than they would have if there had been no association between delinquency and socioeconomic status.

Our next problem was to determine the association, if any, between socioeconomic deprivation and white and nonwhite racial populations. A definite association was revealed in that 68 percent of the nonwhite population lived in the below-average socioeconomic areas, IV and V, while 64 percent of the white population lived in the above-average areas, I and II. Less than 2 percent of the nonwhite population was housed in neighborhoods of the highest socioeconomic status, and less than 2 percent of the white population lived in neighborhoods of the lowest socioeconomic status.

These findings would lead us to believe that any correlation between race and delinquency is spurious. Such a correlation is simply another expression of the demonstrated association between delinquency and socioeconomic status. As additional evidence, we computed a partial correlation coefficient in which the association between two variables was measured while the influence of a third variable was held constant. We found the association between juvenile delinquency and race tended to disappear when the effects of socioeconomic status were held constant. Specifically, the correlation coefficient between these two variables was .05 when we controlled for the influence of socioeconomic status. This coefficient, of course, is not significantly different from zero, indicating no correlation. This finding indicated there was no association between juvenile delinquency and race that cannot be accounted for by the differential socioeconomic circumstances of life experienced by white and Negro populations.

The proportion of children living in households with one or both parents absent was used as an indicator of alienation. Of all children in Washington, 30 percent experienced this kind of family life. Those census tracts where the percentage of children in broken families was greater than the city-wide percentage were grouped as an area of many broken families. The area of few broken families consisted of census tracts in which fewer than 30 percent of the children were in households with one or both parents absent. Where there were many two-parent families, the delinquency rate was only 16. Where there were many broken families, the delinquency rate of 41 was more than twice as great. These findings indicated an association between juvenile delinquency and alienation. A coefficient of .64 was obtained when juvenile delinquency rates by census tracts were intercorrelated with the percentage of children in homes without two parents.

Racial composition of the population differed in each of these two areas. Three out of every four persons in the area of many broken families were Negro, while two out of every three persons in the area of few broken families were white.

We computed a partial correlation coefficient to determine the association between race and juvenile delinquency when the effects of a third factor, like family composition, were held constant. The partial correlation coefficient of .13 was small, not significantly different from zero, indicating no association. The apparent association between race and delinquency was spurious; it was accounted for by the higher proportion of broken families among nonwhites.

It would appear, then, that the juvenile delinquency rate in the total Negro population is higher than the rate in the total white population because a higher proportion of Negroes live under unfavorable circumstances. Sixty percent of the nonwhite youth ten to nineteen years of age, but only 10 percent of the white youth, live under conditions of both extreme deprivation and alienation. Thus, a higher proportion of Negro youth live in neighborhoods and under conditions that predispose them to delinquency.

Summary and Conclusion

In summary, the main findings of this study show that: (1) socio-economic status is related to juvenile delinquency—the lower the socioeconomic status level of a neighborhood, the higher the juvenile delinquency rate; (2) family composition is related to juvenile delinquency — the higher the proportion of broken families in a neighborhood, the greater the juvenile delinquency rate; and (3) any association between race and juvenile delinquency may be explained by differences in the socioeconomic status and family composition of white and nonwhite populations.

Therefore, we conclude that the difference in juvenile delinquency rates in white and nonwhite populations would disappear were the circumstances of life similar for white and nonwhite persons.

The conditions of alienation and deprivation as defined in this study need closer scrutiny. The variables selected for analysis are not exhaustive of all dimensions of these concepts. Moreover, there are certain limitations imposed by the data and the ecological method of analysis. Nevertheless, these findings have indicated some specific conditions which merit special consideration both in terms of further research and action programs designed to reduce delinquency.

Notes

Revision of a lecture delivered at the twenty-seventh annual conference of the Division of the Social Sciences, Howard University, 24 April 1963. Acknowledged with appreciation are data on juvenile delinquency by census tracts made available by Dr. Hylan Lewis. Dr. Willie was associate professor of sociology, Syracuse University, and on leave when study was conducted in Washington.

1. Leslie T. Wilkins, "Criminology: An Operational Research Approach," in A. T. Welford et. al. (eds.), *Society, Problems and Methods of Study* (London: n.p., n.d.) p. 329.

2. Albert J. Reiss, Jr., and Albert Lewis Rhodes, "The Distribution of Juvenile Delinquency in the Class Structure," *American Sociological Review* 26 (October 1961): 727.

3. Ibid., p. 729.

4. Richard A. Cloward and Lloyd E. Ohlin, *Delinquency and Opportunity,* (Glencoe: Free Press, 1960), pp. 161–186.

5. Erik H. Erikson, "Youth: Fidelity and Diversity," *Daedalus* 91 (Winter 1962): 5–27.

6. Charles V. Willie and Morton O. Wagenfeld, *Socioeconomic and Ethnic Areas, Syracuse and Onondaga County, New York* (Syracuse: Syracuse University, Youth Development Center, 1960), p. 2.

CHAPTER 9

The Relative Contribution of Family Status and Economic Status to Juvenile Delinquency

A review of the literature indicates two basic conditions associated with juvenile delinquency that have been confirmed in several studies. They are (1) poverty and poor living conditions and (2) broken homes and inadequate family life [1]. It is sometimes assumed that poverty and family instability are so closely intertwined that one is but a reflection of the other. Probably the best summary on the association between family instability and economic insecurity is provided by Abram Kardiner and Lionel Ovesey. They state that "the broken home in the lower-class family is very commonly attributed to the precarious economic conditions under which these families live. This statement is not untrue; it is merely incomplete" [2].

The general hypothesis of this study is that economic status and family status make both joint and independent contributions to deviant behavior. Family instability is aggravated by economic insecurity but is not limited to poor households. Also, inadequate family finances do not always result in broken marriages. It is of particular importance to study this hypothesis (1) since doubt has been cast upon the assumption that family instability and economic insecurity are but different reflections of the same phenomenon, and (2) because of the recent debate surrounding the Moynihan Report on *The Negro Family* [3, 4] which discusses the relationship between family instability, economic insecurity, and deviant behavior.

Daniel Patrick Moynihan concluded that federal government programs should be designed to enhance the stability and resources of the Negro family. What is unclear in this conclusion is the relationship between stability and resources. Belton Fleisher in a recent study of the eco-

Reprinted from *Social Problems*, Vol. 14, No. 3, Winter 1967, pp. 326–335.

The author was affiliated with Syracuse University and the Laboratory of Community Psychiatry of the Harvard Medical School at the time this article was published.

nomics of delinquency stated that "when family income increases...the number of women over 14 who are separated or divorced will decline..." [5]. It was suggested by Fleisher that family stability is a function of economic security. But Moynihan implied that upward mobility and economic security would continue to elude Negroes "unless the viability of the Negro family is restored" [6]. Moynihan, of course, does not rule out increasing the economic resources of the Negro family as a way of contributing to its viability; but it is clear that his focus is upon the social integration of family members.

So a study is needed not only of the independent contributions of family status and economic status to deviant behavior such as juvenile delinquency but also of their interaction effect. Which comes first — family stability or economic security? Does one give rise to the other? With reference to juvenile delinquency, this question might be asked: Is the rate higher among children of poor stable families than among children of affluent unstable families?

Because the findings to date about the correlation between delinquency rates and race are ambiguous, as pointed out by Roland Chilton in his study of Baltimore, Detroit, and Indianapolis [7], a study of the relative contribution of economic and family status to juvenile delinquency should attempt to study whites and nonwhites separately to determine if the association (if there is any between race and delinquency) is similar or different in these two populations. Unequivocally, Fleisher has stated that "in areas of high tendency toward crime, a 10 percent rise in income might well result in a 20 percent decline in delinquency" [8]. It should be determined, if possible, whether this phenomenon would be true both of white and nonwhite populations.

Chilton has wisely pointed out that "questions concerning the relationship of delinquency to the degree of organization of an area or to the degree of agreement on norms cannot be adequately answered with delinquency area data and procedures" [9]. Social area data and ecological correlations are basic to the analysis in this study and therefore limit the kinds of inferences that may be drawn. No attempt is made to correlate delinquent behavior with certain sociological conditions such as anomie. This investigation has two goals which are quite modest: (1) to determine whether or not earlier findings regarding the association between economic status and juvenile delinquency, and family status and juvenile delinquency hold when populations of whites and nonwhites are analyzed separately, and (2) to determine the joint effect, if any, of these two variables.

Data and Method

The study area was Washington, D.C. The basic unit of analysis was the census tract. Analysis of the association, if any, between juvenile delinquency and economic status and juvenile delinquency and family status was determined by computing Pearsonian correlation coefficients for 115 of the 125 census tracts in the city (the 10 tracts eliminated were sparsely settled or consisted of institutional populations).

There are, of course, dangers in using ecological correlations, which W. S. Robinson has discussed [10]. The dependent variable, juvenile delinquency, accounted for only 3 percent of the youth population 10 to 17 years of age in the total city and varied from census tracts in which less than 1 percent of the youth had been referred to court during the course of a year to a high-rate tract in which 11 percent of the youth had been referred to court. The small proportion of the population in each census tract that was delinquent means that caution should be exercised in interpreting the findings. However, some of the problems of ecological correlations were guarded against by relating the dependent variable to independent variables such as socioeconomic status (which was a composite value that characterized most of the people in a census tract) and the proportion of children in broken families (which varied from a small minority to a large majority of the families in many census tracts). Because the number of census tracts in the predominantly white area and in the predominantly nonwhite area of Washington was relatively small (41 predominantly white and 51 predominantly nonwhite tracts), this would further complicate a correlational analysis. And so patterns of variations within racial populations by socioeconomic and family status were determined by using the methods of social area analysis [11].

Data for the study are records of 6,269 youth referred to the District of Columbia Juvenile Court for reasons other than traffic offenses and dependency during a 33-month period from 1959 to 1962. Another study conducted by this author in Washington and using the data of a single fiscal year, 1963, revealed a high correlation between the rates for youth who came in contact with police only and youth who were referred to court; the Pearsonian correlation coefficient for 113 census tracts included in that study was .90. This means that a strong socioeconomic bias, which could result in a much higher proportion of police contacts being referred to court in the poorer than in the more affluent neighborhoods, does not appear to contaminate these data. For the city as a whole, 37 percent of the youth contacted by police were referred to court; the percentage in a more affluent socioeconomic area was 32 and in a low-income area, 40. This was not a large difference in percent of court referrals between populations of high and low socioeconomic status. While the bias was not completely eliminated, it was controlled. This may be because Washington has a separate youth aid division in the police department staffed by officers who give full-time attention to youth and who must be consulted on all police contacts that are referred to court.

The 1960 census population 10 through 17 years of age was used as the base for computing rates. The base was limited to these particular age levels because less than 5 percent of court-referred youth were under 10 years. Because these youth are not as vulnerable as those over 10 years, their inclusion in the population base would have distorted the actual incidence of delinquency by depressing the rate. Data for three years (33 months) were used to increase the reliability of rates since only a small proportion (about 3 percent) were referred to court each year. The population base was multiplied by 2.75 to make it comparable to the 33-month study period so that annual rates could be computed for each census tract. The total city population in 1960 was approximately 764,000, about 45 percent white and 55 percent nonwhite.

The economic status and family status of the population, the former of which is more appropriately called socioeconomic status in this study, was measured by a composite index score for each census tract and the percent of broken homes. Five highly correlated variables were used in the index [12]: (1) percentage of the employed in the combined categories of operatives, service workers, and laborers; (2) median number of years of school completed by the population over 25 years of age; (3) estimated market value of owned homes; (4) the gross monthly rental for tenant-occupied dwellings; and (5) percentage of sound dwelling units. (The first factor was inverted so that it varied directly with the other four.) Distributions of each of the five variables were converted into standard scores with assigned means of 50 and assigned standard deviations of 10. The five standard scores for each census tract were simply averaged into a socioeconomic status composite score. The percent of children under 18 years of age not living with both parents was computed as an indicator of the family status of a census tract. Studies of indices of social status, such as one conducted by John Haer, indicate that a composite index of several variables is a better predictor of differentiation within a population than a single variable [13]. In delineating family status, a gross indicator like the number of children in one-parent families was believed to be sufficient. While one parent may be absent from the household due to death, divorce, or desertion, the functional consequence for the child — particularly if the absent parent is the father, which is usually the case — is more or less the same. No one is present who has a primary responsibility, as Malinowski has described it, of orienting the child to the community at large [14].

Census tracts were classified as white and nonwhite for the social area analysis; tracts in which two out of every three persons were white were classified as part of the white area. A similar procedure was followed in delineating the nonwhite area. In spite of the criterion used, 95 percent of the total population in the white area was of Caucasian racial stock and 90 percent of the total population in the nonwhite area was of that color category. Most of the census tracts in Washington are racially homogeneous; only about one-fifth of the population lives in racially mixed residential areas.

White census tracts were grouped into poor and affluent areas and into areas of few and many broken homes. Those census tracts above the city-wide socioeconomic composite standard score of 50 (that is, those tracts in which the median family income was above $4,500) were included in the affluent area. The median family income for some census tracts in the affluent area were well above $10,000. Those census tracts below the city-wide average composite score (that is, those tracts with median family incomes below $4,500) were classified as part of the poor area. Several of the tracts in this area had medians that were below the $3,000 level of extreme poverty. The area of few broken homes consisted of those tracts in the affluent and poor areas in which the percent of children not living with both parents was above the city-wide percentage. There were four area types into which census tracts with predominantly white populations were grouped: area A, the affluent area characterized by few broken homes; area B, the affluent area characterized by many broken homes; area C, the poor area characterized by few broken homes; and area D, the poor area characterized by many broken homes. The number of delinquents and the population 10 through 17 for all census tracts in an area were totaled. With these summations, delinquency rates per 1,000 youth were computed for each. Area A had 32 census tracts, area B, 4 census tracts, area C, 4 census tracts, and area D, 1 census tract classified as white.

The same procedure was followed in delineating areas for the nonwhite population and in computing area delinquency rates. Area A had 6 census tracts, area B, 2 tracts, area C, 5 tracts, and area D, 38 census tracts.

Classifying white and nonwhite populations into these four types of social areas made possible a comparative analysis controlled for variations in socioeconomic and family status that tend to differentiate these two populations. The conditions of the populations in each of the areas were, of course, not identical because of the crude technique of dichotomizing the economic and family status variables above and below the city-wide average.

About 18 percent of the total population of juvenile delinquents was eliminated from that part of the study which compared white and nonwhite areas. These were the youthful offenders who lived in racially mixed areas. The remaining population of 5,148 delinquents was divided this way: 737 or 14 percent in the white areas and 4,411 or 86 percent in the nonwhite areas. The large imbalance of delinquency within the different racial areas is further indication that any meaningful comparison of whites and nonwhites must control for socioeconomic and family status. Although the number of census tracts was few in one or two of the four areas among white and nonwhite populations, no area had a base population of less than 300. Thus, the rates that were computed for comparative analysis were reasonably reliable.

Findings

As reported in a previous study, the correlation coefficient for juvenile delinquency rates and socioeconomic status scores was significantly different from zero and so was the correlation coefficient for delinquency rates and the percent of children with one or both parents absent from home [15]. In this city-wide analysis, the correlation coefficient for juvenile delinquency and socioeconomic status was -.65 and the correlation coefficient for juvenile delinquency and family instability was .64. This means that juvenile delinquency rates tended to increase as the socioeconomic status level of census tracts decreased, and that juvenile delinquency rates tended to increase as the percent of broken homes in the census tracts increased. These findings are in accord with those of other investigators mentioned at the beginning of the paper.

Although socioeconomic and family status variables both correlated highly with juvenile delinquency rates (having coefficients of a similar magnitude), this did not mean that the two variables were identical. To determine the degree of association between these variables, socioeconomic status scores were correlated with the percent of children in broken homes; the correlation coefficient was -.65. This coefficient indicated that slightly more than 40 percent of the variance in the ecological distribution of the family instability factor could be attributed to variation in levels of socioeconomic status. While this was a high degree of association, the correlation coefficient also indicated that nearly 60 percent of the variance must be attributed to factors other than socioeconomic status. Clearly, the two variables did not duplicate each other. Although there was some overlap, they were not simply different ways of measuring the same phenomenon.

A multiple correlation coefficient was computed to determine the independent and joint contribution of economic and family status to the pattern of variation in juvenile delinquency on a city-wide basis. These two variables correlated with the dependent variable — juvenile delinquency — at .71. The multiple correlation coefficient accounted for a larger proportion of the variance in the ecological distribution of juvenile delinquency than either family status or economic status separately correlated with the dependent variable.

Beta weights were obtained to continue the analysis of the independent and joint effects of these two factors upon the dependent variable. They indicate that about 16 percent of the variance in the ecological distribution of juvenile delinquency rates could be attributed to variation in levels of socioeconomic status; approximately 14 percent could be attributed to variation in the distribution of the percent of youth who lived in broken families; and about 20 percent of the variance was due to the joint effect of these two factors. The finding that socioeconomic and family status make a joint contribution to the pattern of variation of juvenile delinquency within an urban community is important. It may help explain why the debate over whether economic status should be upgraded or family stability secured initially, as a way of dealing with deviant behavior, has not been resolved satisfactorily for advocates of either form of action.

This finding suggests that some juvenile delinquency is associated with unstable family life which is unstable because of impoverished economic circumstances; and some juvenile delinquency is associated with families which are economically impoverished and that these families are impoverished because they are unstable. Nevertheless, family status and economic status are independently associated with juvenile delinquency too. This fact should be remembered when assessing the joint effects of these variables. Obviously, the relationship between delinquency, family life, and economic circumstances is complex. A major error in many discussions about the relative importance of different independent variables in preventing deviant behavior has been the tendency to oversimplify.

The contribution of socioeconomic and family status to variations in the pattern of juvenile delinquency in separate white and nonwhite populations is presented now. Fourfold tables were constructed for this analysis.

The data in Tables 9.1 and 9.2 indicated both similar and different ecological patterns of distribution for juvenile delinquency in white and nonwhite populations. The white and nonwhite areas are similar in that circumstances contributing to the lowest and highest delinquency rates were the same for both races. The area of affluent socioeconomic status in which there were few broken homes (as seen in cell A of Tables 9.1 and 9.2) tended to have the lowest delinquency rate in the city, while the highest rate was found in that area characterized by low socioeconomic status and many broken homes (as seen in cell D of Tables 9.1 and 9.2) for white and nonwhite populations. These areas provided the least favorable and most favorable circumstances for the development of delinquent behavior. Apparently, these circumstances affect whites and nonwhites in similar ways.

Table 9.1.

Juvenile Delinquency Rate Per 1,000 Youth 10 Through 17 Years of Age in Nonwhite Area, by Family Status and Socioeconomic Status, Washington, D.C., July 1959–March 1962

	Juvenile Delinquency Rate Among Nonwhites	
	Area of Few Broken Homes	Area of Many Broken Homes
Affluent Area	a 19.7	b 20.9
Poor Area	c 26.5	d 42.4

Table 9.2.

Juvenile Delinquency Rate Per 1,000 Youth 10 Through 17 Years of Age in White Area, by Family Status and Socioeconomic Status, Washington, D.C., July 1959–March 1962

	Juvenile Delinquency Rate Among Whites	
	Area of Few Broken Homes	Area of Many Broken Homes
Affluent Area	a 10.6	b 30.4
Poor Area	c 19.6	d 44.3

White and nonwhite populations differed in the way in which delinquency rates were distributed between affluent areas characterized by many broken households and poor areas consisting of many stable or intact families. Data for this analysis are found in cells B and C of Tables 9.1 and 9.2. Among the affluent, the absence of one or both parents from the home tended to be associated with a higher delinquency rate for whites than nonwhites. And among the poor, the presence of both parents in the household tended to be associated with a lower delinquency rate among whites than nonwhites. It would appear that family status had a greater affect upon the white than nonwhite population in contributing to a lower delinquency rate.

Differences between rates for comparable white and nonwhite areas are not great, never exceeding 11 points. This means that one should exercise caution in drawing inferences from these data. A persistent pattern, however, does merit attention. Further analysis of the data is pursued to confirm or cast doubt on tentative conclusions based on analysis of patterns discussed above.

The goal of this analysis was to examine further the differential contribution of family and economic status to delinquency among white and nonwhite populations alluded to, especially the possibility that family status may be more specifically and immediately associated with delinquency among whites than nonwhites. Since the most favorable circumstance for the development of juvenile delinquency was similar for both racial categories — that is, a low-income area characterized by many broken families — cell D in Tables 9.1 and 9.2 was identified as the high-rate area, having a similar juvenile delinquency rate for both races, i.e., 44 and 42 for whites and nonwhites respectively.

The analysis was designed to determine which area type exhibited the greatest difference in delinquency rate between it and the high-rate area. Rates for areas A, B, and C, therefore, were subtracted from the rate in area D for both white and nonwhite populations. For the white population, the greatest difference was between areas D and A; this was also the case for the nonwhite population. The delinquency rate in this low-rate area was 76 percent lower in the white population and 54 percent lower in the nonwhite population than the delinquency rate in the high-rate area (Table 9.3). In this respect, the two racial populations were similar as mentioned above. They differed, however, in the kinds of areas that resulted in the second and third greatest difference. For the white population, areas D and C exhibited a 56 percent difference in rates while areas D and B revealed a 51 percent difference in rates among nonwhites. The second greatest difference for

Table 9.3.

A Comparison of the Juvenile Delinquency Rate in the High-Rate Area with the Rates in Three Other Social Areas, for White and Nonwhite Populations, Washington, D.C., 1959–1962

	Percent of Change in Delinquency Rate for Three Social Areas Compared with the High-Rate Area[a]			
	White Areas		Nonwhite Areas	
	Percent of Change from High-Rate Area	Rank	Percent of Change from High-Rate Area	Rank
High family stability and high economic status[b]	76	1	54	1
High family stability and low economic status[c]	56	2	36	3
High economic status and low family stability[d]	31	3	51	2

a. The high-rate area is Cell D in Tables 9.1 and 9.2
b. Cell A in Tables 9.1 and 9.2
c. Cell C in Tables 9.1 and 9.2
d. Cell B in Tables 9.1 and 9.2

whites occurred in an area characterized by high family stability and low economic status, while among nonwhites the second greatest difference occurred in an area characterized by high economic status and low family stability. Although the economic circumstances were relatively favorable, the white population had a delinquency rate that was only 31 percent lower than the high-rate area, when there was a considerable amount of family instability in the area. But nonwhite households that lived under similar affluent economic circumstances tended to exhibit a 51 percent difference in delinquency rate below that of the high-rate area even though the area consisted of many unstable households. The area among nonwhites which registered the smallest difference in delinquency rate between it and the high-rate area was the one characterized by high family stability and low economic status.

Thus, it would appear that the extremes — those circumstances that were the most and least favorable for the development of delinquent behavior — had similar consequences for white and nonwhite populations. But between these most and least favorable circumstances, whites were more affected by family composition while nonwhites were more affected by economic circumstances. Because of the kinds of data and methods used in this analysis, these differential effects cannot be stated with certainty. But the findings do suggest that different approaches may be needed for white and nonwhite populations in the United States to solve some problems of deviancy, like juvenile delinquency.

There are, of course, no innate differences between these two races that could cause one to be more affected by economic or family circumstances than the other. One possible explanation of the differential affects of family and economic status in white and nonwhite populations is their different positions in the opportunity system as described by Cloward and Ohlin [16]. In Washington, D.C. 80 percent of the white population lives in economically affluent areas while 67 percent of the nonwhite population lives in neighborhoods of poverty or marginal economic condition. Since poverty was no longer an overwhelming problem for most white people, family instability was a major remaining and outstanding problem contributing to the incidence of juvenile delinquency.

Although the percent of nonwhite children growing up in one-parent families was greater than the percent of white children who had this kind of experience, the impoverished economic circumstances of nonwhites was overwhelming. In the light of the data and analysis of this study, it is hypothesized that nonwhites may be able to deal with the family instability factor which is associated with juvenile delinquency only after notable improvements have been experienced in their economic circumstances. The hypothesis is advanced on the basis of the findings in this study, particularly the findings pertaining to the white population which is largely beyond the pale of poverty.

Out of this analysis, then, has come the sociological principle that the solutions of some social problems occur in a serial pattern, that the solution of one problem makes possible the solution of another. There is an ordering of social events into a sequential pattern. Obviously, white and nonwhite populations are in different stages of the series. Most whites have passed beyond the stage of economic insecurity.

This means that efforts to strengthen family ties and increase family stability in the nonwhite population probably will not be very successful until opportunities for economic upgrading are provided. This society may have the possibility of helping a population achieve greater family stability to prevent delinquency only after it has assisted a population to achieve greater economic security. The longitudinal unfolding of life in the social system needs to be studied in a much more refined way. This study has suggested the significance of this kind of investigation and called attention to the inadequacy of explanation that does not take into consideration a serial or developmental view of social conditions.

Conclusions

A general conclusion emerging from this study is that juvenile delinquency will not be greatly reduced in Washington, or in cities like Washington with a large nonwhite population, until there is a substantial increase in the nonwhite population's economic status. The low rate of delinquency among white youth who are members of a population that has achieved economic affluence is further evidence supporting this conclusion. Other conclusions of the study are these:

Socioeconomic and family status are phenomena that have overlapping but different ecological patterns of distribution in an urban community.

Socioeconomic and family status make independent as well as joint contributions to variations in the ecology of juvenile delinquency.

The preventive potential of two-parent households against juvenile delinquency tends to be impaired by circumstances of poverty.

The preventive potential of affluent economic status against juvenile delinquency tends to be impaired by family instability.

Delinquency rates are similar for members of white and nonwhite populations who live in the most disadvantaged environment characterized by many broken homes and low income.

Community programs designed to prevent juvenile delinquency associated both with family instability and economic insecurity will probably have greater success if they focus first upon increasing the economic status of a population.

The full answer, however, to the question of whether community programs should attempt first to create more economic security or develop greater family stability depends upon the target population and the stage through which it is passing. More than four out of every five youth referred to juvenile court in Washington, D.C., are Negro. If a community is really interested in reducing delinquency in this kind of a city, it would appear, according to the findings of this study, that much assistance must be rendered to the nonwhite population, in the form of increased economic opportunities.

Notes

The author was Associate Professor of Sociology at Syracuse University and on leave serving as Visiting Lecturer in Sociology at the Harvard Medical School, Department of Psychiatry (Laboratory of Community Pschiatry). Data for this study were gathered while the author was Research Director of Washington Action for Youth, a delinquency prevention project in the District of Columbia, sponsored by the President's Committee on Juvenile Delinquency and Youth Crime. Data on delinquency were secured from Dr. Hylan Lewis of Howard University. His assistance is acknowledged with appreciation, and so is the help of the research staff of Washington Action for Youth. This is a revised version of a paper presented at the Eastern Sociological Society Annual Meeting, New York, N.Y., 10 April 1965.

1.   Leslie T. Wilkins, "Juvenile Delinquency: A Critical Review of Research and Theory," *Educational Research* 5 (February 1963): 104–119.

2.   Abram Kardiner and Lionel Ovesey, *The Mark of Oppression* (Cleveland: World, 1962), p. 344.

3.   U. S. Department of Labor, *The Negro Family— A Case for National Action* (Washington, DC: Government Printing Office, 1965).

4.   Lee Rainwater and William L. Yancy, "Black Families and the White House," *Transaction* 3 (July–August 1966): 6–11, 48–53.

5.   Belton M. Fleisher, *The Economics of Delinquency* (Chicago: Quadrangle 1966), p. 117.

6.   U. S. Department of Labor, *The Negro Family,* p. 30.

7.   Roland J. Chilton, "Continuity in Delinquency Area Research: A Comparison of Studies for Baltimore, Detroit and Indianapolis," *American Sociological Review* 29 (February 1964): 75–78.

8.   Fleisher, *The Economics of Delinquency,* p. 117.

9.   Chilton, "Continuity in Delinquency Area Research," p. 83.

10.   W. S. Robinson, "Ecological Correlations and the Behavior of Individuals," *American Sociological Review* 15 (June 1950): 351–357.

11.   Eshref Shevky and Marilyn Williams, *The Social Areas in Los Angeles* (Berkeley: University of California Press, 1949); Wendel Bell, "Economic, Family and Ethnic Status: An Empirical Test." *American Sociological Review* 20 (February 1955): pp. 45–51; Eshref Shevky and Wendel Bell, *Social Area Analysis* (Stanford: Stanford University Press, 1955).

12.   Charles V. Willie and Morton O. Wagenfeld, *Socioeconomic and Ethnic Areas, Syracuse and Onondaga County, New York, 1960* (Syracuse: Syracuse University, Youth Development Center, 1962).

13.   John L. Haer, "Predictive Utility of Five Indices of Social Stratification," *American Sociological Review* 22 (October 1957): 541–546.

14.   Bronislaw Malinowski, "Parenthood — The Basis of Social Structure," in Marvin B. Sussman (ed.), *Source Book in Marriage and the Family* (Boston: Houghton Mifflin, 1955), p. 25.

15.   Charles V. Willie, Anita Gershenovitz, Myrna Levine, Sulochana Glazer, and Roy J. Jones, "Race and Delinquency," *Phylon* 26 (Fall 1965): 240–246.

16.   Richard A. Cloward and Lloyd E. Ohlin, *Delinquency and Opportunity* (New York: Free Press of Glencoe, 1960).

CHAPTER 10

Two Men and Their Families

A Story of Low-Income Earners in the Nation's Capital and Their Need for Intercessors

One of the basic facts of social existence is that we are all interdependent. One person must do for another what the other cannot do for oneself. But the needs of some may not be known, or if known, others may not know how to respond. This, then, is the responsibility of an intercessor, a person who brings individuals and a community together so that they embrace each other in helpful response.

Compassion and justice seldom appear spontaneously; they are cultivated characteristics. The intercessor contributes to their cultivation by prodding the advantaged to assume responsibility for the disadvantaged and by pushing those who are considered outcasts into the mainstream of community life so that each may help and be helped by the other. Working in behalf of families of great need, the intercessor encourages the community to develop a retraining project, or to modify its educational system, or to revamp its welfare program, or to do any number of things that can contribute to the quality of life for the low-income citizen. It is expecting too much to ask the person or family in marginal circumstances to confront our gigantic bureaucracies alone.

One of the tragedies of modern life is that a disturbingly large number of families live out their time in closed and shuttered worlds. They are cut off from the larger community (often from their own neighborhood) and without an intercessor who could be both a prod and a link to the outside.

Reprinted from Irwin Deutscher and Elizabeth J. Thompson, editors, *Among the People: Encounters with the Poor,* New York: Basic Books, 1968, pp. 53–66. The author was affiliated with the Department of Sociology and the Youth Development Center of Syracuse University when this article was published.

117

This is the story of two such families, families with limited resources and on the brink of difficulty. They are residents of Washington, D.C., citizens of the nation's capital. Sometimes these families have bread enough, but never any to spare.

The names used, of course, are fictitious, but the families and their problems are real. These are young families, hidden from the sight of the community at large, cut off from its compassion. Their plight has only recently come to public view through a community survey conducted by Washington Action for Youth, a federal-local delinquency prevention project sponsored by the President's Committee on Juvenile Delinquency and Youth Crime.

Armed with questionnaires, ten interviewers called on a random sample of 1,000 households in the Cardozo High School district, a four-square-mile area in the northwest section of Washington. The families of this area have diversified backgrounds, although most are low-income and Negro. During a two-month period in the summer of 1963, interviewers elicited confidential information about the way of life of family members, the organizations and associations to which they belonged, and their connections with the community at large, including public and private programs and services.

In a real sense, this survey has become a spokesman for unknown, hidden, and forgotten families whose problems and possibilities are ignored. The facts derived from the survey are the basis for several action programs for the benefit of poor youth in the community.

This, then, is the story of two families, their hopes, aspirations, and worries, and with some observations on their concrete problems and possibilities. Meeting these families, one is convinced immediately of their terrific push to make a go of it. But one also becomes aware of the community's responsibility to pull the family members along. This story is one of courageous push that has not yet found the compassionate pull.

The Peter Paul Family

Both Mr. and Mrs. Paul are natives of Georgia. Though "just kids" when they were married—he was seventeen and she was fifteen—this was the second marriage for Mrs. Paul. It has been successful, however, and the couple recently celebrated their tenth anniversary. There are four Paul children, ranging in age from 3 to 7 years. Mrs. Paul describes the family as "real close."

The Pauls moved to Washington two years after their marriage. Mr. Paul works as a cement finisher with a construction firm, earning about $65 a week. The neighborhood in which the Pauls have lived for the past two years is "not as nice" as some of their former residences, but rental for their three-room apartment is only $50 a month—all this family of six can afford. They have thought of moving to a larger dwelling in a residential section, since Mrs. Paul considers this neighborhood to be dangerous and the streets and buildings unclean. She knows there is some juvenile delinquency in the area. But finding housing elsewhere at a price the family can afford has not been possible, so Mrs. Paul has resigned herself to being "satisfied" with the neighborhood. Moreover, there is a "good back yard in which the children can play."

Mr. and Mrs. Paul share joint responsibility in disciplining the children. However, Mr. Paul is home very little because of his long working hours. He eats neither breakfast, lunch, nor dinner at home, and since he does not take his meals with the family, Mrs. Paul and the four children have no specific mealtime. Mrs. Paul does not work; she stays at home with the children. They appear to be well-behaved youngsters, but when questioned, Mrs. Paul has no advice on child-rearing methods that may help children to grow up without getting into trouble.

The Paul family members are engaged in a valiant effort to "make it" on their own. From time to time, however, they have had to turn to the Salvation Army for clothes and to the Welfare Department for surplus food. They have also attended clinics at the D.C. General Hospital and the Children's Hospital. Other than for occasional use of these facilities, the Paul family has depended little on the community for assistance.

Although Mr. Paul completed only nine years of school and Mrs. Paul has less than a fifth-grade education, both have high aspirations for their children. Mrs. Paul wants the children to work in a profession, such as nursing for the girls and law for the boys. But she has little idea of how much education is required to attain these lofty goals. An "average" education is what she thinks may be necessary. Inadequate information about requirements for these vocations is coupled with inadequate financial resources. According to Mrs. Paul, there is not enough money even now for the school needs of the children. The seven-year-old has never attended school, so is already one year behind.

Mrs. Paul, who is at home all day, knows from twenty to thirty persons in the neighborhood well enough to stop and chat. One of these, a housewife who lives next door, is her best friend, the person to whom Mrs. Paul would turn if she had a serious problem requiring outside help. In general, however, the Pauls have few connections with community organizations and associations, except for a neighborhood Baptist church. The family attends Sunday School and morning and evening worship services, and Mrs. Paul sings in the choir. Going to church on Sunday is a family affair.

The Pauls have heard about one or two civic action groups, but do not participate in any. Mr. Paul does not hold membership in a union nor is he, his wife, or his children connected with any political, recreational, social, or fraternal organization. They have no contact with casework social services in the community, with character-building agencies, or with group-work programs. The family is connected to the community at large only through Mr. Paul's job, the church, the daily newspaper, and television.

In summary, one might describe the Pauls as a hard-working, God-fearing family that is hammering out an existence, a family that is stable but also highly vulnerable. With only a slight change in the circumstances of life, the Pauls could go under.

The Bernard Brown Family

Mr. and Mrs. Bernard Brown have been married five years and have two sons, aged two and three. Mr. Brown, twenty-five at the time of the survey, is a native of the District of Columbia; his wife, twenty-seven, was born in Mississippi. The family has lived in its present neighborhood, a low-income district near the downtown section of Washington, for more than four years. Mr. Brown is a gasoline service station attendant with an income of less than $3,500 a year.

The family would very much like to move to Maryland, near Mr. Brown's mother. It is "nicer back in Maryland" and "a better place to bring up the children," according to Mrs. Brown, who is "somewhat dissatisfied" with their present location. But the Browns continue to live in a three-room apartment; they know the owner, and the rent of $100 a month is normal for what they are receiving. These rental payments, however, are relatively high for Mr. Brown, taking 37 percent of his monthly earnings. The family has thought about moving for more than a year, but cannot see how to follow through financially. Even though Mrs. Brown is unhappy with the present neighborhood, she doesn't quite know what ought to be changed. She does know that the steps in their apartment building are unsafe for children.

Obviously, money is a major problem for the Browns. Mr. Brown dropped out of school at the eighth grade and has no special vocational skills. His wife completed high school, but her job is to be at home with the children; Mr. Brown is the breadwinner. In the light of these circumstances, Mrs. Brown is uncertain about what the future holds for her two small boys and is unwilling to hazard a guess as to what they might do when they grow up. About all she can plan on, Mrs. Brown thinks, is to "teach the children right from wrong." She also wants to build some regularity into their lives. The family therefore has a regular mealtime, although the father cannot eat with his wife and children because of his work schedule. Mrs. Brown describes the family as "close" but not "real close."

A next-door neighbor is Mrs. Brown's best friend. Aside from this neighbor, Mrs. Brown does not know anyone in the community who can "really get things done," except the police. Moreover, she knows no one to whom her family could turn for help in improving neighborhood conditions, although she has a vague idea that "business people" could be of some assistance.

At home all day with the children, Mrs. Brown knows only five to ten persons in her neighborhood. And other than the bowling club in which Mr. Brown participates each week, none of the family members is involved in community organizations or activities. Though both husband and wife are Baptists, they seldom attend church. Sundays are devoted to visiting the grandmother in Maryland in the afternoon, having an early evening dinner, and watching television. Mrs. Brown has little, if any, knowledge of any civic action groups in the community and no contact with casework services. During the past year, some members of the family were "treated" at the D.C. General Hospital and the Washington Hospital Center. This is the only contact the family has had with the health and welfare services of the community, public or private. The Browns are connected to the "outside" only through the husband's job and bowling team, the television set, and one daily newspaper. There is no radio or telephone to extend family knowledge of the world.

In summary, the Brown family is one that is very much on its own, with small children, limited income, and a nagging sense of uncertainty. The Browns appear to be drifting in the present and afraid to plan for the future. Nevertheless, and in spite of several inadequacies, the family is making a go of it. But the present equilibrium will remain only if the future is unchanged from the past. To the extent that the future is different, this family may not survive.

Community Responsibility

The problems of the Bernard Browns and the Peter Pauls must be shared by the total community if such families are to be sustained at a self-supporting level and redeemed should they fall below it. Both the Browns and the Pauls stand on the brink of difficulty. The immediate, urgent challenge to the community is how to prevent these families from plummeting to the depths of disaster and settling down in perennial despair.

Race, some readers have undoubtedly noticed, has not been mentioned in this report. It is not important. But for those who need to know, one family is Negro and one is white—which one really doesn't matter. What does matter is that these are families who are passed over by private agencies and turned away from the public services because they have bread enough. Who cares if there is none to spare? The answer, of course, is that all of us must care. The Browns and the Pauls have the will; we in the larger community must provide the way.

Of all the lessons that can be learned from this story, three seem paramount. The community must (1) extend jobs and job training to the unskilled, (2) revise the administration of public welfare so that it becomes an instrument of prevention, and (3) provide new family services that seek out families in need of help rather than waiting for their services to be sought.

In an economic system increasingly dominated by technology, men and women need technical skills if they are to earn enough to meet the needs of their families. While both men in our story have jobs, they are unable to obtain better ones because of their limited education. These men should be candidates for retraining. They cannot teach themselves.

The community must provide new training experiences. Indeed, it has to be a community responsibility; for the community must subsidize retraining of the unskilled worker or subsidize his inadequate family income tomorrow. We are reminded of the testimony of Secretary of Labor Willard Wirtz in support of expanding the Manpower Training Program. He informed a congressional committee that the average cost of training a person under the manpower program is $1,000, as compared with a possible cost of $1,000 per year that the community may pay to support a family when the breadwinner is not trained for work that is in demand [1]. John W. Gardner, Secretary of Health, Education, and Welfare, suggests that men and women enroll in one or another kind of educational program throughout their lives—for example, to acquaint themselves with new technological developments. He recommends that this become an accepted practice [2].

It is clear from the foregoing discussion that school dropouts must be considered a community problem as well as a personal tragedy. A recent three-year study of dropouts in the District of Columbia conducted by Washington Action for Youth revealed that one-third of the high school youth who drop out of school do so to go to work. In a real sense, these youths may be classified as pushouts. They are pushed out of school by a community unwilling to provide a subsidy sufficient for them to remain in school until they have received the kind of training required in a technology-dominated economy. Also, they are pushed out of school by a system too rigid to modify itself to accommodate both part-time and full-time students.

The Manpower Development and Training Act provides an opportunity for communities to upgrade the skills of their workers through retraining. The community should insist, however, that these training programs be available for younger as well as older workers, and that training allowances be provided. What does it profit a community to provide training programs for older workers only, when more than one-fifth of its out-of-school youth are unemployed? What does it profit a community to establish elaborate training programs based upon assessments of community job needs, with no arrangement for financial compensation, when one-third of the youngsters who leave high school do so because they need money?

This story of two men and their families also indicates a need for revamping local welfare regulations if public welfare is to prevent family disintegration. When the father in a family with marginal means becomes unemployed, the outlook is bleak. It is hard to save money for a rainy day when one earns less than $65 a week. Yet with a father in the family, a household in the District of Columbia is ineligible to receive aid to families with dependent children to tide it over a "bout with bad weather." As pointed out by Senator Abraham Ribicoff, "We force men to desert their families so their wives and children can become eligible for help" [3]. According to District of Columbia welfare regulations, aid to families with dependent children is provided if children are living with their mother and there is no father or substitute father living in or frequenting the home [4]. Reporter Bill Davidson has pointed out that this rule "does not distinguish between a man who will not work and a respectable husband who cannot get a job" [5]. Peter Paul and Bernard Brown, for example, are respectable husbands devoted to their families. These are low-wage earners who from time to time may need public assistance to tide them over minor difficulties. Such aid could prevent further dependency by keeping a family together.

The importance of keeping families together has been demonstrated by a study of the neighborhood distribution of juvenile delinquency in Washington conducted by the research staff of Washington Action for Youth [6]. A high relationship was found between the proportion of families without fathers and the rate of juvenile delinquency in a neighborhood. In the neighborhood with the highest juvenile delinquency rate (a neighborhood in which one out of every ten youngsters 10 to 17 years of age is referred to court each year), nearly half of the youth were growing up in households in which one parent was absent. Thus, public welfare could help promote family stability if families with fathers were eligible for assistance. Public welfare could even help prevent juvenile delinquency by facilitating the staying together of family members and discouraging their drifting apart. Public welfare could become a preventive service.

Finally, the story of two men and their families indicates the need for a comprehensive family service to help with practical, concrete problems. I have in mind a family service that provides homemaking consultants, helps with budgeting problems, gives information about health, welfare, educational, and legal resources, assists in finding housing for families in special circumstances, seeks out educational and job-training opportunities, and advises family members on the alternative ways to solve personal problems and refers them for specialized guidance. I have in mind a modified model of the Philadelphia Homemaking Consultants, who provide short- and long-term service ranging from two or three months to a year. The service proposed, however, should help fathers as well as mothers better meet the responsibilities of their roles. A generalized and comprehensive family service would be of particular help to marginal families out of contact with both public and private specialty agencies.

Existing family-service agencies have been oriented largely to solving psychological problems. The practical problems of living are sometimes overwhelming for low-income families. Where can they turn for help? Where can they go for guidance? If the community has compassion for these families, it would appear to be in eclipse.

The Intercessor: A Present Help in Time of Trouble

The theoretical implication of this analysis for planners of community services is that the role of the intercessor must be extended and strengthened as an essential function in the community. Intercession is a marvelous concept. It has to do with "the act of interceding; mediation; prayer, petition or entreaty in behalf of another," according to *Webster's Seventh New Collegiate Dictionary*. In recent years, intercession has been limited largely to religious activity and has been viewed as a passive approach to problem solving. We think of intercession as prayer in behalf of another — an activity that does not involve direct confrontation with the oppressed or the oppressor, the victim or the victimizer. Because of this, intercession is seen as having little effect upon everyday problems; thus, it has fallen into disrepute in the minds of many as a useful method in community action.

Intercession, however, can be an active approach to problem solving. It can be an act of mediation between the oppressed and the oppressor, between the individual and the community; an experience of direct confrontation with all becoming involved with each other. In the case of the Brown and Paul families, an intercessor is needed to bring the burdens of these households to the attention of the total community and to engender within the community a sense of responsibility to share collectively what could become overwhelming for an individual or a single family.

The essential function of the intercessor was revealed in a research-demonstration study of problem families in a public housing project conducted between 1960 and 1962 in Syracuse, New York. A social worker was retained to give intensive help to half of the 54 households identified by the manager as being in need of immediate help. Since the social worker could handle only about 22 families on an intensive basis during the course of a year, the remaining households were observed as a control group. One goal was to determine whether the social worker (or family consultant, as she was called) had an effect upon the rent-paying patterns of problem families; that is, did she help these families pay their rent in full and on time each month?

When families are delinquent in paying their rent, they may be served an official precept, petition, or warrant. The findings of this study pertaining to the effect of the social worker are the following:

> ... 41 percent of the families in the study group and 52 percent of the families in the control group received one or more precepts, petitions, or warrants during the study period. However, *none of the families seen by the worker was evicted* during this period. [Italics added.] Often she discussed their problems with representatives of the Housing Authority and of other agencies, and she succeeded in making special arrangements in behalf of her clients. Though at times the worker encouraged some families to make their own special arrange-

ments in accordance with their unique situation, she often acted as an intercessor for them. Housing Authority personnel apparently reacted differently to families that had someone to speak in their behalf, and when the consultant acted as intercessor, they showed a willingness to continue working with families whose rent payment had been a problem.

Families in the control group had to "go it alone." No one interpreted their situation to others or sought special help for them. No one supported them as they faced their daily problems. More than 20 percent of these families were evicted or moved because of a threat of eviction when their rent-paying behavior, or some other behavior, became unacceptable to the management of the development.

A specific test was made of the intercessory function of the worker. Without knowing that five families in the control group had been evicted or threatened with eviction, the worker was asked to identify the families in the study group that she judged would have been evicted if she had not intervened. She identified six families, almost the same number. The rent-paying patterns of the families that were saved from eviction and those that were evicted were very similar. ... There is reason to conclude that the six families in the study group were retained in the housing project ... because of the worker's intercession in their behalf. She interceded for them not only with the project manager but also with other agents of voluntary and public organizations, including the Department of Social Welfare [7].

The study further revealed that the evicted families returned to unsound dwellings in the slums of the city. Thus, their condition of slum living was a function not only of their own actions but also of those of the Housing Authority, which, as a representative of the total community, evicted these families. The fortunate ones were those who had an intercessor; they remained in a clean and protected housing development. Standing alone before the Housing Authority, poor and marginal families are unable to resist its decisive judgments.

William Stringfellow, who practiced law for several years in the East Harlem slums of New York City, tells of his first case in court as a novice in law practice. The case involved four boys arrested on the charge of illegal possession of narcotics. As Stringfellow explains:

... the amount was sufficient to warrant a felony charge if the "stuff" belonged to just one of the boys arrested. If, however, the four jointly and equally owned the drugs, then the charge against each would be only a misdemeanor. I interviewed all of the boys and was satisfied that they had all participated in the procurement of the drugs and were partners in its possession and intended use. But they had decided among themselves that it would be best if, as they put it, just one of them "took the weight." As they saw it, it was better for one to plead that the stuff was entirely his own and therefore be charged with a felony and risk a long prison sentence than for each of them to admit part ownership and each be charged with a misdemeanor, with the prospect of much shorter sentences for each other. ...

On the day the case came up for pleadings, I left my tenement early. ... I had decided, partly on the advice of another attorney, to go to court before it convened and discuss the case with the prosecutor and try to persuade him to reduce the charge, in exchange for a guilty plea. There were not any serious legal grounds for the district attorney to agree to this. ...

When I arrived at the court room, several other lawyers were standing in line, waiting to speak to the D.A. I overheard their discussions of other cases on the day's calendar. They were terse, to say the least, and seemed to me to be quite disinterested and even indifferent to the merits of the cases being negotiated. Finally my turn came. I identified myself to the district attorney, whom I had never met before, this being my first court case.

I told him whom I represented, and then he said, "Well, counselor, what do you want?" "I want a misdemeanor," I replied. And then to my astonishment he said, "O.K. When the case is called, we'll talk to the judge."

We did. The judge agreed to the guilty plea to a misdemeanor and the defendant was sentenced to seven months in prison. ... I did not have to persuade anybody, either the D.A. or the court, that the charge should be reduced. I just had to go in and ask for it. It all seemed wrong — some great sham was being made of the law and of the legal system. Yet it all seemed right. ... Maybe this is just the kind of world that is: upside down, broken, foolish, wasteful, and filled with irony. Maybe so [8].

Maybe another boy has been arrested. Maybe he should have been tried for a misdemeanor but has been convicted for a felony. Maybe this has happened because no one interceded for him, because no one was there simply to ask that the charge be reduced. There is no justice for many in poor or marginal circumstances often because there is no one to intercede. As pointed out in one proposal for a legal service agency for the poor that was filed with the federal Office of Economic Opportunity: "The poor are seldom aware of their legal rights in relationship to governmental agencies, landlords, merchants and the like. Unchallenged procedures often create abuses which are accepted by the poor as part of life [9]. The poor or marginal person cannot challenge these procedures alone.

Intercession Plus Self-Help

At a time when self-help programs are being launched in many communities, it is important to highlight the continuing need for the intercessor — one who labors in behalf of another. There are some things none of us can do for ourselves. The intercessor role is not intended as a displacement of self-help programs. Actually, it is a necessary complement, with intercession preceding self-help. This sequential pattern is frequently forgotten. We want people to help themselves, but overlook the fact that the capacity to help oneself is a function of once having been helped. In 1964, in Syracuse, New York, for example, the Syracuse Community Development Association was established to help the poor organize to make their needs known to the community at large and to become participating members of that community. Essentially, this association was established to foster self-help programs among the poor and to enable them to identify their problems. Initial funds for the program, however, came from the Office of Economic Opportunity through the intercessory activity of Syracuse University. Representatives of the university prepared the original application in which the Syracuse Community Development Association was described as a fieldwork extension of the university's Community Action Training Center. Although the Syracuse Community Development Association is no longer affiliated with the university, this self-help program of autonomous organizations of the poor needed an intercessor to come alive.

There is much that poor and marginal families such as the Bernard Browns and the Peter Pauls can do for themselves. But there is much that others must do in their behalf. While poor and low-income families may seize the opportunities that are available, only the community at large can provide the new and different opportunities that these families may need. Our inability to comprehend the role of the intercessor as a necessity in community life may be based in part upon our inability to deal effectively with dependency. As stated elsewhere, "Independency is not a virtue and dependency is not a vice. We all must experience both at some period in life. ... It is time we acknowledged ... that our feet are all caught up *together* (as Langston Hughes has put it) in 'the sweet flypaper of life.' All are sheep and all are shepherds. Each must minister and be ministered unto" [10].

Notes

1. *Washington Post,* 9 July 1963.
2. John W. Gardner, "From High School to Job," reprinted from the Annual Report of the Carnegie Corporation of New York, 1960, pp. 11–12.
3. Bill Davidson, "The Mess in Washington — A City in Trouble," *Saturday Evening Post,* 13 July 1963, p. 22.
4. *Characteristics of State Public Assistance Plans Under the Social Security Administration.* Public Assistance Report No. 50 (Washington, DC: Government Printing Office, 1962).
5. Davidson, "The Mess in Washington," pp. 21–22
6. Charles V. Willie et al., "Race and Delinquency," *Phylon* 26 (Fall 1965): 245.
7. Charles V. Willie, Morton O. Wagenfeld, and Lee J. Cary, "Patterns of Rent Payment Among Problem Families," *Social Casework* 45 (October 1964): 467–468.
8. William Stringfellow, *My People Is the Enemy* (New York: Holt, Rinehart and Winston, 1964), pp. 48–51. © 1964 by William Stringfellow. Reprinted by permission of Holt, Rinehart and Winston, Inc.
9. Crusade for Opportunity, "Legal Service Proposal for Syracuse, New York " (mimeo., 1965).
10. Charles V. Willie, "Our Changing Nation," in General Division of Women's Work of the Executive Council of the Episcopal Church (ed.), *Knowing the Time* (New York: Episcopal Church in USA, 1965), p. 38.

Chapter 11

Intergenerational Problems of Poverty for Blacks and for Whites

Several years ago, I conducted an ecological investigation of the distribution of a middle-sized city population by age and discovered that a "significant number of adults in all socioeconomic areas move at least once in 20 years to a neighborhood of higher status." This finding indicated that a tendency toward upward mobility existed in all segments of the population [Willie 1960:264]. There seems to be a natural tendency for families and individual households to improve their circumstances in time.

Yet poverty has not been eliminated in the United States. Why the nation has been unable to eradicate poverty is an issue about which there is much conjecture. Some analysts argue that the upward social mobility described above was largely a function of the motivation, value orientation, and social organization of immigrant communities that fought their way up as ethnic groups from the bottom of the economic ladder [Glazer and Moynihan 1964]. This same style of reasoning is used to explain why lower-class blacks remain impoverished. The circumstances of many black Americans are frequently explained as a function of the intergenerational transmission of poverty.

Poverty Among Blacks: Moynihan Thesis

In the United States Department of Labor report on *The Negro Family,* Daniel Patrick Moynihan maintained that "a national effort towards the

Reprinted from Charles V. Willie, *A New Look at Black Families,* Second Edition, Bayside, New York: General Hall, Inc., 1981, Chapter 10, pp. 193–206. The chapter was first published in *Poverty and Human Resources Abstracts*, Volume 4, Number 1, (January–February 1969), pp. 5–15. The author was Professor and Chairman, Department of Sociology, Syracuse University, when this article was first published.

problems of Negro Americans must be directed towards the question of family structure." He looked upon the weakness of the family structure as "the principal source of most of the aberrant, inadequate, or antisocial behavior that ... perpetuates the cycle of poverty and deprivation." He concluded that "the present tangle of pathology [among lower-class blacks] is capable of perpetuating itself" [U.S. Department of Labor 1965:47, 30]. In effect, Moynihan is saying that motivation, value orientation, and family organization of racial or ethnic group members contribute to the perpetuation or elimination of poverty within that population. The implication is that the family organization and cultural values of blacks differ from those of other ethnic groups and that these differences account for the persistence of poverty among the members of this racial category. This assertion has been advanced as a basis for social action as if it were supported by empirical evidence. In fact, assertions about the intergenerational transmission of poverty among blacks, such as Moynihan's, are inadequately documented.

Trends in the Proportion of Poor People in the Total U.S. Population

The evidence shows that the proportion of the total United States population that is poor today is less than half of the proportion that was poor three or more decades ago. Clearly, some Americans have escaped the poverty that their parents experienced only one generation ago.

Research into the circumstances associated with poverty has not kept pace with policymaking needs because too many policy-makers have been more interested in justifying the presence or absence of poverty among "their people" rather than explaining it. Thus, the search for solutions to poverty has proceeded within the context of varying ideological orientations.

Moynihan has been identified with the hypothesis that poverty is perpetuated intergenerationally largely because of deficiencies in the family structure. In the United States Department of Labor report, he asserted that employment reflects educational achievement, which depends in large part on family stability [U.S. Department of Labor 1965]. This trinitarian association, however, must be understood for what it is — an assertion and not a conclusion based on evidence. In fact, the evidence appears to point in another direction.

Mollie Orshansky raised a serious question about the strength of the association assumed to exist between poverty and family instability when she pointed out that "two-thirds of all children in the families called poor do live in a home with a man at the head" and that "more than half of all poor families report that the head currently has a job." It would seem on the basis of the Orshansky analysis that many poor families are not unlike affluent families [Orshansky 1965].

Poverty and Family Characteristics

A study of income and welfare conducted by the Survey Research Center of the University of Michigan found that characteristics of parents did have a substantial effect on the amount of education their children completed, but that this effect accounted for less than half — 41 percent of the variance in years of school completed [Morgan et al. 1962:383]. The contribution of a combination of nonfamily factors to the amount of schooling received by children, therefore, was found to be more important than variables pertaining to the structure and process of the kinship system.

A Census report revealed that "six out of every ten college students in the United States were receiving higher education despite the fact that their fathers did not have this opportunity" [Miller 1964:26]. It is true that youth from higher-income families that have college-trained heads are more likely to complete school than are poorer youth. Yet it has been stated also that college youth come from all levels of American society. These data mean that no definitive answer is available concerning the extent to which insufficient education received by parents results in limited education and consequently low earning power for their children.

Because family characteristics have some association with the economic status of households, it might be helpful to consider characteristics that could have a significant intergenerational effect. The presence of one or both parents in the household is easily observed and usually is pounced upon as a quick and easy explanation. But because some low-income families are two-parent households, other variables should be considered too. A more subtle, but possible influential, variable is the education of the wife and mother in the family. The University of Michigan study discovered that "an average education attained by children is also influenced by the educational achievement of the mother. The more education the wife has relative to her husband, the more education the children attain. ... Where the wife has less education than the head, achievement of the children is impeded but not so much as they are advanced when the wife has more education than the head" [Morgan 1962:374–375].

Promiscuity, Illegitimacy, and Poverty

Probably the behavior that has caught the attention of the public more than any other, and that is believed to be eminently responsible for the intergenerational transmission of poverty among blacks, is illegitimacy. The Department of Labor report authored by Moynihan stated that "the number of illegitimate children per 1,000 live births increased by 11 among whites during a period of two decades but by 68 among non-whites." The report further stated that of the million or more black illegitimate children in the nation most of them did not receive public welfare assistance. Nevertheless, illegitimacy was used as one of several indications of family breakdown among blacks that was assumed to be associated with the perpetuation of poverty. Why illegitimacy among whites was not declared to be a circumstance indicative of family breakdown was never clarified. The report stated that "the white family, despite many variants, remains a powerful agency not only for transmitting property from one generation to the next, but also for transmitting no less valuable contacts with the world of education and work. White children without fathers at least perceive all about them the pattern of men working. Black children without fathers flounder" [U.S. Department of Labor 1965:8, 12, 34].

Again a series of assertions has been presented with little evidential base. The implication of these assertions is that part of the source of intergenerational poverty among blacks could be eliminated if illegitimate births could be prevented.

The conception of children out of wedlock is often described as a way of life for low-income women, a cultural norm. William Goode believes that many low-income women have few attributes other than sex at their disposal in the process of bargaining for husbands. He arrives at this conclusion based on his study of illegitimacy in the Caribbean Islands [Goode 1960:20–30]. It should go without saying that lower-class women often are exploited by men who have no intention of marrying. But the fact remains that the illegitimate child is sometimes a by-product of the women's search for a husband. In these cases, the woman misunderstands the paramour and miscalculates, with tragic results.

The Culture of the Poor

In general, persons who hypothesize that poverty is intergenerationally transmitted because of deficiencies in the person, family, and clan believe that there is a "culture of the poor" [Lewis 1962:2]. This concept, which may help organize our thoughts about the poor, also may tend to inhibit our perceptions of the great variations in behavior among poor people. A range of behavior patterns exists among poor people just as a range of behavior pattern exists among the nonpoor. Thus, it is inappropriate to look upon the poor as constituting a subculture that reinforces and perpetuates itself, including the condition of poverty. Our studies, which revealed diversified behavior in rent payment practices and in family activities among households in a low-rent public housing project in Syracuse, New York, cast doubt upon the concept of a culture of the poor [Willie, Wagenfeld, and Cary 1964:465-470]. Of course, there are deficiencies in the life-style of some poor people as there are deficiencies in the life-style of others in the society. But these deficiencies should not be interpreted as an internally consistent, normative, and integrated pattern or a system of beliefs that guide and give direction to behavior that perpetuates poverty.

Poverty and the Social System

A hypothesis in opposition to the one discussed above is not formulated to explain whether or not poverty is transmitted intergenerationally. However, it does focus upon deficiencies in social systems and in the community at large. This alternative hypothesis is that change in social organization tends to be associated with change in individual behavior. According to this hypothesis, poverty is a function of inadequacies in the operations of social systems; thus, systemic changes are necessary to eliminate poverty among individuals. By implication, then, this hypothesis is relevant to the debate about intergenerational transmission of poverty. The background for this hypothesis is what has happened in this nation, as well as what is known to date about the intergenerational transmission of poverty.

The significant reduction in the proportion of low-income families during the past three decades has occurred largely because of change in the economic system. This sytem has continued to grow and expand, increasing in productivity and efficiency, and has brought more income to people through the years. Thus, much of the poverty that might have been perpetuated intergenerationally was eliminated as a consequence of systemic change — the growth and expansion of the economy.

Certain specific studies of intergenerational poverty also cast doubt on its transmission through families. One, for example, conducted by Lawrence

Podell in New York City, discovered that only "15 percent of a citywide sampling of mothers on welfare rolls ... had parents who also had been relief recipients." Moreover, Podell found that "eight out of ten believed their children would not become dependent adults." In the light of the experience of the mothers included in this study, there is reason to believe that their predictions might be realized; less than 2 out of 10 of current recipients came from families that received welfare assistance [*New York Times* 1968]. (Failure to receive welfare, however, does not indicate automatically that 85 percent of the mothers came from nonpoor families. In spite of public concern about increasing welfare rolls, it is a well-known fact that a large majority of poor families do not receive needed assistance.) Limiting the analysis to welfare families, however, one finds little evidence to support the contention that poverty is transmitted intergenerationally. The evidence indicates that intergenerational transmission is experienced in only a few families.

Education: Pro and Con

Many analysts who subscribe to the system change hypothesis as a more fruitful approach to an adequate explanation of poverty believe that the best way to eliminate it is to move on the educational system. For instance, a report issued by the Upjohn Institute for Employment Research stated that "the keystone of any attempt to broaden the employment possibilities for blacks is obviously education — not only the formal programs of kindergarten through high school but also education that is now available in the form of training programs financed by various federal agencies" [Sheppard and Striner 1966:22]. However, psychiatrists Abram Kardiner and Lionel Ovesey have not held much hope for manipulation of the educational system as a way of dealing with poverty, especially among blacks, unless there is also a corresponding change in the education of white people. They state that "the psychosocial expressions of the black personality are the ... end products of the process of oppression. They can never be eradicated without removing the forces that create and perpetuate them. What is needed by the black is not education but re-integration. It is the white ... who requires the education. ... There is only one way that the products of oppression can be dissolved," according to Kardiner and Ovesey, "and that is to stop the oppression" [Kardiner and Ovesey 1962: 387]. These two psychiatrists consider the inadequate education of blacks — and whatever association may exist between their poverty and education — to be the result of antiblack prejudice and discrimination.

Robert Merton, in his essay "The Self-Fulfilling Prophecy," supports this view in an illustration of the mechanism at work: "Whites who prophesy that blacks are incompetent and incapable of benefiting from formal education withhold support from black schools [making them inferior] and then point to the smaller number of black high school or college graduates [which the inferior schools produce] as justification for not providing greater support for the education of blacks" [Merton 1949:179–195]. In his commentary on schools in metropolitan areas, James B. Conant observed that "we now recognize so plainly but so belatedly [that] a caste system finds its clearest manifestation in an educational system" [Conant 1961:11–12].

If the educational system in this country is to change so that it serves the needs of black people better, those people who established and continue to maintain a system of inferior education for blacks must change. They must support an educational system that equips blacks with the skills to participate productively in the mainstream of a technology-dominated economy. This, however, is not likely to occur unless whites are reoriented in their education and general socialization to relate to blacks as human beings, divested of any belief that whites are superhuman. Kardiner and Ovesey [1962:379] point out that blacks were subjected to pure utilitarian use during the period of slavery in this country. "Once you degrade someone in that way," they remind us, "the sense of guilt makes it imperative to degrade the object further to justify the entire procedure." Merton doubts the efficacy of education as a way of dealing with the prevailing patterns of race relations. His belief is that "education may serve as an operational adjunct but not as the chief basis for any but excruciating slow change in the prevailing patterns of race relations." What is likely to be more effective, according to Merton, is "deliberate institutional change" designed to destroy discrimination [Merton 1949:183, 193].

Racial Discrimination and Poverty

Economist Herman Miller, who also subscribes to the hypothesis of institutional change as a way of dealing with poverty among disadvantaged minority groups, maintains that "racial discrimination is a key cause" of the black's perpetually low estate. He refers to a study of the Council of Economic Advisers that estimated that during a single year billions of dollars more than they received would have been placed in the hands of blacks had there not been any racial discrimination in employment [Miller 1965:32]. He points out that black people with the same amount of education as whites usually earn less money. In an analysis of the Census, Miller discovered that "non-white men earn about three-fourths as much as whites with the same amount of schooling," and that "blacks who have completed four years of college education can expect to earn only as much in a lifetime as whites who have not gone beyond the eighth grade." Thus, Miller concludes, "there is some justification for the feeling by Puerto Ricans, blacks, and other minority groups that education does not do as much for them, financially, as it does for others" [Miller 1964:140–153].

It would appear that racial and ethnic discrimination more than inadequate education is one of the chief factors contributing to the low-income status of many blacks. For example, among whites of limited education (with eight or fewer years of schooling), 50 percent are likely to have jobs as service workers or laborers at the bottom of the heap, while nearly 80 percent of black workers with limited education are likely to find work only in these kinds of jobs [Miller 1964:140–153].

James Tobin has pointed out that the low earning capacity of blacks and their inferior education "both reflect discrimination" [Tobin 1965: 878–898]. The point I continue to emphasize, however, is that even when work capacity and education are equal of those of whites, discrimination still persists and results in a lower family income for blacks. The Moynihan thesis that the lack of improvement in opportunities for a large mass of black workers is correlated with a serious weakening of the black family, therefore, obscures the issue of discrimination and white racism in the United States, and so does his statement that "equality, as a fundamental democratic disposition, goes beyond equal opportunity to the issue of equal results" [Moynihan 1965:746–747]. The Census data analyzed by Miller indicated that equal opportunity has not yet been realized for black Americans; thus discussion of equal results is indeed premature.

We know that the rise in income in the past 20 to 30 years has been shared by black and by white families, and that the percentages of black and of white families below the poverty line have been significantly reduced, according to the U.S. Bureau of Labor Statistics [1967:18]. The two populations, however, started from different bases. Of black families, 65 percent were poor two to three decades ago, compared with only 27 percent of white families. The proportion of blacks in poverty was two to three times greater than the proportion of poor whites two to three decades ago, and this ratio has remained constant over the years, even though the number of poor families has been reduced in each racial population [1967:18].

Different Approaches for Eliminating Poverty Among Whites and Among Blacks

Because there are more than twice as many poor blacks proportionately as there are poor whites, and because racial discrimination has been identified as a key cause that keeps blacks at the bottom (an experience that they do not share with poor whites), it could very well be that different hypotheses are needed for explaining the continuation of poverty in the two racial populations. Failure to explore the possibility that different explanations of poverty may be required for different racial populations, which have had essentially different experiences, may have contributed to the contemporary controversy. It is conceivable, for example, that the hypothesis that may contribute to a better understanding of poverty among whites is one that seeks to determine the association, if any, among low-income status, motivation, aspiration, and life orientation. For blacks, however, a more powerful explanation of poverty might proceed from an examination of the hypothesis that seeks to determine the association, if any, among low-income status, racial discrimination, and institutional oppression.

The findings of another study that I conducted in Washington, D.C. are the basis for suggesting the possibility of differential explanations of poverty in white and in black populations. The study dealt with juvenile delinquency among whites and among blacks. I discovered that reducing family instability would probably contribute to a greater reduction in delinquency among whites than among blacks, and that increasing economic opportunities would very likely contribute to a greater reduction in delinquency among blacks than among whites. While a good deal of family instability existed with the black population in Washington, economic insecurity was overwhelming. It appeared, according to the data collected, that we would not get at the family instability factor and its association with delinquency without first dealing with economic insecurity and its association with delinquency. Because a higher proportion of whites were not poor, family instability was their outstanding problem. But economic insecurity was the salient problem for blacks, and it could not be circumvented in favor of family instability [Willie 1967].

The same principle may apply to the issue of poverty. Institutional changes during the past three to four decades have resulted in a substantial reduction in the proportion of whites who are poor. External changes in social organizations have upgraded most of the white population beyond the poverty level. The few who remain poor probably have problems that are more personal and less susceptible to mass amelioration through institutional manipulation. These whites may be the individuals with insufficient motivation, low aspiration, and a fatalistic orientation unreached thus far by changes in the institutional systems of society that create new opportunities. The proportion of poor blacks, however, remains at a higher level and may still be amenable to ameliorative mass efforts. Apparently, the kinds of institutional changes needed to upgrade the black population are somewhat different from those required to upgrade the white population. In addition to deliberate institutional changes that may increase economic opportunities, blacks require deliberate institutional changes that will prevent racial discrimination. Until these are put into effect, we cannot know how large the residual proportion of black poor people might be who need such individualized attention as the few poor whites may now require. To date, two-thirds of the black population have been upgraded beyond poverty. There is every reason to believe that more can and must be done.

A Problem with the Moynihan Proposal

In the light of this discussion, it would seem that one problem with the Moynihan proposal for dealing with poverty is that it projects a solution more appropriate for the white than for the black poor. One essential difference between blacks and whites with reference to poverty is that blacks also experience a great deal of discrimination and that the institutional changes that helped pull more than 9 out of every 10 whites above the poverty line have not run their full course for blacks. That is why the Moynihan concern about equal results is premature until there are equal opportunities.

Conclusions

On the basis of the foregoing analysis, we may derive the following conclusions:

1.   There is some intergenerational transmission of poverty, though not as much as is generally assumed.
2.   Upward social mobility is a more common experience in the United States than is the continuation of intergenerational poverty.
3.   The perpetuation of poverty from one generation to the next is likely to be a function of personal and family-connected circumstances as well as of patterns of institutional organization.

4.   Personal and family-connected circumstances are likely to be more powerful explanations of poverty among whites than among blacks.

5.   Institutional arrangements and patterns of racial discrimination are likely to be more powerful explanations of poverty among blacks than among whites.

The latter two conclusions are stated tentatively and should be further tested as hypotheses. The reason for suggesting a differential explanation for the continuation of poverty by race is the fact that whites and blacks have dissimilar patterns of participation in the economic system of the United States. As stated by Louis Kriesberg [1968: 5–6], "generational change in the proportion of the population which is poor is largely determined by economic developments and public policies regarding income maintenance and distribution." Racial discrimination has prevented blacks and other nonwhite minorities from participating fully in the benefits of an expanding economy. Changes in institutional arrangements have been largely responsible for preventing poverty among whites, and there is reason to believe that such changes will aid in the prevention of poverty among blacks if the benefits of these changes are made available to all sectors of society.

Because whites, in general, have had free access to the opportunities produced by institutional change, the residual number of poor people in this racial category might well be a function of personal and family-connected deficiencies. It is not concluded that poverty among whites cannot be further reduced by more changes in the institutional systems of society. Rather, it is suggested that new manipulations of social institutions will probably net a smaller rate of change in the proportion of poor whites as compared with poor blacks, for most whites who could benefit from these major institutional changes probably have already taken advantage of them.

References

Conant, James B. 1961. *Slums and Suburbs*. New York: McGraw-Hill.

Glazer, Nathan, and Daniel Patrick Moynihan. 1964. *Beyond the Melting Pot*. Cambridge, MA: M.I.T. Press and Harvard University Press.

Goode, William J. 1960. "Illegitimacy in the Caribbean Social Structure." *American Sociological Review* 25 (February): 20–30.

Kardiner, Abram, and Lionel Ovesey. 1962. *The Mark of Oppression*. Cleveland: Meridian Books.

Kriesberg, Louis. 1968. "Intergenerational Patterns of Poverty." Paper presented at the annual meeting of the Eastern Sociological Society, Boston, 6 April.

Lewis, Oscar. 1962. *Five Families.* New York: Science Editions.

Merton, Robert K. 1949. *Social Structure and Social Theory.* New York: Free Press.

Miller, Herman. 1965. "The Dimensions of Poverty." In Ben E. Seligman (ed.), *Poverty as a Public Issue.* New York: Free Press.

_____. 1964. *Rich Man, Poor Man.* New York: Crowell.

Morgan, N., et al. 1962. *Income and Welfare in the United States.* New York: McGraw-Hill.

Moynihan, Daniel Patrick. 1965. "Employment, Income, and the Ordeal of the Negro Family." *Daedalus* 94 (Fall): 745–770.

New York Times. 1968. "Survey of Relief Shows Tie to Past." 24 March.

Orshansky, Mollie. 1965. "Consumption, Work, and Poverty." In Ben E. Seligman (ed.), *Poverty as a Public Issue.* New York: Free Press.

Sheppard, Harold L., and Herbert E. Striner. 1966. *Civil Rights, Employment, and the Social Status of American Negroes.* Kalamazoo: W. E. Upjohn Institute for Employment Research.

Tobin, James. 1965. "On Improving the Economic Status of the Negro." *Daedalus* 94 (Fall): 878–898.

U. S. Bureau of Labor Statistics. 1967. Bureau of Labor Statistics and Bureau of the Census, *Social and Economic Conditions of Negroes in the United States.* BLS Report No. 332, Current Population Reports, Series P–23, No. 24. Washington, DC: Government Printing Office.

U. S. Department of Labor. 1965. *The Negro Family. A Case for National Action.* Washington, DC: Government Printing Office.

Willie, Charles V. 1960. "Age, Status, and Residential Stratification." *American Sociological Review,*(April).

_____. 1967. "Family Status and Economic Status in Juvenile Delinquency." *Social Problems* 14 (Winter): 326–335.

_____; Morton O. Wagenfeld; and Lee J. Cary. 1964. "Patterns of Rent Payment Among Problem Families." *Social Casework* 45 (October) 465–470.

Chapter 12

Theoretical Implications:
Disease, Mortality, Delinquency, and Poverty

In the foreword to Janice Perlman's prize-winning book about the people of poverty in Rio de Janeiro, Fernando Henrique Cardoza praised the author for demystifying a social problem such as poverty. He was particularly pleased with her rejection of the "ideology of the culture of the poor" because it tends to stigmatize and hold the poor responsible for not being affluent. Cardoza noted that there is a dialectical relationship between the world of the disinherited and the affluent that Perlman's analysis illuminates [Cardoza 1976:xi-xiii]. Such a relationship, according to Perlman, is masked by the affluent as a way of denying that the problem of poverty is, in part, a function of their reluctance or unwillingness to share their privilege [Perlman 1976:102].

After reviewing the findings of several studies and her own data, Perlman concluded that poor people do not have an economic life of their own but are linked with the larger community in many ways [Perlman 1976:101]. In answering the question — why does poverty exist — one must examine the way of life of the affluent as well as the customs and characteristics of the poor. Perlman's study reveals that the two populations are interrelated. The study also revealed that low-income families are diversified in attitudes and behavior. Thus, their common social problems cannot be attributed to common characteristics, since there is great variation among poor people. Observing the interaction between the poor and the rest of the community, Perlman described the poor as often humiliated and defeated when they attempt to make use of social services. They find the system generally closed to their interests [Perlman 1976:140].

Yet the labor of the poor is welcomed. Most are employed in the service sector. The jobs they perform need to be done. Moreover, the poor generate income that recirculates throughout the economy. Far from being a drain, Perlman said, "the economy benefits doubly from purchases by lower sector residents because they must often buy on credit" [Perlman 1976:154]. The dialectical relationship between poverty and affluence, then, is "[the poor] are integrated into [the economy] on terms detrimental to them"; this gives rise to "a stable system which is balanced to the advantage of some precisely through the explicit or implicit exploitation of others" [Perlman 1976:245].

Clearly, the relationship between the poor and the affluent that Perlman found in Brazil is not limited to that setting. The myths about poverty there are similar to those found elsewhere. In general, these myths assert that the poor are inadequate and their poverty is self-perpetuated. These myths, in Perlman's opinion, "fulfill the ideological-political function of preserving the social order which generates them" [Perlman 1976:246].

Essentially, Perlman sought the reasons for poverty. Then she determined how poverty is distributed. Both questions of why and how must be asked in the scientific study of humanity and social problems. When humanity is studied as if it were just a phenomenon of nature and not composed of thinking, feeling human beings who are free to act or not to act with a purpose, then the researcher asks only questions concerned with what or how, but not why. Why is a metaphysical question of causation. As Whitehead pointed out, knowledge of nature can be described only as "the 'what' of knowledge"; in other words, "we can analyze the content and its internal relations" [Whitehead 1957:32]. But he added, "there is need of a metaphysics whose scope transcends the limitation of nature" [Whitehead 1957:32]. Sociology should be recognized as a science that asks questions about why one population group is treated the way it is by another. With an answer to this question of causation, one is better able to understand how social problems are distributed among the various racial, ethnic, and socioeconomic groups. The why and how questions are essential in the study of humanity because even though human action is in nature, it also transcends nature and its limits of time and space.

When questions concerning social problems such as disease, delinquency, and poverty are asked only about what these phenomena are and how they are distributed, researchers are limited to studies of covariation of these phenomena with characteristics of the population. Despite the sophisticated statistical and other analytical techniques used, such studies end up "playing the dozens with path analysis," to use Howard Taylor's phrase [Taylor 1973]. The dozens is a word game of one-upmanship played by black people in which the adversary is cleverly insulted by derogatory remarks about his or her ancestors, usually the adversary's mother [Taylor

1973:433]. Path analysis is a statistical technique for handling social data. Studies that ask questions of what and how tend to investigate patterns of covariation between social phenomena and heritability characteristics. Such studies, as pointed out by Taylor, do not tell us anything about the way one is treated in one's own environment. Moreover, said Taylor, "the IQ scores of the members of any given pair have no direct causal effect on each other" [Taylor 1980:211]. As mentioned in a previous chapter, the differences among racial and ethnic groups reflect how they act and the way they are treated. To understand the treatment of one group by another, one must answer the why question, which is the question about human choice and purpose.

The genetic scientist Theodosius Dobzhansky defined inequality as a human, not a biological, problem. He said, "it can be withheld from, or bestowed upon, members of a society ... regardless of how similar or diverse they are" [Dobzhansky 1973:4].

In general, our criticism is that a nature-bound social science perspective is a deficient social science that studies how racial, ethnic, and other groups react to their environments in terms of incidence and prevalence rates of social pathology, but does not also study why such environments are created for varying populations. As stated by Dobzhansky, "genes have determined the intelligence (or stature or weight) of a person only in the particular sequence of environments to which that person has been exposed in his upbringing and life experiences" [Dobzhansky 1973:8]. The why question is essential not only in gaining an understanding of the reasons environments vary for different racial and ethnic groups, but also for determining the multiple reactions of members of a specific group to the same environment. Our tendency to consider information about norms as more important than information about coefficients of variation has blinded us to the overlapping ranges of behavior and characteristics in distributions of all racial, ethnic, and socioeconomic groups, and to the various reactions of the members of a specific group who are exposed to different environments.

Studies presented in this volume demonstrate that black populations and white populations tend to have similar rates of mortality, disease, and other disorders when family income and other socioeconomic status conditions of life are held constant. Yet, the similar economic circumstances of different populations may be attributed to different reasons, as the report of the President's Commission on Mental Health [1977] declared. For example, troubled emotions and thoughts of individuals and the disruption or diminution in earning power associated therewith may be experienced by one group because of race discrimination, by another because of sex discrimination, and still by another because of isolation and lack of participation due to migration. Although the disordered behavior manifested by various groups may be similar, the reasons for the behavior may be different. Thus a social science that asks and answers the why question in the diagnosis of social problems is able to offer group-specific prescriptions for their solution. When questions of why are not posed along with questions of how, one group (usually the dominant group) tends to project upon other groups prescriptions that are appropriate for its own circumstances. This is precisely what a social scientist who also was a federal government administrator did in the mid-1960s. As reported earlier, Moynihan said, "it is clearly a disadvantage for a minority group to be operating on one principle, while the great majority of the population and the one with the most advantages to begin with, is operating on another" [United States Labor Department 1965:25]. This assertion does not acknowledge the validity of group-specific principles and approaches to solving social problems. Note that the prescription offered (the way of life of dominants) was not based on a determination of why the environments for minority and majority populations differ. If disadvantaged circumstances have been created for the minority by the majority, in part, to perpetuate its advantaged circumstances, then a minority that adopts the principles of the majority as valid (as Moynihan said it should) will contribute to its own oppression and continue the advantaged and disadvantaged circumstances as they are. The prescription of what should be done to overcome social problems and other adversities in society should be based on knowledge of why adversity exists. Not to determine why is to offend subdominants by disregarding their unique circumstances and by ignoring the fact that their way of life is a complement to that of the dominants. The latter fact means that the dominants also are responsible, in part, for the way of life of subdominants.

In terms of the solution of social problems, such an understanding gives validity to the assertion that a serial approach is needed. If the condition of subdominants is, in part, a function of the actions of dominants, then dominants first must change as a way of influencing subdominants to change. To the assertion that "the keystone of any attempt to broaden the employment possibilities for blacks is obviously education" [Sheppard and Striner 1966:22], Abram Kardiner and Lionel Ovesey are on target when they state that there must be a corresponding change in the education of white people. Specifically they say, "the psychosocial expressions of the black personality are the ... end products of the process of oppression. They can never be eradicated without removing the forces that create and perpetuate them. What is needed by the black is not education but reintegration. It is the white ... who requires the education. ... There is only one way that the products of oppression can be dissolved, and that is to stop the oppression" [Kardiner and Ovesey, 1962:387]. When poverty is analyzed as a covariant with race as if it were a natural occurrence without intention and purpose, then prescriptions of how it may be solved are imprecise if not faulty. The Joint Commission on Mental Illness and Mental Health, for example, not wishing to engage in the faulty practice of projecting the way of life of the majority upon the minority but at the same time not wishing to ask questions about why a higher incidence of all kinds of illnesses are found among people who are deprived by reason of race or poverty, presented this ambivalent response. The Commission members were reported to be uncertain as to whether a person from the ghetto who is depressed or paranoid is reacting normally or abnormally, compared to a person who is adjusted and happy in similar surroundings. If the Commission first had diagnosed why the ghetto exists, then its members could have determined what is an appropriate or an inappropriate response to an environment purposefully created. To determine why the ghetto exists, the Commission members would have had to acknowledge their own complicity. Having admitted this, they could have been more certain about what to do to overcome poverty. They would have examined their own behavior and how it affects the behavior of poor people and racial minorities.

Such an analysis gives rise to the concept of the intercessor if a society is serious about helping the disadvantaged to confront the established ways of doing things and to negotiate a solution. As Perlman [1976] found, the system that is controlled by the dominant people of power is generally closed to the interests of subdominants. The intercessor helps open the system to fuller participation so that the dominants and the subdominants may negotiate toward a mutually acceptable end. In nature there are winners and losers; but in humanity, there is the ever-present potential of achieving a double victory of mutual fulfillment.

For this reason, thoughtful natural scientists have urged social planners not to use nature as a model for solving the problems of society. With reference to physiology, René Dubos said, "the wisdom of the body is often a short-sighted wisdom." He cites the production of scar tissue as an example: it heals wounds and helps in checking the spread of infection; but in the liver or the kidney, scar tissue means cirrhosis or glomerular nephritis; in rheumatoid arthritis, it may freeze the joints [Dubos 1972:248]. People differ from the animal kingdom, said Dubos, not by their biological endowments but by the use they make of them, usually in a conscious way.

People think and reflect about what they see; they interpret and try to find meaning in what they encounter. Dubos was critical of social scientists who develop the homeostatic attitude of nature toward humanity. He said this causes such scientists to be insensitive to the potential for social change. Finally he concluded that "the concept of homeostasis in sociology and economics ... is a postulate which hardly ever fits reality" [Dubos, 1972:248–249]. Racial, ethnic, and socioeconomic status groups tend to maintain traditions and customs but they also tend to transcend these, reach out beyond present circumstances, and change. For this reason, Whitehead declared, "there is a need for a metaphysical science that has as its object [the exhibition] in its utmost completeness our concept of reality" [Whitehead 1957:32]. Such a sociology asks questions about why as well as how; it should enable us to understand better the cause and distribution of social problems and how to overcome them.

References

Cardoza, Fernando Henrique. 1976. "Foreword." In Janice E. Perlman, *The Myth of Marginality*. Berkeley: University of California Press.

Dobzhansky, Theodosius. 1973. *Genetic Diversity and Human Equality*. New York: Basic Books.

Dubos, René. 1972. *A God Within*. New York: Scribner's.

Kardiner, Abram, and Lionel Ovesey. 1962. *The Mark of Oppression*. Cleveland: Meridian Books.

Merton, Robert K. 1949. *Social Theory and Social Structure*. New York: Free Press.

Perlman, Janice E. 1976. *The Myth of Marginality*. Berkeley: University of California Press.

President's Commission on Mental Health. 1977. *Preliminary Report to the President*. Washington, DC: Government Printing Office for Public Committee for Mental Health.

Sheppard, Harold L., and Herbert E. Striner. 1966. *Civil Rights, Employment, and the Social Status of American Negroes*. Kalamazoo: W. E. Upjohn Institute for Employment Research.

Taylor, Howard F. 1973. "Playing the Dozens with Path Analysis." *Sociology of Education* 46 (Fall 1974): 433–450.

_____. 1980. *The IQ Game*. New Brunswick, NJ: Rutgers University Press.

U. S. Labor Department. 1965. *The Negro Family, A Case for National Action*. Washington, DC: Government Printing Office.

Whitehead, Alfred North. 1957. *The Concept of Nature*. Ann Arbor: University of Michigan Press. First published in 1920.

PART III

INSTITUTIONAL AND COMMUNITY STUDIES

FAMILY, SCHOOL, AND COMMUNITY: STABILITY AND CHANGE

Chapter 13

A National Population Policy
and the Fear of Racial Genocide

Some people in the black community are deeply suspicious of any family-planning program initiated by whites. Whites probably have heard about but not taken seriously the call by some male-dominated black militant groups for black females to eschew the use of contraceptives because they are pushed in the black community as "a method of exterminating black people." While black females often take a different view about contraceptives than their male militant companions, they are also concerned about the possibility of black genocide in America.

The genocidal charge is neither "absurd" nor "hollow," as some whites have contended. It is also not limited to residents of the ghetto, whether they are young black militants or middle-aged black moderates. Indeed, my own studies of black students at white colleges indicate that young educated blacks fear black genocide, too [11].

This statement from a black female student is representative of the thinking of so many other blacks. She said: "The institutions in society are so strong. The C.I.A. is everywhere. I believe that America desires to perpetuate concentration camps for political opponents of the system of this country. People who speak out against the system are being systematically cut down." She concluded her recitation of despair with this depressing thought: "I wouldn't say that this society is against all-out genocide for black people" [11, p. 7]. While there is uncertainty in her accusation, there is no mood of hope.

Reprinted from Charles V. Willie, *Black/Brown/White Relations,* New Brunswick, New Jersey: Transaction Books, 1977, pp. 27–33. This is a revised version of a position paper presented to the Commission on Population Growth and the American Future, Washington, D.C., April 13, 1971. The author was affiliated with Syracuse University as Vice President for Student Affairs when this article was written.

149

I designate the death of Martin Luther King, Jr., as the beginning of this serious concern among blacks about the possibility of genocide in America. There were lynchings, murders, and manslaughters in the past. But the assassination of Dr. King was too much. Many blacks believed that Dr. King had represented their best. He was scorned, spat upon, and slain. If America could not accept Dr. King, then many felt that no black person in America was safe. For none other could match the magnificent qualities of this great man. Yet his achievements and character were not enough. So he was cut down by the bullet of a white assassin in a crime that remains mysterious when considering the help that the assassin received in escaping to a foreign land.

I dwell upon this event of our modern history because the Commission on Population Growth and the American Future must consider the present as well as the recent past, which is the context within which it must plan for the future. This context cannot be ignored. The American society must assure black people that it is committed to their survival with dignity and equality. The Commission on Population Growth must demonstrate that participation in any national plan will serve the self-interests of blacks.

The Commission will have difficulty demonstrating that a national population policy will fulfill the self-interests of black people. To some blacks, any call today by a federal commission for a national population policy, especially if it focuses on family planning, sounds similar to a call some years ago by a federal official for a national program to stabilize the black family. That call was set forth in *The Negro Family, A Case for National Action,* which was prepared by the U.S. Labor Department [10]. Its chief author was Daniel Patrick Moynihan. I need not remind you of the negative reaction of blacks to the Moynihan Report. Many blacks got the idea that the national policy Moynihan was advocating was designed to make over blacks in the image of whites. They got this idea from his allegation that the matriarchal family structure that exists among blacks has seriously retarded their progress *"because it is so out of line with the rest of the American society"* [10, p. 29, italics added]. In an article published later in *Daedalus,* Moynihan described the black family as being in a state of "unmistakable crisis." He concluded that the crisis was acute because of "the *extraordinary rise* in Negro population" [7, p. 299, italics added].

While Moynihan may not have intended to give this impression these two statements seem, to me, to call for a national policy to obliterate any family forms among blacks that might be different from the family forms found among whites. Moreover, he suggested that the nation should act quickly to refurbish blacks in the image of whites because blacks were gaining on whites in numbers. These statements came from someone who has been an intimate consultant to presidents. Blacks were suspicious of Moynihan's call for a national policy that focused upon the black family. The Moynihan Report, therefore, is excess baggage that the Commission (or any other national planning and policy-recommending group) does not need and from which it should separate itself.

If the Commission on Population Growth and the American Future is to promulgate a national policy that will gain the cooperation of black people, such a policy must fulfill the goals and aspirations that blacks themselves have identified as important. A national population policy must demonstrate that it is more concerned about the *health and wealth* of black people than it is about the number of children they have.

Let me explain why some blacks believe that a national population policy that focuses upon limiting the number of black children born is a desperation move on the part of whites to remain in control. Whites were not concerned about the size and structure of black families centuries ago. Then blacks were nearly one-fifth (18.4 percent) of the total population. This, of course, was during the age of slavery before 1820. Then blacks were not free. They were not a challenge to whites. Although they represented one out of every five persons in the United States, and although the family assumed even more functions for the growth, development, and well-being of individuals then, than it probably does today, American whites were not concerned about the fertility or stability of the black family at that point in time. Indeed, there were attempts to breed healthy black male slaves with healthy black female slaves, disregarding any family connections and, in many instances, even prohibiting marriage. Gunnar Myrdal wrote, "most slave owners ... did not care about the marital state of their slaves. ... [In fact,] the internal slave trade broke up many slave families" [8, p. 931]. Neither the size of the black population nor its circumstances of family life worried white Americans before black people were free.

But with the emergence of the Freedom Movement among blacks, there is a continuing call for self-determination. White Americans have become concerned about the size, the structure, and the stability of the black family. Moynihan alerted blacks about what was in the minds of some whites when he described the situation as "acute" because of the "extraordinary rise in Negro population." The size, structure, and stability of the black family were of no concern to some white Americans when black people were enslaved. The size, structure, and stability of the black family are cause for alarm among some white Americans, requiring a national program of control, now that black people are beginning to achieve freedom and equality.

Blacks, of course, would not claim that there has been an extraordinary rise in their population. Blacks in America have increased from 9.9 percent in 1920 to approximately 11.4 percent in the early 1970s — hardly "extraordinary." But then maybe an increase of between one and two percentage points of the total population is an extraordinary rise if one believes it is. Sociologist Robert Merton has written that "self-hypnosis through one's own propaganda is a not infrequent phase of the self-fulfilling prophecy" [4, p. 185].

Moreover, a population increase of one to two percentage points of the total creates an "acute" situation and is cause for alarm if the ultimate national goal is to eliminate black people; for such an increase, although small, indicates that they will not go away.

The genocidal fears of blacks, therefore, are anchored in facts. These facts are: (1) that a leading governmental spokesman declared that an increase of black people of one to two percentage points of the total population is "extraordinary"; (2) that over the years the greatest contributor to family instability among blacks has been the death of the male spouse rather than divorce or desertion; and (3) that the major control upon the fertility rate of blacks in the past has been the deaths of their very young children.

Back in 1910, 27 percent of black females were members of broken families because their husbands were dead. During that same year, only 6 percent of black families were broken because of divorce or desertion of the male spouse. Thus, death was four times more frequently a contributor to family disruption than other social causes. I should add that death of the husband was the chief cause for marital breakup for black families compared with desertion or divorce as late as 1963. Thus divorce and desertion, which were highlighted by Moynihan as reasons why a national program to stabilize the black family was needed, are newcomers as chief causes of family breakup for black people. The information on trends in marital status comparing the relative contributions of death, desertion, and divorce to family breakup among blacks was obtained from findings by Reynolds Farley [2, p. 175].

It would seem that whites were not concerned about the stability of the black family when it was broken largely because black men were dying prematurely. Whites now are concerned about the size, structure, and stability of the black family when the number of black men who are dying prematurely is decreasing and the number of black live-born children who survive is increasing.

Irene Taeuber, a distinguished demographer, has said that "the test of future population policies, planned and unplanned, will be in the speed and the completeness of the obliteration of those demographies that can be categorized by the color of the skin or the subcultures of origin" [9, p. 37]. A national population policy cannot succeed if it focuses only on reproduction and family size of one category of people. Past experiences have revealed that family planning, particularly with reference to size, is often a function of other socioeconomic opportunities. Clyde Kiser and Myrna Frank have discovered that black women over 25 years of age who have a college education or who are married to professional men tend to have a fertility rate that is much lower than that for whites of similar circumstances [3, pp. 42–43]. Irene Taeuber also refers to the socioeconomic facts of life. She states that "trends in the fertility of the blacks in future years will be influenced both by rapidity of the upward economic and social movements and by that complex of factors that influences national fertility, white or black ... " [9, p. 37]. It can be stated, in general, that an inverse relationship exists between fertility and socioeconomic status factors. People of higher income, occupation, and education tend to have fewer children.

However, the association between fertility and socioeconomic factors is a bit more complex when one is dealing with blacks. Reynolds Farley relates that among urban blacks a general increase in fertility has occurred that has involved all social classes. He concludes that this is probably due to improved health conditions resulting in decreased death rates, particularly infant and maternal mortality [1, pp. 189, 194–195].

These facts should help the Commission understand why some blacks who only recently have begun to receive the kind of health care that whites have received for years are lukewarm to any discussions about reducing fertility when they have begun to exhibit modest gains in fertility only because of increased health care. Because so little trust exists among the races in the United States, when whites speak of limiting fertility or controlling the family in any way, many blacks believe that these whites wish to return to a modified Malthusian plan that has controlled black family life in the past. Blacks know that their families have been disrupted and limited in the past because of deaths. They, therefore, are suspicious of any program that does not assure them that death again will not be the chief controlling variable.

In a jocular vein, Moynihan, writing for *America* magazine, the National Catholic Weekly Review, said, "while the rich of America do whatever it is they do, the poor are begetting children" [6, p. 392]. I should point out in a not so jocular vein that many of the children begotten by the black poor in the past died before reaching manhood or womanhood and that children begotten by these blacks today are beginning to live, so that the proportion of black people in the total population is increased by one to two percentage points of the total. The increase in fertility due to the achievements in health care therefore is no cause for alarm. Indeed, the Commission on Population Growth should urge and encourage a fertility that is not impeded by disease and death.

If the poor beget children, if the number they beget is counterproductive for the future welfare of the total nation, and if there is an inverse association between fertility and socioeconomic status, then it would seem that a national population policy should have as a major plank a program to guarantee equality in economic and educational opportunities for all people in this nation. This means that a national population policy must come out strongly against racial and ethnic discrimination. Herman Miller of the U.S. Census Bureau offers that "the average Negro earns less than the average white, even when he has the same years of schooling and does the same kind of work." This conclusion comes from the analysis of income figures that, according to Miller, "provide the unarguable evidence on which public policy should rest" [5, p. *xxi*].

It is for this reason that I conclude that a national population policy that would serve the best interests of blacks as well as the other citizens of this nation should focus on enhancing the *health* and *wealth* of every household in America as well as controlling family size, structure, and stability.

References

1. Reynolds, Farley. 1970. "Fertility among Urban Blacks." *Milbank Memorial Fund Quarterly* 48, part 2 (April).
2. _____. 1970. "Trends in Marital Status among Blacks." In *The Family Life of Black People,* edited by Charles V. Willie, Columbus, Ohio: Merrill.
3. Kiser, Clyde V., and Myrna E. Frank. 1970. "Factors Associated with Low Fertility of Nonwhite Women of College Attainment." In *The Family Life of Black People,* edited by Charles V. Willie, Columbus, Ohio: Merrill.
4. Merton, Robert. 1949. *Social Theory and Social Structure.* New York: Free Press.
5. Miller, Herman. 1964. *Rich Man, Poor Man.* New York: Crowell.
6. Moynihan, Daniel P. 1967. "A Family Policy for the Nation." In *The Moynihan Report and the Politics of Controversy,* edited by Lee Rainwater and William L. Yancy, Cambridge, MA: MIT Press. First published in *America.*
7. _____. 1970. "The Ordeal of the Negro Family." In *The Family Life of Black People,* edited by Charles V. Willie, Columbus, Ohio: Merrill. First published in *Daedalus* 94 (Fall 1965): 745–770.

8. Myrdal, Gunnar. 1944. *The American Dilemma.* New York: Harper and Brothers.
9. Taeuber, Irene. 1970. "Discussion at Milbank Memorial Fund Roundtable on Demographic Aspects of the Black Community." *Milbank Memorial Fund Quarterly* 48, part 2 (April).
10. United States Department of Labor. 1965. *The Negro Family, A Case for National Action.* Washington, DC: Government Printing Office.
11. Willie, Charles V., and Arline McCord. 1972. *Black Students at White Colleges.* New York: Praeger.

Chapter 14

Dominance in the Family:
The Black and the White Experience

By examining data that are controlled for race and social class, this analysis not only refutes categorically the myth of the black matriarchy but indicates that the equalitarian pattern of decision making appears to be the norm for American households, and that the cultural lag, if any, is found not among blacks but among middle-class white households that now are struggling toward the equalitarian goal.

In May of 1960, the *American Journal of Sociology* published a study by Russell Middleton and Snell Putney that should have put to rest for all time the theory of the black matriarchy—the domineering woman in the black nuclear family [Middleton and Putney 1960-1970]. Later, Delores Mack studied 80 couples in their homes and used methods similar to those in the Middleton and Putney study. Mack concluded that "marital dominance is not a trait but a context-dependent function of the relationship between two marriage partners" [Mack 1978:148]. Warren TenHouten studied 148 black families and 138 white families from higher and lower socioeconomic levels and concluded that most of the families were equalitarian [TenHouten 1970:145-173].

Robert Staples [1970] and Jacquelyne Johnson Jackson [1973] have called "the black matriarchy" a myth. Jackson stated that even in the presence of evidence against it, some white social scientists continue to write about "black female dominance over black society" [Jackson 1973:186-199]. The purpose of this discussion is twofold: (a) to examine patterns of dominance in black and white families by social class, and (b) to speculate on the reasons why white social scientists continue to ignore these findings.

Reprinted from *The Journal of Black Psychology,* February 1981, Vol. 7, No. 2, pp. 91-97. Copyright © 1981 by the Association of Black Psychologists. All rights reserved. The author was on the faculty of Harvard University at the time this article was published.

Many studies about the effect of race upon various forms of behavior are not comparative. Interpretations about race and race-related events are likely to be erroneous when limited to an examination of only one racial population. Even when comparative studies are undertaken, social scientists must guard against the Ingroup/Outgroup Syndrome—the tendency to study the positive adaptations in the racial population with which one identifies and the negative adaptations in the other groups.

Fortunately, Middleton and Putney steered clear of this syndrome. For this reason, it should be of value to reexamine their data. These two social scientists analyzed the decision-making experience in nuclear families, while controlling both for social class and race. Despite the small size of the sample, the careful way in which Middleton and Putney designed their study and the absence of biased assumptions cause this to be a valuable investigation into the association, if any, among race, socioeconomic status, and authority practices within the family.

A reexamination of the Middleton and Putney data provides an opportunity to confirm or cast doubt on the presence of a matriarchy not only in black families but also in white families. Essentially this is the reason for a reexamination of these old data. Our concern is with determining the dominance pattern, if any, in family decision making in minority and majority racial populations. A comparative analysis is of value in determining the relative effect of race and social class.

Specifically, 40 families were studied—20 black and 20 white. Each racial study-group was divided equally between white-collar and blue-collar workers. Ten college professors were selected in a random way to represent the black middle class, and ten tradesmen were randomly selected to represent the black working class. A similar procedure was followed in obtaining a sample of whites for the two social classes. Only two-parent households were included in the study. The spouses were American-born, had been married two or more years, were 20 to 49 years of age, had at least one child, and all resided in the same small town.

A fifteen-item questionnaire was filled out separately by each spouse in a household. Later the spouses conferred and then filled out the same questionnaire jointly. Questions had to do with child care, family purchasing activity, decisions about standard of living, recreation, and role relationships. An example of the questions is the following: "If you were buying a house, would you prefer to buy a small new house or a large but older house costing the same amount?" When filling out the questionnaire jointly, the couple was asked to arrive at a family decision if answers for each spouse were not the same. If the husband won two-thirds or more of the "joint decisions" — that is, if the wife changed her answer to that indicated by the husband — then the dominance pattern for the family was classified as patriarchal. If the wife won two-thirds or more of the "joint decisions," the family was labeled matriarchal. An equalitarian family was one in which there was a considerable amount of give and take in decision making, so that one spouse prevailed less than two-thirds and the other more than one-third of the times when they differed with respect to a decision about a family activity.

The most outstanding finding is that middle-class and working-class black families tend to be equalitarian. Seventeen of the 20 black households in this study made joint decisions in which the husband tended to win about as often as the wife, when there was a difference of opinion between them. Among blacks, the middle class was the most equalitarian, nine out of 10 of these families resolved their differences with neither the husband nor the wife always dominating. Of the three black families out of the 20 that were not equalitarian, two in the working class were matriarchal and one in the middle class was patriarchal. In terms of this analysis, 85 percent of nuclear families among middle-class and working-class blacks are equalitarian in household decision making. The myth of the black matriarchy — the domineering wife — is refuted by these data.

This experience of equalitarian decision making in black households differed sharply from what was observed among whites. Most white families were equalitarian too. But the proportion was down to 65 percent, or 13 out of the 20 nuclear white families in the study. Of the seven white families out of 20 that were not equalitarian, four were matriarchal (two in the middle class and two in the working class) and three were patriarchal (two in the middle class and one in the working class).

Among whites, the most outstanding finding had to do with the middle class. There was equalitarian agreement in family decision making at this social class level in only six of the 10 households. The other four were dominated in decision making either by the husband or the wife. This tug-of-war between spouses in many middle-class white households clearly differed from the decision-making experience in middle-class black households, where nine out of 10 were classed as equalitarian.

Although nuclear white families were moving toward the goal of an equalitarian pattern of decision making, they had residuals of both matriarchal and patriarchal dominance. Competition between these two forms of decision making was most pronounced among middle-class whites. The strong identification of male and female role responsibilities in some middle-class white households is an example of the absence of a universal equalitarian experience. White women in this class category tend to dominate in child-care decisions, and white men tend to prevail in decisions regarding the standard of living and household purchases. This separation in role behavior and household responsibility for husband and wife is more rigid in middle-class nuclear white families than in any other race-class group.

My own case studies of middle-class and working-class black families confirm the presence of equalitarian decision making and reject the notion of a matriarchal or female-dominated household. Specifically, I found that "Middle-class status for most black families is a result of dual employment of husband and wife," and that "The economic foundation for most middle-class black families is a product of the cooperative work of the husband and wife." One could call their way of life "a genuine team effort." I found that "Few if any family functions, including cooking, cleaning, and shopping, are considered to be the exclusive prerogative of the husband or the wife." I called the black woman in the middle-class family "the best example of the liberated wife in American society" because "she and her husband have acted as partners out of necessity and thus have carved out an equalitarian pattern of interaction in which neither husband nor wife has ultimate authority." In general, one may describe black middle-class families as "achievement-oriented, upwardly mobile, and equalitarian. They immerse themselves in work and have little time for leisure. Education ... hard work and thrift are accepted as the means for the achievement of success" [Willie 1981:48].

Among the black working class, I found that "Family life ... is a struggle for survival that requires the cooperative effort of all—husband, wife, and children." I found that "Cohesion in the black working-class family results not so much from understanding and tenderness shown by one for the other as from the joint and heroic effort to stave off adversity. Without the income of either parent or the contributions of offspring from part-time employment, the family would topple back into poverty." Household chores have to be shared because husbands and wives sometimes are engaged in what has been described as "tandem parenting." For example, "In some households the husband may work during the daytime and the wife, during the evening hours. Such work schedules mean that the family as a unit is not able to share any meals together." I found that despite these and other hardships, "There is a constancy among the members of black working-class families that tends to pull them through." The black working-class husband or wife knows that "his or her destiny is dependent upon the actions of the other." While there is a tendency for the spouses to have assigned roles, I found that "in time of crisis these roles can change"; and crisis is a perennial in working-class black families. Thus, there is a good deal of role exchange between family members, including older children who may take on some parental responsibilities of socializing younger members of the household. To sum up, one could say that "Black working-class families with limited education and occupational opportunities are ingenious in their methods of coping, surviving, and overcoming adversity. ... The means used to cope are tailor-made for each household and are most innovative. ...They probably are the best manifestation of self-reliance in American society. They are sustained by few institutional supports beyond the kinship system. By hook or crook they make it when others say, 'it can't be done.' " [Willie 1981:50–54].

My case studies of white middle-class families also confirm the findings of Middleton and Putney regarding the rigid role responsibilities assigned to each member. I found, for example, that "the job of the head of the household of the white middle-class family is the major mission of the family. All else is subordinate to it." I found that "work opportunities for the wife or whether the wife will work at all tend to be conditioned by the effect or the perceived effect of such activity on the advancement of the husband." I concluded that "the husband and father in the white middle-class family is given an almost impossible task of being the sole provider for the physical well-being of his family. Most white men in their moments of reality realize how vulnerable they are as individuals and immediately attempt to extend their strength through linkages with institutions. Thus they tend to measure their success in terms of their capacity to control the institutions which, in turn, can help care for their family members." On the basis of this analysis, I concluded that "the symbol of success of the white middle-class family, then, is the job of the husband and father, and the power and authority that it carries in society."

The children and wife in white middle-class families are free to do whatever they wish to do as long as their activity does not jeopardize the work of the husband and father. Seldom is there a common mission that unites the whole family. "In effect, the middle-class white family has made a deal which has resulted in a rather rigid division of labor in the household. If the male head will make an extraordinary effort to provide resources for the physical well-being of the family, the wife will make extraordinary effort to attend to his pleasure and not distract him with her personal concerns or those of the children" [Willie 1978:15–17].

The analysis does more than refute the myth of the black matriarchy; it indicates that the tendency, if any, toward a matriarchy (or wife dominance in household decision making in American society) is most visible among whites, especially in the middle-class nuclear white family. It is not the purpose of this analysis to contribute to a new myth of the white matriarchy while disposing of an old myth about the black matriarchy. Clearly the equalitarian pattern of household decision making is the prevailing pattern among whites as well as blacks. Among whites, however, this pattern is under attack by residual practices of matriarchal and patriarchal dominance.

These residual practices give a clue as to why some white social scientists, as charged by Jackson, continue to make assertions about the black matriarchy. Possibly they are projecting upon blacks their own experience of households dominated by females, as the data presented above indicate. The act of projecting, of believing others have thoughts, feelings, and experiences similar to our own, is probably one of the greatest impediments to the development of valid social science knowledge and understanding. The distorting effects of projecting occur most frequently among those social scientists who believe that any behavior of blacks that is not imitative of whites is deviant. It is appropriate to conclude, on the basis of facts presented in this analysis, that Daniel P. Moynihan's statement that "the Negro community has been forced into a matriarchal structure ..." is a form of projection upon blacks of what he had seen among whites [U.S. Department of Labor 1965:29]. Rather than blacks being modeled in the image of whites, as Moynihan suggested they should be, to facilitate their progress, the evidence indicates that white families are moving in the direction of equalitarian decision making that has characterized black households.

The process of projecting has caused other social scientists to commit the same error that Moynihan committed. Howard Taylor said that "Jencks ... takes considerable liberties in discussing the effects of integration, segregation, race, etc., upon occupational and income equality." According to Taylor, Jencks "clearly infers that education is not related to success for black people; that if blacks want more money, then more education will not get it." Then Taylor introduced a surprising piece of evidence against Jencks. He said that inferences by Jencks were based on a statistical technique called path analysis, and that data used in the analysis were obtained from "native white non-farm males who took an armed forces IQ test!" Taylor discovered that "Not one single path analysis in the entire report on [*INEQUALITY*] is performed on even one black sample." The fallacy of "studying whites and then generalizing to blacks without studying blacks directly is consistently made in 'important' social science research documents," according to Taylor [Taylor 1977:245–246].

Overcoming the fallacy of projecting will encourage social scientists to study all racial populations directly and to learn from them the beneficial and harmful effects of various patterns of adaptation. By examining data that are controlled for race and social class, this analysis not only refuted categorically the myth of the black matriarchy but indicated that the equalitarian pattern of decision making appears to be the norm for American households, and that the cultural lag, if any, is found not among blacks but among middle-class white households that now are struggling toward the equalitarian goal.

References

Jackson, J. J. "Black Women in a Racist Society." In C. V. Willie, B. M. Kramer, and B. S. Brown (eds.), *Racism and Mental Health.* Pittsburgh: University of Pittsburgh Press, 1973, pp. 185–268.

Mack, D. "The Power Relationship in Black Families and White Families." In R. Staples (ed.), *The Black Family.* Belmont, CA: Wadsworth, 1978.

Middleton, R., and S. Putney, "Dominance in Decisions in the Family: Race and Class Differences." *American Journal of Sociology* 65; no. 6 (1960): 605–609. Also in C. V. Willie (ed.), *The Family Life of Black People.* Columbus, OH: Merrill, 1970, pp. 16–20.

Staples, R. "The Myth of the Black Matriarchy." *Black Scholar* 1 (1970): 8–16.

Taylor, H. F. "Playing the Dozens with Path Analysis." In R. L. Hall (ed.), *Black Separation and Social Reality.* New York: Pergamon Press, 1977.

TenHouten, W. D. "The Black Family: Myth and Reality." *Psychiatry* 25 (1970): 145–173.

U. S. Department of Labor. *The Negro Family: A Case for National Action.* Washington, DC: Government Printing Office, 1965.

Willie, C. V. *A New Look at Black Families.* 2nd. ed. Bayside, NY: General Hall, 1981.

———. "Black and White Middle Class Families: What They Can Teach and Learn from Each Other." *Interaction,* Winter 1978, pp. 12–20.

Chapter 15

School Desegregation and Public Policy:
The Boston Experience

Because the court order for [school desegregation in] Boston and public reaction to it have been discussed often in the mass media, a more detailed analysis of some of the public policy issues is presented in this chapter. Particular attention is given to an analysis of the role of social scientists in the making of public policy and of public officials in maintaining public order pertaining to school desegregation. I begin by linking the present with the past.

Queen Elizabeth II of Great Britain, a descendant of King George III, came to Boston to celebrate the bicentennial anniversary of the United States. With 200 years of hindsight, she tried to explain what went wrong. The queen's version of the American Revolution is that England lacked the statesmanship to know the right time and the manner of yielding what was impossible to keep. The vicar of Old North Church in Boston, where the candles to alert the colonists were placed, liked what he heard and echoed the queen's ideas in his Sunday sermon. The Reverend Robert Golledge said, "Stubborn pride shouted out in every situation is nonsense and evil, not bravery and steadfastness." Then he said, "Knowing when and how to relinquish something you have but cannot hope to keep in the face of another's fair claim is a strength found in brave [people], not a weakness." This was his commentary on the school desegregation revolution in Boston during the bicentennial year. Unfortunately, many of the residents of Boston heard neither the vicar nor the queen; and if they heard them, they—like the queen's ancestors—would not listen. And so the school desegregation revolution flamed in Boston and elsewhere in the nation, fueled by stubborn pride, nonsense, and people fearful of losing their ethnic purity.

Reprinted from Charles V. Willie, *The Sociology of Urban Education,* Lexington, MA, Lexington Books of D.C. Heath, 1978, Chapter 7, pp. 77–87.

There is common ground and similarity among the queen's analysis of Britain during the last trimester of the eighteenth century, the vicar's analysis of Boston during the last trimester of the twentieth century, and the sociological analysis of social conflict. My purpose here is to focus on the latter and to examine selected aspects of the school desegregation issue in Boston in the light of some sociological principles.

There is and indeed must be a place for sociology in public policy pertaining to school desegregation plans and their implementation. The determination of guilt and innocence or what is legal and illegal is a matter of law and not sociology in disputes that are settled in the court. The responsibility of the court, however, is not limited to making such a determination. If the court arrives at a decision based on law that is in favor of the plaintiff and against the defendant, then the court has the added responsibility of fashioning a remedy or a means of granting relief to the person or persons who were treated unfairly. Blacks and other racial minorities, according to the court, were treated unfairly and not granted equal protection of the laws in public education. Public officials intentionally created a racially segregated or dual public school system that was educationally harmful. Blacks and other racial minorities could not be treated fairly until the harmful social arrangement was changed. How to change a segregated system is a sociological as well as a legal and political problem.

The court knows something about justice and interpretations of the law. Sociologists know something about social organization and social change that may be required to fulfill the law. The remedy in school desegregation cases must provide for new social arrangements in the public school system to replace those that were found to be illegal. Sociologists are experts in understanding social arrangements and should participate in the formulation of school desegregation plans. Often they do not because the court cannot determine which sociologist to believe.

Whose advice should the court act upon? This is a major problem. The answer thus far has been elusive. It is a problem, however, not limited to sociology or to sociologists. Indeed, the law is similarly confronted. Five justices of the Supreme Court may believe one thing, and four others may believe another thing. Yet the common opinion of the majority is the law, despite the differing opinions of the minority. Thus, justices of the Supreme Court differ even as sociologists differ. But our society has developed a procedure for handling the varying opinions of a panel of judges. The opinion of a Supreme Court justice is followed only when it is concurrent with that of a majority. This procedure enables the Court to cope with diversity in the opinions of its members. I am not suggesting that this is the only procedure for dealing with diversity of expert opinion. Indeed it may not be the best way and probably would be the wrong procedure for dealing with the diversity of expert sociological opinion, which seldom is unanimous. In our society, then, we have no agreed-upon procedure outside the court for determining when to accept or reject expert opinion in the making of public policy. In the absence of agreed-upon procedures, we rely upon unreliable indicators such as the race, religion, or reputation of the expert and his or her Ingroup or Outgroup status. Members of the Ingroup, for example, tend to doubt the expert opinion of members of the Outgroup.

The issue is not whether sociology can make a valid contribution to court-authorized plans for remedy and relief in school desegregation cases. The main problem is the development of a procedure for determining which expert opinion to use. Herein lies our difficulty. Social science advice is necessary and needed. But our society knows neither which social science advice to use in the development of school desegregation public policy nor how or when to use it. Even if our society developed an acceptable procedure for determining which social science advice to use, that procedure could rule in advice that is wrong, and rule out advice that is right. We should not forget that a decision of a majority of the justices of the Supreme Court is lawful and legal, but could also be inhumane, such as the Dred Scott decision of 1857 that decreed that a black person whose ancestors were sold as slaves had no rights of citizenship or standing in the court.

Sociologists should not wait until their knowledge is perfect before offering it to the court and other institutions in society. Neither they, the justices, nor other professions ever will be perfect. There are no ultimate guarantees in human society. In the absence of an agreed-upon procedure, our best protection against error is a self-correcting approach — one which seeks the advice of many different people rather than that of a single individual. This approach may escalate confusion because of the competing versions of truth that must be considered, but is better than not seeking any social science advice.

There are competing versions of social science truth. School desegregation plans and practices, like other social events, are subject to various interpretations that may be valid or erroneous. Errors may be a function of analytic technique, perspective, or the time-frame considered. What is called for, then, is not the dismissal of sociology from the public policy process, but a rational way for the public to determine when an opinion is informed and the conditions under which an informed opinion should be used.

The consequence for Boston of rejecting sociological principles in the implementation of school desegregation is the focus of this analysis [1].

The Boston experience in school desegregation revealed a phenomenon that is increasingly characteristic of the entire nation — the tendency to view achievement in education in terms of performance on standardized tests of communicating and calculating skills [2]. These are skills of efficiency. Michael Katz has said that order and efficiency, values that have permeated public education since the nineteenth century, have strong social class overtones [3]. Thomas Pettigrew has complained about this focus in formal education, too: "Achievement-test scores are surely not the sole goal of education," he said. On the basis of his own research, he concluded that "desegregated schooling does in fact prepare its products — both black and white — for interracial living as adults" [4]. The achievement of harmonious interracial living also is a skill that can be learned in school, although standardized tests for its measurement are not available. Maybe the development of this skill is what the Supreme Court had in mind when, in *Brown* v. *Board of Education,* it described an equitable education, in part, as one in which a student of one racial group is able "to engage in discussion and exchange views with other students." Obviously racial segregation prohibits this kind of learning and, therefore, is a harmful educational arrangement.

Living effectively in an interracial society consisting of majority and minority populations of unequal power because of their numbers, organization, or resources requires the development of systems of justice and equity. It was Reinhold Niebuhr who said that "a simple ... moralism counsels [people] to be unselfish; [but] a profounder ... faith must encourage people to create systems of justice which will save society ..." [5]. Thus justice and equity are major goals of the educational system in a free society. And if they are not, they ought to be.

We have witnessed in Boston and elsewhere in this nation what Aaron Wildavsky has called the *principle of goal displacement,* in which "the process subtly becomes the purpose" [6]. By focusing upon the effects of schooling for individuals (in terms of their communicating and calculating skills development) and ignoring the social consequences of segregated or integrated education (for the quality of racial interaction in community life), justice and equity, which have to do with purpose in society, have been deemphasized or displaced in favor of order and efficiency, which have to do with method of social organization. Reading, writing, and arithmetic, once upon a time identified as the methods of education, how have become goals or ends in themselves — so much so that they sometimes are classified as "the basics" in education. These are clear and present examples of goal displacement.

When the Boston news media were taking stock of the second year of court-ordered school desegregation, Muriel Cohen, a staff member of the *Boston Globe,* wrote the following as the lead sentences of her article: "The Boston schools are on their way up. Slowly. Reading scores are holding the rise of last year." Clearly, such improvement was considered a favorable outcome. The article continued, "Preliminary reading test results for the year ... show improvement in a number of district high schools, gains for minority children but no loss for whites [7]. In other words, school desegregation had benefited blacks and had not harmed whites, if test scores are taken as an indicator of educational benefit or success. There was no discussion of whether Boston school children had gained a better understanding of the functions of the court in a democratic society or developed a better understanding of justice and equity by going through the school desegregation experience.

Even under conditions of our present situation, where efficiency and skills development are exalted, something beneficial has come out of desegregation in Boston. The benefit has been in favor of some whites as well as blacks and is directly attributable to their interracial experience. For example, South Boston whites profited from court-ordered school desegregation. Initially, they opposed school desegregation. South Boston is an ethnically homogeneous, largely working-class community. James Dougherty, a school official, told a newspaper reporter that the second year of desegregation at South Boston High School had its positive side. Said he, "The 'in' thing with blacks is going to college, and that was a boon to Southie, where almost no one goes [to college]." Dougherty further said, "the very feeling [blacks] had about going on to college had a good effect on the white kids." According to him, "The white kids have downgraded themselves, felt college was too tough or that they didn't have the ability." And, "Now there is a feeling [among whites]," reported Dougherty, "that if blacks are going [to college], why can't we?" The school official said, "It's rubbed off on the white kids [of South Boston]," meaning, of course, the desire to go on to college [8]. Nowhere in any of the analytical discussions of desegregation success or failure is there acknowledgment of this fact as a benefit for whites.

Judge Garrity found that the Boston public school system was characterized by racial segregation and that the defendant, the Boston School Committee, did not dispute this central fact. Indeed, the School Committee had encountered administrative sanctions by the federal government for alleged violations of the Civil Rights Act of 1964 and had been hauled into court several times for rulings on whether or not it had complied with the State Racial Imbalance Act of 1965. Thus, the children of Boston were presented with a model of massive resistance to school desegregation public law for at least ten years prior to Judge Garrity's comprehensive plans for citywide desegregation.

After years of defeat in its attempt to enforce the Racial Imbalance Act, the Massachusetts Board of Education moved against the Boston School Committee and its dilatory tactics and began to withhold state funds. The State Board also demanded that Boston develop a plan to eliminate racially imbalanced schools. Winning on some fine procedural points, the Boston School Committee managed to get state action impounding city school funds overturned, although it never developed a comprehensive school desegregation plan. Frustrated by the flagrant violations of state law, both the State Board of Education and the National Association for the Advancement of Colored People (NAACP) charged the Boston School Committee with violation of the United States Constitution. Formal proceedings were brought by black parents and their children against the Boston School Committee in federal court in 1972. Meanwhile, the State Board of Education decided to draft its own plan for eliminating racial imbalance in the Boston public schools.

The State Board of Education's plan for Boston included some but not all sections of the city. It was not a systemwide approach. It reduced the number of predominantly black schools in Boston from seventy to forty-four. The initial response of the Suffolk Superior Court was that the plan was too limited. The State Board of Education made some modifications and it eventually was accepted by the State Supreme Judicial Court, which concluded that "the time for prompt action to implement ... is at hand." Judge Garrity's finding that the Boston School Committee had deliberately maintained a dual school system for whites and blacks and other racial minorities was issued the last day of the school's spring term in 1974. With only the summer months available to prepare for desegregation, the judge ordered the Boston School Committee to implement the partial desegregation plan that was prepared by the State Board of Education.

Because so many neighborhoods of Boston were excluded from the partial desegregation plan implemented in Phase I of Judge Garrity's order, some behavioral scientists and long-term desegregation watchers such as Robert Coles called it an imposition "on working class people exclusively" [9]. Further, Coles said that social change cannot just occur in one area while everyone else is let off the hook. The partial plan was implemented because the Boston School Committee had refused to prepare a comprehensive plan and also because the state and the court had not consulted social scientists to determine the consequence of implementing a partial versus a comprehensive plan. The outcome was great bitterness on the part of both blacks and whites in the affected communities. A comprehensive desegregation plan was not implemented until the second year, or Phase II, of court-ordered school desegregation.

It was as late as June 1976, the end of the second year of court-ordered school desegregation, and after the Supreme Court had rejected a petititon to review the appellate court's affirmation of Judge Garrity's order, that the mayor of Boston finally told the people of that city the facts of life: "That the process of desegregation will continue, ... that schools that are now integrated will remain integrated," and that "where segregation remains, it will be eliminated." He further said that "busing will continue," and that "any who tell you otherwise ... that the courts will change their minds ... or that violent resistance will succeed ... mislead you." One may wonder why it took the mayor of Boston so long to tell the people what he knew to be true.

Of the South, Ralph McGill said, "History already is drawing a harsh indictment of those political leaders who ... took a decision delineating the rights of children ... and dishonestly distorted it ... " [10]. Shortly after the Court's decision in 1954, McGill believed that had public officials spoken out "when ears ached to hear from the ... leaders," there would have been a different story [11]. This did not happen decades ago in the South and it did not happen in the North and in Boston.

McGill explained the violence in the South this way: "Before the winter of 1954–55 was done ... the hoodlums were fired up by the hot defiance from ... city halls. ... If the power structure could damn the courts and describe their actions as illegal, then the [people] who wished to dynamite or burn ... felt ... approved" [12].

The mayor of Boston, in his brief filed with the Supreme Court requesting a review of the district court's school desegregation decision and plan, indicated that the pairing of some communities would be acceptable in the redrawing of school districts, but that the pairing of others such as Roxbury and South Boston would not. Such an argument was at variance with the reasoning by Judge Garrity based on previous court decisions that "a preference ... for neighborhood schools ... can be validly maintained by school authorities only if it will not interfere with the authorities' constitutional duty to desegregate" and that "no amount of public ... opposition will excuse avoidance by school officials of constitutional obligations to desegregate and [that] constitutional principles which mandate duty to desegregate cannot be allowed to yield simply because of disagreement with them." The mayor did not tell the people of Boston this until it was too late to avoid the violence caused by those who thought that they could resist a court order if they disagreed with it. The violence undoubtedly was stimulated by the actions of public officials that cast doubt on the legality of the court order.

The Supreme Court rejected the mayor's petition for review and the mayor eventually spoke out. He spoke in a forthright manner and taught the children of Boston a good lesson about constitutional democracy and the separate powers of the executive, the legislative, and the judiciary branches of government. It was a lesson in civics far better than those of yesteryear — a lesson that came late but still one worthy of remembering.

When public officials of northern or southern communities do not tell their constituents the facts and do not urge them to obey the law to desegregate the public schools, the result is the same: mob rule and violence. Hostility and hatred, prejudice and discrimination are the same whether found in the North or the South. This is another way of saying that the North could have learned from the South, that Boston could have avoided the experience of Little Rock. The South had experienced the futility of massive resistance to the constitutional requirement to desegregate public schools; but the mayor of Boston did not tell his people that massive resistance to a court order was futile until the end of the second year of court-ordered school desegregation.

The mayor of a community is responsible for and to all the people, whites, blacks, and other minorities, those in favor and those opposed to desegregation. It is not the privilege of one who occupies the position of the chief executive officer of a community or country to be selective in the rules and regulations enforced. The Boston community, like other communities in the United States, is based on law. These laws are for the purpose of maintaining social order in a pluralistic population. They are enacted by legislative bodies, interpreted by the courts, and enforced by an executive branch of government. Obedience of the laws of the community, then, is the ultimate basis of social order in the city. Antinomies are eternal. Always there will be people who disagree with some practices in community life such as school desegregation. But such people can be persuaded to abide by that which they dislike if they believe that the activity is lawful. The law, then, is the basis for achieving accommodation among people of the same community who have disparate interests. This principle is true for southern and northern communities, for Boston as well as for Little Rock and other urban areas.

When the mayor of Boston appealed the school desegregation order of the United States District Court, he let it be known to the citizens of Boston that he believed the decision was unlawful. By his actions, the mayor lost any legal basis for asking those who disliked the school desegregation court order to obey the law because he already had indicated his doubt of its legality. By officially expressing doubt, the mayor placed in jeopardy his law-enforcement authority regarding this matter. As proof that this indeed was what happened, one need only look at the violence which came like thunder and lightning. Ralph McGill said it is an old lesson that "the white Southerner will not join in mob violence unless he believes that laxity in law enforcement will make it possible [13]. The same may be said of the North. Sociologically, what we have learned from the Boston experience is that the appeal of a school desegregation court order is a proscribed policy for the mayor or any chief executive officer of the total community. Plaintiffs and defendants may appeal; citizens who are affected and are parties to the case may appeal; but mayors may initiate appeals at their peril.

A further example that race relations, northern and southern style, are similar came from Dallas, Texas, which behaved years ago in ways quite similar to the way Boston behaved recently. Before 1940, all blacks in Dallas attended one high school, Booker T. Washington. From East Dallas, West Dallas, and South Dallas, they used public transportation to go to North Dallas to Booker T. Washington High School, and the costs for this transportation to maintain segregation were assumed by the minority students and their parents.

There is a limit to the capacity of any school to accommodate one more student, even a black high school. Already Booker T. Washington was in double session. Finally, the Dallas Independent School District erected a new high school building in South Dallas for blacks. What was unique about this move in the 1930s is that a *new* structure was erected for blacks. In the past, when practicable, new structures had been erected for whites and the abandoned white schools had been reassigned to blacks. The new Lincoln High School for blacks in South Dallas near white neighborhoods was a new development in school construction policy in that city. What do you think happened? Whites in Dallas were so outraged over the fact that a new building near their neighborhoods was to be occupied first by blacks that they went into court and obtained an injunction which prevented Lincoln High School from opening at the beginning of the academic year. In the end, the blacks obtained a just decision. The injunction was lifted and they marched into Lincoln High School for the spring semester, singing "God Bless America."

What happened to Dallas in the South decades ago is no different from what happened in Boston in the North in recent years. In September 1973 English High School, which is located in the Back Bay Fens section of Boston, was scheduled to move into a new $24 million facility, the first new high school opened in Boston in thirty-five years. When the new building was planned as a replacement for old English High six years earlier, the student body was 20 percent black. When the new structure was ready for occupancy, the English High School student body was 80 percent black. Although the structure was erected as a replacement for old English High, the Boston School Committee by majority vote reneged on the commitment to rehouse English High in the new structure and reassigned it to Girls Latin School. At that time, only 5 percent of the student body at Girls Latin was black; in fact, it was 89 percent white. If the new building had been assigned to Girls Latin, the only structure available for English High was the antiquated structure from which Girls Latin would have moved, since the old English High School building had been razed. The plaintiffs (blacks in Boston) obtained a court ruling that prevented the reassignment of the new building to Girls Latin.

The similarity between the North and the South in these cases is that whites believed that any new and modern building for educational purposes ought to be assigned first to whites. The difference between the North and the South in these cases is the use made of the court. The court was used by whites in Dallas in an attempt to maintain discrimination and the court was used by blacks in Boston in an attempt to eliminate discrimination.

And what of the future? Two social scientists, Robin Williams and Margaret Ryan, found that "few communities can sustain, over protracted periods of time, intense bitterness and tension involving only one of the functions of the community" [14]. Little Rock and other cities emerged from a state of turmoil after desegregation was accepted as lawful, and so will Boston and other cities.

The mayor pointed toward the new Boston at the close of his speech in June 1976. He said, "If we choose to accept our realities, and to build on those realities toward a society in which tranquil equality is accompanied by real opportunity, then I know enough of this city's possibilities to believe that in a generation, Boston — and its way of life — will be the envy of the nation." The sociologists are inclined to agree with him and would make but one correction. The new Boston may come more quickly than he realizes, in less time than a decade, now that public officials are stating that the school desegregation law will be enforced.

Consider, for example, this 1976 report from Central High School, Little Rock, Arkansas, where federal troops were deployed around that building in the 1950s to maintain public order due to the uproar over court-ordered school desegregation. As late at 1959, black and white students were kicking each other in the corridors of Central High. But in 1976, a *New York Times* reporter found Central High School in Little Rock "one of the most effectively desegregated schools in the United States," with perhaps a slight majority of blacks. Reporter Roy Reed explained that "racial violence has practically disappeared. Athletic teams, cheerleader squads, and several ... student organizations are integrated. ... Both races participate vigorously in student government. Tension seemed to be nonexistent. ... A few black and white students walked and talked together between classes, although a large majority still gathered with members of their own race. ... Many of Central's white students are bused in ... over the objection of some parents. ... [The] School Superintendent, ... who is white, said ... that the district had done many things to try to make desegregation work. ... A new principal, the second black principal since the school was desegrated, ... enjoys exceptional rapport with black and white students and is spoken of with respect in and out of the school" [15]. All of this has occurred in less than a generation where the officials did "many things to try to make desegregation work."

Florence Levinsohn summed up the desegregation situation for the nation this way: "Since 1954, there has been more peaceful integration of schools than violent" [16]. John Egerton, an education writer who has studied the South in depth, concluded that "there has been no decrease in the quality of education as a consequence of desegregation" [17]. These statements also apply to Boston, Louisville and other cities; but few realize that this is so because they have not seen or been told about it. Florence Levinsohn said, "These successful and peaceful efforts have not been brought dramatically to the attention of the American public ... [because] television newspeople have not learned how, have not made the effort to dramatically convey these peaceful transactions" [18].

The court-appointed masters were partially successful in fashioning a desegregation plan for Boston that united the goal of education with the method. Moreover, in granting relief to the minorities, the masters were interested also in promoting interracial harmony. Their plan and the modified version that was implemented were defective in some ways. Yet the Boston school desegregation plan achieved a measure of success beyond that expected because the assumptions on which it was based were sociologically sound. To recapitulate these assumptions, the masters believed that:

1. Busing is a phony issue.
2. There is no correlation between how students go to school and what they learn in school.
3. Big-city schools cannot be desegregated without using some form of transportation.
4. Whites need not be the majority to receive a quality education.
5. Unique educational benefits accrue to people of the minority which whites should be permitted to experience.
6. Integrated education benefits whites as well as blacks.
7. A systemwide desegregation plan is essential.

Notes

1. Ralph McGill, *The South and the Southerner* (Boston: Little, Brown, 1964), p. 246.
2. "Report of the Masters", in *Tallulah Morgan, et al.,* vs. *John Kerrigan, et al.,* 31 March 1975.
3. Michael B. Katz, *Class, Bureaucracy and Schools* (New York: Praeger, 1971), p. 108.
4. Thomas F. Pettigrew, *Racially Separate or Together* (New York: McGraw-Hill, 1964), pp. 246, 248, 249.
5. Charles V. Willie, "The American Dream: Illusion or Reality," *Harvard Magazine* 78 (July–August 1976): 37.
6. Aaron Wildavsky, *Can Health Be Planned* (Chicago: University of Chicago, Center for Health Administration Studies, Graduate School of Business, 1976), p. 3.
7. Muriel Cohen, "Report Card on Boston Schools: Slow Steady Gain for Students," *Boston Globe,* 4 June 1976, p. 56.
8. George Croft, "Graduate Joy Missing for Many South Boston Seniors," *Boston Globe,* 4 June 1976, p. 56.
9. Mike Barnicle, "Busing Puts Burden on Working Class, Black and White," *Boston Globe,* 15 October 1974, p. 23.
10. McGill, *The South and the Southerner,* p. 246.
11. Ibid.
12. Ibid., p. 248.
13. Ibid., p. 265.
14. Robin M. Williams and Margaret W. Ryan (eds.), *Schools in Transition,* (Chapel Hill: University of North Carolina Press, 1954), pp. 237, 238, 242, 243.
15. Roy Reed, "Little Rock School Now Integration Model," *New York Times,* 8 September 1976, pp. 1, 16.
16. Florence H. Levinsohn, "TV's Deadly Inadvertent Bias," in Levinsohn and Benjamin D. Wright (eds.), *School Desegregation, Shadow and Substance* Chicago: University of (Chicago Press, 1976), p. 93.
17. John Egerton, *School Desegregation, A Report Card from the South* (Atlanta: Southern Regional Council, 1976), p. 47.
18. Levinsohn, "TV's Deadly Inadvertent Bias," p. 93.

Chapter 16

Corpus Christi: A Triethnic Nonviolent Experience in School Desegregation

Corpus Christi is a community with a calm exterior that is at war with itself. The shoreline and flowering plants that surround the homes of the affluent and the poor throughout the city present a beautiful setting for much of the Spanish-style architecture. There is affluence and wealth in Corpus Christi. The metal industry is a source of steady employment. The city has a deep-water port and natural resources. Yet, there is considerable poverty that is disporportionately experienced by the black and the Mexican-American populations.

The Mexican-American population has a range of individuals in terms of social class. There is an increasing number of lawyers, physicians, educators, and public administrators. Also, Mexican-Americans are strong in organized labor, especially among the steel workers. The total population for this group balances that of the Anglos. Together, they are 90 to 95 percent of Corpus Christi, which has a total population of about 200,000.

Blacks are a small minority of only about 5 percent. The blacks who have lived elsewhere in the United States, where they were the largest minority, have difficulty accepting the fact that issues pressed by Mexican-Americans get priority attention. The blacks are angry over losing a favored minority status that they have had elsewhere. Moreover, the black community is isolated residentially from the other citizens of Corpus Christi and has not decided to date to make common cause in coalition with Mexican-Americans. Black neighborhoods are contained by an interstate highway and a water channel, cut off from the rest of the city. Blacks are more compact in terms of socioeconomic status. A few black professionals are in the population. Otherwise, there are few individuals with the time and "know how" to negotiate the system.

There are separate Anglo and Mexican-American neighborhoods, schools, and other facilities. However, there is a considerable amount of

This report is based on a site-visit in 1978 to Corpus Christi by Charles Willie in connection with a National Institute of Education-sponsored study on court-ordered school desegregation in ten communities.

175

racial integration in housing for the more affluent Mexican-Americans. Some Corpus Christi property deeds carry restrictions concerning the race of the person to whom a property can be sold. Such deed restrictions are not enforceable; they are illegal. Yet they are customary, have the force of tradition, and influence some real estate dealers. A few, including realtors of Mexican-American background, abide by the restrictions.

Deeds that are restricted to white ownership may or may not exclude Mexican-Americans. There is confusion in racial self-designation and in racial designation by others of Mexican-Americans. Part of the internal warfare in Corpus Christi, then, is a conflict within the Mexican-American community as to whether it should identify itself as white or otherwise. The U.S. Census Bureau has classified Mexican-Americans as whites. As members of the dominant race in terms of numbers, Mexican-Americans enjoyed opportunities denied blacks. The U.S. Court has ruled that Mexican-Americans are an identifiable ethnic minority. As an identifiable minority, the population is protected by public law designed to overcome racial discrimination by a majority population against blacks and other minorities. The Mexican-American population has accepted at varying times majority and minority designations. This has contributed to separation within the population and alienation between Mexican-Americans and other racial minorities such as blacks. There are Mexican-Americans throughout the United States who designate their population as brown, Chicano, Latino, Hispanic, Spanish-speaking, and white.

When Mexican-Americans are identified as a minority, they are eligible for recompense due to discrimination. Blacks believe that they are taking the "goodies" that belong to them as a racial minority. When Mexican-Americans are identified as white, blacks see them as part of the majority enemy that oppresses. Thus, some but not all blacks have developed a hostile posture against Mexican-Americans, often accusing them of rejecting blacks, while Mexican-Americans are aggrieved over the fact that they are rejected by Anglos.

Mexican-Americans prefer to refer to whites as Anglos so that a determination of whether Mexican-Americans should be classified as white or otherwise is eliminated as an issue. All Mexican-Americans accept the fact that they are not Anglos; but there is disagreement over whether they should or should not be classified as whites. Blacks, who may be unaware of the oppression visited upon Mexican-Americans by Anglos, resent the fact that Mexican-Americans classify themselves as a minority, and believe that the members of this group are trying as legally protected minorities to "have their cake and eat it too."

It is all a puzzlement filled with misconceptions and misunderstand-ings. Meanwhile, Anglos do not help disentangle the problem. Many of their actions are roadblocks to a resolution. One could say that Anglos are temporary beneficiaries of the disunity in that both Mexican-Americans and blacks solicit white favors for themselves and against the other. Beneath the calm and noncombative appearance of the Corpus Christi community, then, is a deep channel of triracial fear, mistrust and suspicion that could shatter the facade of good will. At the same time, the city has an unusual opportunity to effect intergroup harmony, because no group is a numerical majority, and Mexican-Americans can identify with both blacks and whites.

Moody High School is an excellent example of misunderstanding, mis-trust, and misperception. School officials identify the construction of this school building as "the straw that broke the camel's back," and precipitated Corpus Christi into extended litigation over school desegregation. The Cor-pus Christi Independent School District had been asked to build new struc-tures in locations that would facilitate desegregation. It ignored this request and erected Moody High School in an area that was heavily populated with Mexican-Americans. To overcome charges of segregation, the school system assigned blacks and Anglos as well as Mexican-Americans to Moody. The Anglos petitioned to withdraw. All such petitions were approved. School authorities contended that the school was desegregated because of the presence of blacks, since it classified Mexican-Americans white. The Mexican-Americans were upset by this action. The blacks thought that Mexican-Americans were upset because the black racial group had been assigned to Moody when in reality the Mexican-Americans were upset because the white (Anglo) racial group had been permitted to withdraw from Moody. The blacks thought that the Mexican-Americans resented their presence and had rejected them. The Mexican-Americans resented the sanc-tioned withdrawal of Anglos and interpreted this as a rejection of Mexican-Americans. The Anglos thought that the Mexican-Americans were upset simply because the new school had been placed in a Mexican-American area, and appeared to be a form of containment.

With such misconceptions and misunderstandings, a court case prob-ably was the only means of sorting out the issues and achieving justice. Actu-ally, the case of *Cisneros* v. *Corpus Christi Independent School District* was based upon a number of issues and not the Moody High School situation only.

The National Association for the Advancement of Colored People (NAACP) had assigned national staff to examine the school situation in Corpus Christi as early as 1958 and, on the basis of this investigation, had requested the integration of school faculties and the hiring of more blacks. There was little if any affirmative action by school authorities on these requests.

A decade later, in 1968, José Cisneros, an auto mechanic by trade and a member of the powerful United Steel Workers of America, became concerned about the conditions of the public schools. Previously, his children had attended parochial school. He was in a position to know the difference in physical plant of parochial and public schools and he acted upon what he saw. He and several fathers, his friends and neighbors, who were members of the United Steel Workers Union, asked the principal to have the toilet fixtures and broken windows repaired. The principal of the public school attended by Cisneros' children and their friends refused to honor their request for these and other maintenance improvements. He indicated that the central administration of the school system might not look with favor upon a request for funds for such purposes. He let it be known that his concern was about how such a requisition might affect his future as a professional school administrator in the Corpus Christi school system. Nothing was done.

And so the parents escalated their action beyond that of a simple request to a local school principal for better maintenance. Since there was an inappropriate response, they decided to initiate a court case. The complaint was that discrimination existed throughout the system. The case was initiated largely because of the recalcitrance of a local school principal who was afraid of his superiors and because of the courage of a local auto mechanic who knew from previous experience with parochial schools that the learning environment need not be as dismal and delapidated as it was in his child's public school. Cisneros also knew that the union was strong at the state level and that if it could be persuaded to back the bid of local members for better educational opportunities, there could be few if any reprisals against individuals.

Cisneros shared his concern with Paul Montemayo, also a Mexican-American, and a well-respected local, state, and national union leader. Montemayo had been appointed to the National Civil Rights Committee of the United Steel Workers. The chief staff person for this national unit of the union was black. Montemayo won approval at all levels for financial support by the union for a court case against the Corpus Christi Independent School District. The Steel Workers Union in Corpus Christi was dominated by Mexican-Americans, although it included blacks and Anglos too. A class-action suit including all three groups was contemplated. The actual plaintiffs finally were 25 to 30 Mexican-Americans and 5 blacks. The civil rights division of the union in the national office in Pittsburgh supervised the case and helped in securing legal assistance and funding.

The developments in the Corpus Christi case as described thus far demonstrate that the alleged alienation between black, brown, and white racial populations of the working class was not present. Some Anglo union members were willing to be plaintiffs in a court case alleging segregation and discrimination by race in education. Moreover, funds to support the litigation, which has been estimated by various individuals as running from $100,000 to $400,000, were supplied by a union whose members included working-class whites throughout the nation, the kind of people who have been labeled "hard hats."

Clearly, the Corpus Christi school trustees and administrators have been obstructionists and have not voluntarily reformed the system by eliminating segregation and discrimination. They are middle class. Indeed, the representatives of this class-interest have resisted change, have insisted that the charges against the schools and remedies requested be tested in the court, and have sought ways of evading the full effect of desegregation following the official finding that the public school system had willfully and deliberately segregated the races and engaged in discrimination in teacher hiring and promotion and in the maintenance and upkeep of facilities provided for the education of children.

The class interest that is associated with resistance to desegregation as a way of overcoming discrimination in education appears to be more characteristic of the affluent who have used the institutional systems of society to do their bidding in a court case filed by working-class union members.

Middle-class people such as church leaders did not use institutional approaches to prevent desegregation. However, they were uncomfortable with, and certainly did not financially support, the legal approach to desegregation as a way of redressing the grievances of minorities as a collectivity in court. The preferred action of middle-class religious leaders in the Corpus Christi area was to address the problem of institutional discrimination by encouraging individual resistance. The only corporate or institutional effort the middle-class religious leaders would embrace was mediation. Thus, a City Human Relations Commission was formed due to the efforts of the Baptists and other humanitarians. Through conciliation and persuasion, the Commission was able to help a few individuals obtain employment and get housing. The Commission investigated and mediated individual complaints of discrimination, but did not welcome and was not equipped to handle a joint complaint of classes, categories, or collectivities. The religious leaders who condemned discrimination and sought relief for individuals on a case-by-case basis usually advocated such an approach as more appropriate. The Human Relations Commission and its members talked with school officials from time to time about various charges of discrimination in education but indicated that it had little influence and almost no effect upon school board actions.

In terms of social class and social action with reference to anti-discrimination activities in Corpus Christi, the union of working-class black, brown, and white members scored higher as advocates than the middle-class school trustees or the middle-class religious leaders. The experience in Corpus Christi indicates that further examination is needed of social theory that postulates a direct association between social class and resistance to desegregation. In Corpus Christi, working-class and poorer people tended to exhibit greater acceptance of the concept of desegregation for the purpose of overcoming discrimination than midddle-class and more affluent people. The latter are alleged to be more liberal. This, however, was not so in Corpus Christi.

Actually, there was little violence between individuals that was associated with school desegregation in Corpus Christi. It cannot be determined from available information whether this is (1) because the cultural traditions of the racial populations in this community supported passive resistance, or (2) because desegregation to date is small, involving only about one-fourth of the 40,000 school-age population, or (3) because of other sociological characteristics or features of Corpus Christi. Thus, it is hard to test a theory about social class and violence on the basis of what has and has not happened in Corpus Christi. However, one can say based on observations of Corpus Christi that collective resistance to racial desegregation tends to be greater among those institutions dominated by the affluent and middle-class people than among those controlled by working-class and poorer people. Indeed, a working-class dominated institution — a labor union — in Corpus Christi actively promoted racial desegregation.

The question of violence probably needs to be separated and analyzed in terms of violence initiated by individuals and violence activated by institutions. Thus, it could be that violence associated with desegregation for the purpose of overcoming discrimination is indirectly associated with social class when it is initiated by individuals (the lower the social class the greater the incidence of violent resistance to desegregation) and directly associated with social class when it is activated by institutions (the higher the social class that dominates the institution, the greater the incidence of violent resistance by the collectivity to desegregation).

Maybe the phenomenon of individually-initiated violence is not so much a function of social class as it is a function of physical isolation from people unlike one's own kind. While there are distinct neighborhoods for Anglos and Mexican-Americans in Corpus Christi, there is a considerable amount of intermingling—much more than the intermingling between blacks and whites in other communities in which blacks are the major minority population. The fact that Anglos and Mexican-Americans more or less balance each other in terms of numbers increases the probability of intergroup contact among these individuals.

We offer this hypothesis: Where there has been frequent intergroup contact over an extended period of time, the individuals affiliated with different groups are less likely to aggress against each other in a violent way. This hypothesis is in need of study and is worthy of immediate investigation in view of the experience of nonviolence in Corpus Christi but of violence occasioned by desegregation in other communities where there is more separation and alienation among ethnic and racial groups.

The Boston metropolitan area, for example, has experienced individually-initiated violence in connection with school desegregation in South Boston, Charlestown, and in Concord. The first two communities are in the central city and consist of many working-class families. The third area is in the suburbs and is recognized as an affluent middle-class community. What Concord, Charlestown, and South Boston have in common is a condition of racial isolation of whites from blacks.

Roxbury High School, predominantly black and located in central-city Boston where many working-class families reside, responded to school desegregation in a calm and peaceful way. As late as the mid-twentieth century, this was a neighborhood in which blacks and whites more or less balanced each other numerically. This fact prevented social isolation and contributed to frequent intergroup contact. The Roxbury desegregation experiences were less violent.

Police were summoned to the campus of the Concord-Carlisle High School the final day of examinations in 1978 in connection with a fight between students that clearly was race related. Annually, about three thousand Boston students are bused to several suburban communities as part of a state-supported program to desegregate the public schools in the central city. Concord has few black and brown families. Less than 40 Boston black student participated in the suburban busing program to Concord. The high school student body then was about 1,700. Such odds contributed to limited contact and little interaction of whites with blacks or other racial minorities. Our hypothesis is that this condition contributed to the individually-initiated violence that was seen in this affluent suburban community; the condition of racial isolation in Concord was similar to that which existed in the white working-class communities in Boston's central-city neighborhoods that responded to school desegregation in a violent way. The social-class levels of the central city and suburban communities were different. But their violence associated with school desegregation was similar, as was their experience of racial isolation.

The race relations experience in Mobile, Alabama, when desegregation began, is further evidence that suggests a connection between racial isolation and violence. At the beginning of the 1970s, whites were about 60 percent of the total Mobile population. Nevertheless, the tradition of state-sanctioned racial discrimination had resulted in segregation and a rigid pattern of separation of the races by residential areas, occupations, and public facilities, including schools. Thus, when desegregation was initiated, there was violence in several schools. One school that experienced a considerable amount of violence was the elite, almost all-white Murphy High School, that had had, prior to desegregation, the reputation of being the best school in the city. The white students who attended it came from affluent families and a high proportion of its graduates attended college. Their contact with blacks had been quite limited and highly regulated in dominant and sub-dominant patterns in the past with whites as dominants. School desegregation was a new occasion; the previously isolated black and white students were not prepared to fulfill the new duties of this occasion. And so they acted violently against each other.

All of these examples point in the direction of identifying racial isolation as a key condition associated with intergroup violence in school desegregation. The experience of nonviolence in Corpus Christi in comparison with the violence that accompanied desegregation in other cities suggests this conclusion.

Chapter 17

White Students in Black Colleges

The Southern Regional Educational Board authorized in 1977 a study of whites in predominantly black public colleges and universities [Standley 1978]. The principal investigator was Nancy V. Standley of Florida A. and M. University, a predominantly black public institution of higher education. The study included twenty predominantly black schools all located in the South in which approximately 10 percent of graduate and undergraduate students enrolled were white. The study analyzed the attitudes and self-reported experiences of white students regarding the campus climate and learning environment, including interpersonal relations. The study also obtained information regarding the white students' assessment of the competence of their teachers and of the adequacy of the curriculum, facilities, and support services in their schools [Standley 1978:3].

Data and Method

The twenty southern colleges and universities with predominantly black student bodies were requested to distribute a questionnaire to a sample of one-fourth to one-third of all whites enrolled. Institutions with a white enrollment of less than 100 were asked to include all their white students in the study. A total of 2,550 questionnaires were distributed; 1,189 were returned. This number represented a return rate of 46 percent [Standley 1978:24].

The research instrument consisted of a series of questions regarding the campus learning environment that required a response on a Likert-type scale: strongly agree, agree, undecided, disagree, strongly disagree.

Reprinted from Charles V. Willie, *The Ivory and Ebony Towers,* Lexington, MA: Lexington Books of D.C. Heath and Company, 1981, Chapter 9, pp. 79–90.

Percentages were computed for the range of responses to each questionnaire item and published in the monograph that presented an initial analysis of the data [Standley 1978:36–39]. This chapter presents a reanalysis of these data and further interpretation. The data on which this analysis is based may be found in the appendix to this chapter.

These are some of the characteristics of the students who responded. Seven out of every ten were born in the South, and a similar proportion attended predominantly white high schools. They were older than most college students; indeed, eight out of every ten were twenty-three years of age or over. A majority (about 60 percent) were married. Almost all lived off campus. They attended day classes (56 percent) and evening and weekend classes (44 percent). Three to four out of every ten of the white students were enrolled in a graduate course. Most were performing well at the B level or above. Education was the field in which a majority majored; it was followed by the natural sciences, the social sciences, and business. Of these white students, 41 percent were male and 59 percent were female [Standley 1978:30–35].

Findings

First, we attempted to determine areas of greatest uncertainty for white students in predominantly black colleges and universities. Extracurricular activities created the most uncertainty. A majority of the white students questioned whether student government on campus adequately represented their point of view and were uncertain as to whether they were welcome to participate in campus politics.

Also the white students were undecided about whether interracial dating was acceptable, and they could not quite make up their minds whether they found the campus musical events appealing and entertaining. If such events were not entertaining, then white students could justify not attending these extracurricular functions.

Extracurricular activities are less predictable and can foster random intimacy. Harvey Molotch's study of managed integration in the South Shore area of Chicago discovered that there is great inhibition to random intimacy in most urban settings. Molotch found that people tend to shy away from intimate contexts in which there is uncertainty of the trustworthiness and acceptance of others. He found that people tend to feel interpersonal vulnerability in uncontrolled social situations [Molotch 1972: 177–184]. Even in religious organizations such as churches, Molotch found that integration existed primarily in terms of formal worship, where the role relationships were prescribed and predictable, and less so in the social-life activities of the church outside of worship services. Social activities were virtually completely segregated in the integrated community that he studied.

The white students on predominantly black college and university campuses exhibited great uncertainty particularly about social events. Their uncertainty probably reflected interpersonal vulnerability and fear of rejection. Molotch said that interpersonal vulnerability is an important determinant of racial patterns [Molotch 1972:190]. Apparently the black students on predominantly black campuses had not yet given sufficient signals of acceptance to their white schoolmates to minimize their feelings of social vulnerability [Molotch 1972:198, 184].

The other area in which a majority of the white students on predominantly black college and university campuses expressed uncertainty had to do with personal services. Nearly six out of every ten remained undecided as to whether the counseling and advising services were especially sensitive to the needs of white students. Most white students enrolled in these predominantly black schools were not affluent (only one-third were members of families whose annual income was above the national median); yet they were uncertain whether financial assistance was readily available to them at the predominantly black schools. How much of the uncertainty could be attributed to fear of rejection if they had applied for financial assistance and been refused, and how much was due to reluctance to discuss personal money matters with college-staff members of a racial group that is considered to be a stranger to whites could not be determined from these data. An indication that some of the professional personnel in predominantly black institutions were looked upon as strangers is the high proportion (46 percent) of the white students who said that they were reluctant to use school health services because there were no whites or few whites on the staff. Whereas a similar proportion of white students (48 percent) were not reluctant to go to the campus health clinic, the high proportion who were reluctant to do so is mentioned because their behavior may be part of a pattern of tending to seek like-kind from whom to obtain personal services. The practice is found among blacks in predominantly white settings and among whites in predominantly black settings. In due time, such reluctance may pass away as the black and the white strangers become friends and learn to accept and trust each other. For the nonce, however, race still is a barrier to the revelation of intimate concerns for a large number of whites in predominantly black schools.

Helen Hughes and Lewis Watts studied blacks who moved into white suburbs in the Boston metropolitan area and found that "with astonishing rapidity the self-integrators' lives [took] on the character and tempo of the white suburbanites all about them" [Hughes and Watts 1970:121]. Yet several of these families returned to inner-city black ghetto communities for personal services such as legal, dental, and hairgrooming services. These neighborhood self-integrators who are black are not unlike the school self-integrators who are white.

There is a great deal of uncertainty among white students on black campuses concerning what is expected of them and why they chose these schools. The uncertainty tends to vanish with reference to specific learning experiences. When one discussed behavior in general (what is appropriate and inappropriate) and abstract reasons why one enrolled in one or another school, uncertainty reappeared regarding the choices that white students made.

For example, about 25 percent of the white students said that many black students expected them to adapt to the way of life of blacks; moreover, they felt that blacks on predominantly black campuses made less effort to adapt to others. A slightly higher proportion (about 30 percent of the white students) said that they disagreed with this assessment, and 45 percent were uncertain about how blacks expected them to adapt.

Whites also were unable as a group to state decisively why they had enrolled in a predominantly black school. About one-third said that whites would not have enrolled in such a school if there had not been special programs that attracted whites. Another one-third, however, said that this was not true, that regardless of the programs offered, whites would have enrolled. Still another one-third was uncertain as to whether whites would or would not have enrolled in a predominantly black institution without special reasons.

So new is the experience of racial integration, especially of whites enrolled in predominantly black colleges and universities, that the participants somehow feel that they have to justify their actions. The data show that there is little, if any, consensus among whites as a group regarding why they are present on predominantly black campuses. They probably have been attracted to such campuses for many different reasons. Even though it is true that about one out of every three whites enrolled because of the special offerings of a school, two out of every three are there for other reasons.

Despite the uncertainties, white students on black college and university campuses have derived some important educational benefits. Their most important learnings are that black schools provide a good education, that teachers in these schools help all students and are not partial because of the race of a student, and that the courses that the schools offer can contribute to future job plans.

Beyond specific educational opportunities that may contribute to future employability, the white students enrolled in black colleges and universities have learned a great deal about race relations in this nation. Through their regular social contacts with blacks on the campuses, 80 percent or more of the white students stated that they now have no difficulty communicating with a person of a race that is different from their own. Moreover, through such communication they have learned about the aspirations of blacks, have dismissed old racial stereotypes from their thinking, and have overcome the tendency to deny that prejudice continues to exist. They no longer are apologists for the status quo.

The negative concepts that have been eliminated from the information reservoirs of white students who have attended black schools have been replaced with positive concepts. Of the white students, 75 to 80 percent said that their education on black campuses has heightened their appreciation of different ways of life and caused them to be more concerned about equal opportunity for all. Moreover, they felt that their multiracial, multicultural experiences would help them to be more effective in their careers. These statements indicate that the white students found their education to be liberating and at the same time job-related. The provision of a "career-oriented education in a liberal arts context" is a typical expression used by black college presidents in describing the unique function of their schools [Willie and MacLeish 1978:138].

The white students claimed that they received the comprehensive kind of education described because of a combination of factors. They said faculty on black college and university campuses were highly competent, students were educationally and vocationally motivated, and the campus atmosphere was one of tolerance. Such a setting was conducive to a range of experiences. Whites who attended black schools learned some things that were both similar to and different from what they could have learned on predominantly white college campuses.

Being a minority on black campuses, whites saw themselves for the first time in a different way. They said that they gained a better understanding of their own unique personhood. They developed what W.E.B. DuBois has called "a double consciousness" — the property of knowing who one is but also recognizing oneself in terms of how others see one. The development of a double consciousness is a survival strategem for those in a less powerful status [DuBois 103:3]. DuBois explained that blacks had to learn the life style of whites as well as their own in order to survive. On the black college and university campuses, whites have had to learn the life style of blacks as well as their own. Learning how blacks perceived them helped whites to see themselves in a uniquely different way.

Coming face to face with the consequences of subdominant status, whites on predominantly black campuses recognized the negative effects of having too few people of one's own group on location. In fact, seven out of ten said that the presence of white faculty members and other white students on predominantly black campuses helped one feel as though one belonged. The white students were very aware of the need for a sufficiently large number of whites to facilitate increased participation by whites in the affairs of the school. The proportion of whites on the campuses of the institutions studied was 10 percent. Presumably this percentage was not sufficient. The white students were not sure that they could count on the administration to lead in efforts to break down racial barriers. If they had to rely on themselves, more white students were needed. Four out of every ten whites were uncertain as to whether the administration on the black college campus was making a genuine effort to recruit more nonblacks; 36 percent said the administration was trying to recruit more whites; 43 percent were undecided; 21 percent said the administration was not making genuine recruiting efforts.

Other studies have reported that when the subdominant population on a campus is too small, that group is condemned to "an inadequate social life and intraracial as well as interracial discord" [Willie and McCord 1972:15]. Of the subdominant population, studies note that a school "should enroll a large enough number to ensure an adequate social life and educational experience." There should be enough students present to provide "a range of potentially compatible personalities and social types. Also the number should be sufficiently large so that all need not be known to each other personally. The goal is to have enough ... students to provide freedom in association, flexibility in movement, and anonymity when desirable" [Willie and McCord 1972:109].

The court-appointed masters in the Boston school desegregation case said that "whites need not always be the majority in good schools." Where whites are not the majority, however, they should be "a sufficient minority" to have a meaningful impact upon the system. From my own studies, I have determined that "the participation of less than one-fifth for a specific group in a democratic ... organization is tokenism and tends to have little effect upon its decision-making structure." Thus, I conclude that "20 percent is the lower limit in terms of critical mass for a particular group" [Willie 1978: 20]. The proportion of whites in predominantly black colleges and universities can be significantly increased over the years to the benefit of both black and white populations.

Summary

In summary, the study of whites on predominantly black college and university campuses that was sponsored by the Southern Regional Educational Board revealed that whites were receiving a career oriented and liberal arts education by competent teachers who cared about their students. Moreover, these whites had learned how to communicate with blacks. These experiences had increased multicultural knowledge for whites and heightened their sense of the need for equality of opportunity for all. Even though the white students were pleased with their new experiences, especially those that flowed from their subdominant status on campus, they wished that the schools would recruit more whites and that extracurricular and social encounters were as comfortable as their educational experiences. White students on predominantly black college and university campuses like their teachers and believe that they are getting a good and relevant education, but they have doubts about the sincerity and intentions of the administrators of these schools.

References

DuBois, W.E.B. 1903. *The Souls of Black Folk.* Chicago: McClurg.

Hughes, Helen MacGill, and Lewis G. Watts. 1970. "Portrait of the Self-Integrator." In *The Family Life of Black People,* edited by Charles V. Willie. Columbus, Ohio: Merrill.

Molotch, Harvey Luskin. 1972. *Managed Integration.* Berkeley: University of California Press.

Standley, Nancy V. 1978. *White Students Enrolled in Black Colleges and Universities.* Atlanta: Southern Regional Educational Board.

Willie, Charles V. 1978. *The Sociology of Urban Education.* Lexington, MA: Lexington Books, D.C. Heath and Co.

Willie, Charles V., and Marlene Y. MacLeish. 1978. "Priorities of Presidents of Black Colleges." In *Black Colleges in America,* edited by Charles V. Willie and R.E. Edmonds, New York: Teachers College Press.

Willie, Charles V., and Arline S. McCord, 1972. *Black Students at White Colleges.* New York: Praeger.

Appendix 17: Selected Survey Items and Responses

Table 17.1.

Uncertainties of Whites on Black Campuses

	Response by Percent				
Items	Strongly Agree	Agree	Unde-cided	Dis-agree	Strongly Disagree
1. The student government here effectively represents my point of view	3.1	10.3	71.3	10.9	4.5
2. The musical events on this campus are appealing and entertaining	5.4	21.4	64.6	5.0	3.6
3. Most of the dormitories on this campus appear to be well kept	2.4	23.4	59.5	10.0	4.6
4. I find that the counseling and advising services here are especially sensitive to the needs of white students	3.9	16.4	58.9	17.0	3.9
5. Interracial dating appears to be an acceptable social relationship on this campus	1.2	6.2	58.6	19.2	14.8
6. The campus political structure does not welcome white student participation	4.6	11.4	56.3	20.8	6.8
7. Financial assistance seems to be more readily available here, especially for me	9.8	18.5	50.5	12.1	9.0
8. Most of the people brought to the campus for lectures are stimulating and interesting to me	7.8	35.1	46.7	8.0	2.4
9. I am reluctant to use the services of the health clinic at this school because there are no (or few) whites on the staff	1.3	4.0	46.1	28.4	20.3
10. Many of the black students want the white students to adapt to them; the black students make less effort to adapt themselves to others	4.8	19.8	45.2	25.7	4.4
11. White administrators and white faculty members appear to have their input in the governance of this school	8.8	34.5	44.1	8.7	4.0
12. I feel that the overall administration of this campus makes a genuine effort to recruit nonblack students	8.1	28.4	42.6	15.9	5.0
13. There appears to be sufficient and effective security on the campus to make me feel safe	12.3	50.3	42.4	7.9	5.1
14. I feel a real part of the school spirit	4.1	21.2	40.4	25.8	8.5

Source: Nancy V. Standley, *White Students Enrolled in Black Colleges and Universities: Their Attitudes and Perceptions* (Atlanta: Southern Regional Education Board, 1978), pp. 36–39. Reprinted by permission.

Table 17.2.

Positive Experiences of Whites on Black Campuses

Items	Strongly Agree	Agree	Unde-cided	Dis-agree	Strongly Disagree
		Response by Percent			
1. Most of my instructors do not show any partiality to students on the basis of race	45.9	43.0	4.0	5.9	1.3
2. My courses/educational experiences are closely tied to my future job plans	34.1	51.1	9.8	3.9	1.1
3. I have no difficulty communicating with black students on the campus	26.0	57.5	8.9	6.1	1.5
4. The thing most blacks want is the same as what every other American wants: a chance to get some of the "good things of life"	29.5	54.2	11.9	3.0	1.3
5. A student's race does not affect his/her ability to learn	51.1	37.3	6.7	3.4	1.5
6. My social contacts on campus include both whites and blacks	28.0	54.2	10.6	5.6	1.5
7. In spite of all of the progress in recent years, there is still a great deal of prejudice operative in our society	26.9	52.8	10.3	8.2	1.8
8. My educational experiences here have given me a keener appreciation of different philosophies, cultures, and ways of life	25.1	53.7	13.6	6.3	1.3
9. I am not reluctant to tell people I go to school here	30.1	47.4	7.3	10.4	4.8
10. The cross cultural-multiracial experiences I am having here will make me more effective in my future career	25.7	52.6	15.9	4.4	1.4
11. Having a degree from here will not deter me from getting a satisfying "good" job	21.9	54.9	18.6	3.6	1.8
12. In most instances, on this campus, there is an atmosphere of tolerance and understanding of people and their views	13.6	63.0	16.8	5.0	1.5
13. Being a student here has made me more positively concerned about equal opportunities for all people, especially in education and careers	20.1	54.3	13.8	6.5	0.8
14. My family supported my decision to attend this school	17.6	54.9	16.0	7.8	3.7
15. The faculty members on this campus do demonstrate a high level of competence in their academic specialities	18.7	52.1	17.9	8.1	3.2

Table 17.2. *(continued)*

	Response by Percent				
Items	Strongly Agree	Agree	Unde-cided	Dis-agree	Strongly Disagree
16. Most black students in my classes appear to be motivated toward developing themselves educationally and vocationally	17.5	53.1	14.4	10.8	4.3
17. The presence of white faculty members and other white students on the campus helps me feel like I belong	15.2	55.4	15.6	11.7	2.1
18. My educational preparation here has met my expectations	18.1	51.5	13.5	12.0	5.0
19. I feel uncomfortable when black instructors relate subject matters to activities and ex-periences of the black com-munity and culture with which I have no familiarity	3.3	12.2	14.8	48.4	21.4
20. Most of the faculty of this campus are well qualified both by academic training and ex-perience	18.0	50.9	20.6	7.7	2.7
21. Being a student here has given me the opportunity to under-stand and appreciate my own unique personhood	17.0	50.5	23.6	7.2	1.7

Source: Nancy V. Standley, *White Students Enrolled in Black Colleges and Universities: Their Attitudes and Perceptions* (Atlanta: Southern Regional Education Board, 1978), pp. 36–39. Reprinted by permission.

Chapter 18

Demographic Basis for Social Action
for Urban Educational Reform

There are two theoretical positions that are generally accepted as descriptive of the future of urban educational reform in the United States. One theory is that urban school desegregation will be severely limited in cities, especially large cities, because not enough whites will be left to desegregate their public school systems. The other theory is that urban schools in the future are likely to experience an "exceedingly rapid rise in the proportion of 'high cost' disadvantaged students and a corresponding drop in overall educational performance" since "the central cities are increasingly becoming the domain of the poor and the stable working class" [Wilson 1978:114, 115].

It is probably a coincidence that these two theories have been set forth by two sociologists who are affiliated with the University of Chicago. James Coleman, in a deposition that was submitted to the Dallas Division of the United States District Court, said, "Based on my research, it is my opinion that extensive desegregation of schools within larger central cities has two effects: first, by reassignment of children within the district, it has a direct and immediate effect in eliminating predominantly black schools. Second, it increases the loss of white children from the district, and as a consequence, it has the long-term effect of re-establishing predominantly black schools in the central city" [Quoted in Willie 1978:28]. William Wilson said, "the racial struggle for power and privilege in the central city is essentially a struggle between the have-nots." He characterized "the relatively poorly trained blacks of the inner city" as being "locked in the low-wage sector" with "inferior ghetto schools" [Wilson 1978:116, 121].

It is the contention of this chapter that there are enough whites in central cities now and will be in the future to achieve meaningful desegregation

Presented in Phi Delta Kappa's Spring Lecture Series, Harvard Graduate School of Education, April 26, 1979.

193

of their public school systems. Also, I contend that city populations are diversified, do not consist overwhelmingly of poor people today and are unlikely to be so constituted in the future. These contentions are supported by demographic data and their analysis.

Size of Population and Desegregation

The claim that the white population in central cities is too small to desegregate public schools is an opinion of an increasing number of public policy makers and other professionals, including social and behavioral scientists. It is summarized by Harry Gottlieb, a specialist in housing and finance, who said that "in growing numbers of cities, there are not only too few whites to achieve meaningful racial desegregation: often there are also not enough economically advantaged people to achieve meaningful economic desegregation [Gottlieb 1976: 158]. While this opinion has been repeated often enough to become part of conventional wisdom, it is entirely at odds with the facts. I would like to make this point emphatically. Claims that the central cities in the United States have become black ghettos, devoid of whites, are incorrect. Of the 183 million whites in the United States, 25 percent or 46 million live in central cities. While the proportion of blacks in central cities, 58 percent, is twice as large as the proportion of white city dwellers, the black proportion represents only 14 million people. Thus whites outnumber blacks in central cities 3 to 1. There are plenty of whites to go around for school desegregation or any other purpose.

It is true that whites are not an overwhelming majority in all central cities as they once were and now are in the suburbs. The fact is, however, that in most central cities, they still are the majority. It is true that city whites have dwindled to a relatively small majority and, therefore, must adapt to their new numerical situation. However, no real change has occurred in their status as the majority in most American cities.

Even in the few cities where blacks are a majority, enough whites remain to desegregate the public school systems. When I testified in the Dallas school desegregation case in the mid-1970s, the attorney for the majority-white school board, the defendant, asked me if there was not a danger that Dallas would become like Atlanta, Georgia, if court-ordered school desegregation was implemented. Before answering, I asked the attorney what was the problem of Atlanta and was informed that the student body of that public school system was more than 80 percent black. I replied that such was of no consequence so far as education was concerned, that I had known of several good public school systems that were 80 percent or more white. The point is that good public educational systems may be majority black, brown, or white if they are unitary systems in which resources are equitably distributed among all schools, and student bodies are desegregated.

A desegregated school is one in which a majority are educated in the presence of a minority or minorities of different backgrounds and experiences. A unitary school system is one in which there is equal access to educational opportunities for both majority and minorities and equitable distribution of educational resources. A public school system that is predominantly black, brown, or white can be a unitary and desegregated system. This is what the constitution requires; it does not require whites to be a majority; it does not prohibit whites from experiencing minority status. Thus, enough whites are present to desegregate the urban school systems of this nation, if it is not necessary for whites always to be the majority. The fact is, however, that whites outnumber blacks 3 to 1 in the central cities of the United States. Thus, enough whites are present to desegregate most city systems where they are and will be the majority.

Socioeconomic Status of City Residents

The claim that central cities have become settings of the poor and that the affluent, by and large, have escaped to the suburbs also is in error. William Wilson has observed the increasing black population in cities and he assumes that the blacks are poor. He quotes from *Urban Education* by Hummel and Nagle, who state that cities have lost "valuable human capital to the suburbs," meaning middle-class whites. Then Wilson asserts that "the mounting financial problems of urban schools seem to go hand in hand with their rapidly changing racial composition" [Wilson 1978: 114–115]. Again, the facts do not support these assertions.

While 7 out of every 10 white families in the suburbs have incomes of $12,000 and above, in the central cities, it is 6 out of every 10. Thus, a majority of city and suburban whites are affluent. While blacks in central cities and elsewhere continue to experience racial discrimination and consequently are disadvantaged economically, they still are not poverty stricken. In fact, the percent of affluent black families with incomes greater than $12,000 a year (36 percent) is larger than the percent of poor blacks with incomes under $5,000 (27 percent). Central cities are far from being ghettoes of the black poor, according to these data.

It is true that the proportion of poor people in central cities is larger than the proportion of poor people in the suburbs. However, the number of white poor in the city is one-third larger than the number of black poor. This fact indicates that it is inappropriate to characterize the central cities of America as ghettoes of poor black people. The main fact is that most people in cities *are not* poor. While whites constitute the largest number of poor people in central cities, only 1 out of every 10 white families has an income under $5,000. The proportion of blacks at this low-income level is nearly three times greater but represents less than 3 out of every 10 black families.

It is important to remember these facts when discussing the future of urban education and school desegregation: (1) that whites outnumber blacks 3 to 1 in central city populations, (2) that most people in city populations, blacks as well as whites, are not poor, (3) that among the poor in cities, whites outnumber blacks 3 to 1. These facts indicate that enough whites are available in central cities to achieve meaningful school desegregation and that most cities, in terms of the socioeconomic status of their residents, are capable of financing desegregated, unitary school systems, although some additional help may be needed from non-local sources.

Regional Location of Future Educational Reform Movements

The future is likely to see increased effort in all regions of the nation to achieve unitary school systems consisting of equal access for minority and majority populations and equitable distribution of educational resources. This movement was initiated in the South but has and will continue to spread to the North and West because of the changing characteristics of the black population in cities. I might add that the demographic phenomenon that will enable blacks to marshall the power to press for reform in urban educational systems would not exist if minorities were randomly distributed throughout the nation.

The black population no longer is concentrated in a single region (about half now live in the South and half reside elsewhere in the nation). However, the black population is concentrated in cities of metropolitan areas. The suburbs contain slightly less than one-fifth of the blacks. But, according to Harold Rose, "the most active suburban growth communities (for blacks) are spatial extensions of central city ghettoes" [Rose 1976: 263].

If blacks were dispersed throughout the nation without discrimination, they would be not more than 11 percent of the total population in any locality. Under these conditions, their relative strength in numbers would be diminished below the critical mass necessary to mount effective campaigns for educational reform against community institutions that practice racial segregation and discrimination. By limiting blacks largely to central cities, whites have given this racial minority group more power through concentrated numbers than it would otherwise have. Indeed, by controlling a few cities, urban blacks have obtained a disproportionate amount of power in this nation. With that power, blacks are now shaking the foundation of the nation, demanding reform in public education and other human services.

I offer the following as a theory of the circumstances and conditions that are associated with the increasing power of subdominant populations to press for institutional reform. A subdominant population is likely to intensify its press for affirmative action with reference to equal access and equitable distribution of community resources when it grows in numbers from a small minority to a large minority and when it changes socioeconomically from a homogeneous to a heterogeneous population. Essentially I am saying that the size of a population and its socioeconomic differentiation are interrelated phenomena that must be examined to determine their joint effect, if the pattern of the press for social action by a subdominant population is to be understood.

An assertion by writer William Robert Miller places this discussion in an appropriate perspective. He stated that the most remarkable achievement of Martin Luther King, Jr., was his success in making middle-class blacks "the backbone" of a crusade for human dignity [Miller 1968: 308]. The group most likely to press for social change in education and in other institutional systems is a large minority that consists of people of differentiated status positions.

The history of social action by blacks in this nation has proceeded in accordance with this theory. A century and a half ago the relative size of the black population was larger than it is today; in 1820, nearly 1 out of every 5 people (18.4 percent) was black. Yet there was no social movement initiated by blacks for desegregation and reform because this relatively large minority was largely undifferentiated; most blacks were slaves. Effective social action is possible only when a group has some members who are free to plan and to deal with matters that go beyond the daily requirements for personal survival. The undifferentiated relatively large minority of blacks during the age of slavery was unable to mount and sustain a revolution for reform. But the relatively large minority that was differentiated into middle-class and other socioeconomic levels during the era of Martin Luther King, Jr., was able to mobilize and act effectively. When Martin Luther King, Jr., began his work in the South, one-fifth of the population in that region was black and at least 1 out of every 3 southern blacks was above the poverty line. This proportion that was beyond the clutches of daily worry about personal physical survival apparently was sufficiently large to spark and sustain a revolutionary movement for reform, to become its backbone. This demographic fact is the reason the civil rights movement started in the South when it did.

The northern population of blacks has always been more differentiated in terms of socioeconomic status. As early as 1960, two-thirds of the blacks in the North were above the poverty line, a proportion that would appear to be sufficient to sustain a social movement for reform. However, the relative size of the black population in the North was small, only 7 percent of the total number of northerners. The socioeconomic resources may have been sufficient but the critical mass was not. But with the containment of blacks in central cities of the North because of racial discrimination, their proportion of the urban population has increased to one-fifth and more in several cities, thus providing them with the necessary critical mass and socioeconomic differentiation to mount effective movements for educational and other institutional changes. As reform efforts in education, particularly those involving school desegregation, have surfaced in the North, they have originated in those cities with relatively large black populations of diversified socioeconomic status. Because the practice of residential containment of racial minorities in central cities in the North and West does not appear to be leveling off and because these areas have a sufficient number of middle-class people who tend to serve as the backbone of reform movements, I predict that the social movement among blacks and Hispanics with reference to educational reform and other human services will continue and intensify as long as residential discrimination and its containment and concentrating effects remain.

Minority and Majority Responsibility for Social Action

Ultimately, each group must accept responsibility for the circumstances and conditions under which it lives. The probability is high that a minority group (or any population that is subdominant in terms of power) will continue to suffer the oppression of inequity and blocked opportunities as long as it continues to cooperate in its own oppression. In colloquial terminology, this idea may be expressed this way: they will do it to you as long as you let them.

In most instances, resistance and reform movements are initiated by the oppressed and not by the oppressors, by those with less power and not by the powerful. For this reason, we should study the mood of the minorities and the subdominant people of power for some of the indications of future activities in the reform of urban education. Among most scholars for whom this is a field of study, investigation and analysis are limited largely to the interests and activities of the majority or the dominant people of power. For example, Daniel Patrick Moynihan's policy study of community action in the war on poverty that was entitled *Maximum Feasible Misunderstanding* had not a single reference to Martin Luther King, Jr. It was as if his demonstrations during the 1950s and the 1960s had been of no effect, which, of course, is patently untrue. Moynihan discussed the Johnson Administration's war on poverty as if it had been concocted out of the minds of university professors and as if the main issue were a contest between the Columbia University and Harvard University professors about the appropriate way to fight the war [Willie 1978:35]. In like manner, too many studies of urban education concentrate on the actions and reactions of whites when the shaking of the foundation of this nation over segregated education was initiated by blacks.

Despite all that has been said about minorities, the majority plays a crucial role in social movements; by their actions, minorities are driven to other reactions. If the racial oppression in the Southland had not been as brutal as it was (and this included the absence of opportunities to earn enough for a decent living), blacks would not have fled in droves to the North, thus raising their numbers in that region to a critical mass sufficient to mount a reform movement. If racial discrimination by residential area had not been practiced in the North, blacks and other racial minorities would have randomly distributed themselves throughout the region and would not have concentrated in cities, thereby obtaining a disproportionate amount of power to initiate change in urban institutions. That the reform movement in urban education has expanded from the South to the North and will surface elsewhere in this nation in the future is due to the two demographic factors of concentration and differentiation among minorities. The concentration of minorities in the central cities of metropolitan areas, of course, is due largely to the actions of the majority. Thus, the majority has only itself to blame for the revolution in urban education, initiated by minorities, that has come upon us.

Conclusions

On the basis of this analysis, I conclude that a minority population needs to be at least one-fifth of the total population and have adequate resources beyond those required for survival among at least one-third of its people to mount an effective campaign for educational and other institutional reform. A black population of this size existed in the South a century and a half ago but was insufficiently diversified in terms of socioeconomic status to sustain an effective social movement for reform. When the appropriate population size and diversity came into being in the post-World War II era, rapid changes occurred in the South. Similar action occurred in the North during the 1960s and after, due largely to the fact that a socioeconomically differentiated black population finally achieved a critical mass that was sufficient for effective social action. These movements are likely to continue in all regions of the United States where racial minorities are concentrated in relatively large numbers and diversified socioeconomically.

References

Gottlieb, Harry. 1976. "The Ultimate Solution: Desegregated Housing." In Florence Hamlish Levinsohn and Benjamin Drake Wright (eds.), *School Desegregation.* Chicago: University of Chicago Press.

Miller, Robert William. 1968. *Martin Luther King, Jr.* New York: Avon.

Riesman, David, and Christopher Jencks. 1967. "The American Negro College." In *The Academic Revolution.* New York: Doubleday.

Rose, Harold M. 1976. *Black Suburbanization.* Cambridge, MA: Ballinger.

Willie, Charles V. 1978. *The Sociology of Urban Education: Desegregation and Integration.* Lexington: Lexington Books of D.C. Heath.

Wilson, William J. 1978. *The Declining Significance of Race.* Chicago: University of Chicago Press.

Chapter 19

Conflict, Withdrawal, and Cooperation:
Three Approaches to Social Action

The role of the sociologists in social conflict is difficult to define not so much because of the content of the sociological contribution but because the nation does not know how to handle competing opinions between different experts in a specific discipline. School desegregation is a good example of the dilemma experienced by the public in determining the sociological advice to accept.

Christopher Jencks said that luck and personality factors were more important than formal education in producing differentials between racial groups in income [Jencks 1972]. According to Harold Howe II, these ideas were rapidly parlayed into arguments by others that schools did not matter, particularly as a way of enhancing black individuals for the purpose of achieving equity with whites [Howe 1976]. However, James Coleman said that schools had a definite effect upon the achievement of minorities. He mentioned integrated schools as having a positive effect for blacks [Coleman 1966].

Educational policy probably will differ depending on which sociologist the policy-makers believe. Those who believe in the linkage between luck and success probably will follow one course of action and those who believe in the association between type of school attended and achievement probably will follow another course. As pointed out elsewhere, "we have no agreed-upon procedure outside the court for determining when to accept or reject expert opinion in the making of public policy" [Willie 1978].

In the absence of agreed-upon procedures for accepting or rejecting expert sociological opinion, the public tends to rely upon indicators that may be unreliable such as the race or the reputation of a scholar, or one's in-group or outgroup status. Because there are competing expert opinions, the public should seek the advice of a variety of sociologists who have had

Paper presented at the annual meeting of the Eastern Sociological Society thematic session on The Role of Sociologists in Social Conflict, March 20, 1982, Philadelphia, Pa.

different existential histories, and who are associated with a range of social locations within the social structure, including dominant and subdominant power positions, and many racial and ethnic populations. Human conduct, including that of sociologists, is in part a function of the situations in which one finds oneself. Situations have a great deal to do with the kinds of issues a sociologist chooses to study and the implications for action that are derived from their analysis. Thus sociological advice from a variety of professionals is better than no sociological advice at all.

Options for Social Groups

The essential role of sociologists is to help others understand social conflict and alternative action strategies. One does this by indicating options available and the situational contexts that render one or another option more efficacious. Sociological analysis should determine the situations and circumstances wherein either conflict, cooperation, or withdrawal may be effective for the achievement of self-interests and group-goals. Thus, whether or not one should conflict, cooperate or withdraw depends upon one's power position in the social structure and one's interests and goals associated therewith, and whether the social arrangements are fair.

Daniel Patrick Moynihan said, "it is clearly a disadvantage for a minority group to be operating on one principle, while the great majority of the population and the one with the most advantages to begin with, is operating on another" [United States Labor Department 1965:25]. Such advice encouraged the minority to conform to the way of life of the majority. But conformity to the standards of another group may be contraindicated in terms of the self-interests of minorities.

Self-Interest and Social Goal

Self-interest is the basic motive for human conduct and social goals give purpose to group effort. The self-interests and group goals of minority individuals, the subdominant group, often are not the same as those of the dominant majority-group individuals. When minorities act as if they were the majority, their actions may contribute to a stable social order that may be organized against them. That social organization is best which fulfills the essential and different but complementary needs of each group.

When the various individuals and groups in society fulfill their interests and diligently pursue their goals, they foster both stability and change. A healthy society, of course, is both flexible and stable. Conflict contributes to change and cooperation results in stability.

Both stability and change are of value. Human institutions that help people should be stabilized and retained and those that harm people should be reformed and changed. Thus, it is beneficial both to embrace and to resist change, depending on the outcome of institutional action and the implications of such action for groups and individuals in specific sectors of the society.

Human society, including its stable and changing norms, cannot be understood apart from the self-interests of its individuals and the goals of its groups. Social scientists who urge one group to adopt the norms of another without determining whether the interests and goals of its individuals will be satisfied by such action do a disservice to the total society, as well as to the group that is misadvised.

Conflict and Cooperation: Essential Social Processes

The antinomies within a society and the conflicts associated with them are ways that social organizations self-correct. Georg Simmel said that the individual who lived only according to the norms of the total society without observing other standards is an ethical abnormality [Quoted in Walter 1959:146]. Cooperation and withdrawal also contribute to the self-regulation of society. Both conflict and cooperation are social processes that may have helpful or harmful outcomes.

Alexander Leighton studied the coercive relocation of thousands of American citizens of Japanese ancestry, from their homes in the Pacific coastal region of the United States to camps in the interior of the United States during World War II. He discovered that adaptation to the stressful circumstances of relocation in an aggressive or conflictive way had alternative consequences for the Japanese-Americans. Aggressiveness and conflict sometimes got results and relieved frustrations by causing authorities to alter their ways of doing things. And aggressive and conflictive behavior sometimes resulted in increased repression by camp authorities who felt vulnerable when threatened [Leighton 1946:264–267]. Whether aggressiveness and conflictive behavior were effective in obtaining the desired results depended, in part, on the social context.

Studies of black students at white colleges reveal that most adapt according to the requirements of the situation. For example, black athletes at Syracuse University achieved their goal of a racially diversified coaching staff by withdrawing; they boycotted spring practice for the football team. The Student Afro-American Society at Syracuse University obtained an increase in its appropriation from the student activities fund after an aggressive presentation of its needs in a session of the student assembly. At this university, a black was elected president of the undergraduate student government the same year that a black was elected president of the graduate student organization. Through cooperative actions, these two black students who were elected to high office became advocates for all students. Reported have been three events in which three different adaptations were effective. There was a successful outcome in each situation because the adaptation was appropriate [Willie 1977: 214-217]. If conflict had been used when cooperation was required, the desired outcome would not have been attained. If cooperation had been used when conflict was necessary, it too would have been found wanting. Each adaptation was efficacious in terms of the social location of the group and its goals and the self-interests of group members.

Choice, Freedom, and Constraint

Humanity differs from other animal collectivities in three significant ways. The basic characteristics of human social organizations are choice, freedom, and constraint. Freedom is essential for individual action. Constraint is necessary for community effort. Choice is a way of articulating purpose described as interests or goals. Freedom facilitates the fulfillment of self-interests by individuals; constraint enhances the achievement of goals in groups. Where there is perfect freedom, there is full conflict, anarchy, and absence of the pursuit of group effort. Where there is full constraint, there is more than cooperation; there is oppressive conformity, and an absence of the pursuit of individual interest. Perfect freedom is the enemy of collective activity and full constraint is the enemy of individual initiative.

In the light of this analysis, neither conflict nor cooperation is always better than its opposite. Both are useful methods and should be chosen, depending on one's social location, interests and goals. Conflict is the method by which individuals resist the authority of groups, and minorities the power of the majority and their potential oppression. Cooperation is the method by which groups accommodate individual concerns, and majority groups the goals of subdominants that if ignored potentially could lead to anarchy and rebellion.

The Social Role of Dominants and Subdominants

Conflict is an expected and necessary action or reaction of subdominants that, when effectively exercised, perserves the personal freedom of all — dominants as well as subdominants. Dominant groups in different societies and during various periods in history control social organization and by way of such control may oppress others; they seldom attenuate their control by voluntarily sharing power and authority with subdominants. It, of course, is an axiom of social science that those who attempt to exert complete power and authority over others, ultimately are controlled by those whom they attempt to fully control. Under conditions of full oppression, then, dominants also lose their personal freedom in the process of maintaining such circumstances for others.

When subdominants cooperate with dominants who oppress them, their compliant and submissive behavior tends to permit the continuance of the harmful experience and eventually may erode the capacity of the individual to seek fulfillment of one's own self-interest [Leighton 1949: 263–264]. Liberation is a self-initiated activity. Oppressed subdominants gain their freedom only after they decide to cease cooperating in their own oppression.

Thus, resistance or conflict is the appropriate social role of subdominants who are not free to pursue their self-interests. Subdominants may passively resist dominants by withdrawing and refusing to participate in the oppressive activity. This is the veto power of subdominants that all possess and that none can take away.

Under more propitious circumstances, especially when subdominants have the sympathy and assistance of some dominants, they may aggressively resist oppression by engaging dominants in direct conflict. By gaining their own freedom through passive or aggressive resistance, the subdominants also free the dominant individuals to seek their own self-interests, since they no longer have to be concerned with holding others down. This is why the social role of subdominants is characterized as beneficial for all. Also this is why conflict is identified as a potentially beneficial method of social interaction.

The social role of dominants is to cooperate with those who resist oppression, especially oppression that is a function of the actions of the dominants. The refusal to cooperate with subdominants who are resisting oppression could result in alienation, separation, and rupture in the community. On her visit to the United States during the bicentennial year, Queen Elizabeth II tried to explain what went wrong during the American revolution. She said Great Britain lacked the statesmanship to know the right time and the manner of yielding what is impossible to keep [Willie, 1978:77]. This is another way of saying, the British Empire that was the dominant power, at that time, was not wise enough to cooperate with the subdominant colonies who were resisting oppression. When England failed to fulfill its cooperative role as the dominant, the American branch of the Empire collapsed; the community of interest was ruptured. The breakdown in collective effort and eventually the separation of the colonies overseas from the British community at home came to pass as the dominants responded in a conflictive way to the initiatives of the subdominants. The response of the dominant was out of character for the purpose of achieving a stability that would benefit all.

Thus, conflict is an appropriate action when initiated by subdominants for the purpose of achieving personal freedom and social change that overcome oppression; and cooperation is an appropriate action when initiated by dominants for the purpose of maintaining social stability and a sense of community that benefit all.

The social roles of dominants and subdominants are complementary; one without the other is incomplete. Subdominants can not do for dominants what only the dominants must do for themselves — that is, be cooperative and accommodating to others, especially in face of resistance to oppressive experiences. Neither can dominants do for subdominants what only the subdominants must do for themselves — resist oppressive experiences, especially those that require excessive conformity and that smother personal initiative.

When dominants and subdominants are urged to switch roles, this is an inappropriate recommendation. Dominants should not be urged to be conflictive, to stand firm and make demands as if they were the minority; and subdominants should not be urged to be cooperative, to submissively accept the status quo as if they were the majority. Such advice fails to recognize that social roles are status-specific, unique to the social locations occupied, and not interchangeable. As stated earlier, the roles of dominants and subdominants are complementary and of mutual benefit.

Symmetrical and Asymmetrical Responses

Our tendency to view humanity as if individuals were made in the image of things evokes the metaphor of the machine as a model of social organization. According to this image, *a* balances *b* in "the human equation" and gives rise to such aphorisms as this: you get out of life only what you put into it. According to the principle of asymmetry, one may get out of life more or less than one puts into it.

Herbert Warren Richardson has analyzed the idea of asymmetry as the appropriate strategem for overcoming oppression in social organization. He said there must be an asymmetry between the form in which evil manifests itself and the form of our opposition to it. Such an approach, said Richardson, breaks the series of counterbalancing interactions [Richardson 1968:201–202]. Martin Luther King, Jr., restated this principle in folk language when he said that one should overcome physical force with soul force.

King advocated the asymmetrical approach because of his observation that violent social action to overcome violence often was countereffective in that it tended to strengthen that which it opposed in the very act of opposing it [Richardson 1968: 202].

Using a figure of speech and in lyrical language, Martin Luther King, Jr., expressed the sociological principle of asymmetry this way: "Darkness cannot drive out darkness; only light can do that. Hate cannot drive out hate; only love can do that" (King 1964:45).

The principle of asymmetry explains why subdominant populations may achieve the mutual benefit of freedom and change the effect of oppressive conformity not by responding to initiatives of dominants in a cooperative way which is the symmetrical response, but by engaging the oppressor in conflict and resisting, which is an asymmetrical response. Likewise, dominants may achieve the effect of stability and the collective effort that is necessary not by resisting the conflict of subdominants with their overwhelming power to subdue conflict with conflict; that would be the symmetrical approach. The asymmetrical action required of dominants for the benefit of all is cooperation, especially with those who are attempting to reform society so that it may accommodate the interests of both the high and mighty and the meek and lowly.

In conclusion, I state in a positive way that both conflict and cooperation have intrinsic value that depend on the social location of individuals and groups that use them, and their interests and goals in varying circumstances. Thus, conflict, cooperation, and withdrawal are three valid adaptations in social organization when used in accordance with the requirements of the situation.

References

Coleman, James, et al. 1966. *Equality of Educational Opportunity.* Washington, DC: Government Printing Office.

Howe, Harold, II. 1976. "Educational Research — The Promise and the Problem." Invited address presented at the annual meeting of the American Educational Research Association, San Francisco.

Jencks, Christopher, et al. 1972. *Inequality.* New York: Basic Books.

King, Martin Luther, Jr. 1964. *Strength to Love.* New York: Pocket Book.

U. S. Labor Department. 1965. *The Negro Family, A Case for National Action.* Washington, DC: Government Printing Office.

Richardson, Herbert Warren. 1968. "Martin Luther King — Unsung Theologian." *Commonweal,* 3 May.

Walter, E. V. 1954. "Simmel's Sociology of Power: The Architecture of Politics." In Kurt H. Wolf (ed.), *Georg Simmel, 1858-1918.* Columbus, OH: Ohio State University Press.

Willie, Charles V. 1977. *Black/Brown/White Relations.* New Brunswick, NJ: Transaction.

_____. 1978. *The Sociology of Urban Education.* Lexington, MA: Lexington Books of D.C. Heath.

Chapter 20

Community Development and Social Change

The community-development literature in sociology is under-developed. One suspects that omissions in this field are due largely to the fact that many contemporary social scientists have been handmaidens of and apologists for the establishment.

In his book, *Maximum Feasible Misunderstanding,* Daniel Patrick Moynihan discusses the so-called war on poverty of the Johnson administration as if it were concocted out of the minds of university professors and as if the main issue were a hassle between the Columbia University and the Harvard University professors about the appropriate way to fight the war. According to Moynihan, the Columbia professors won and thus the war on poverty was lost [5]. Although subtitled "Community Action in the War on Poverty," Moynihan's book has not a single reference to the Rev. Martin Luther King, Jr. It is as if King's demonstrations were of no effect. This, of course, is not true. But the establishment-oriented writers of contemporary social science act as if public policy-making is not affected by the action from below, the community development movement.

Marshall Clinard has stated that "reports on urban developments... [throughout] the world have suggested that effective relations between politicians and citizens self-help projects are generally difficult" [3, pp. 275–76]. Maybe this is why the politicians and the professors, when they write about each other, ignore these unpleasant experiences that intrude into the social system and require a redefinition of operating procedures.

Clinard, for example, accepts the idea set forth by Carl Feiss that the basic weakness of slum programs is that slum people have not been storming city hall. Yet he does not see the storm after it begins. Clinard's book discounted protest by the average, American, black-slum dweller as doing anything for himself. From Clinard's perspective, self-help among black-

Reprinted from Charles V. Willie, *Black/Brown/White Relations*, New Brunswick, New Jersey: Transaction Books, 1977, pp. 151–158.

slum dwellers in America should be defined as "self-initiated changes in [their] norms and values ... relating to delinquency and crime, violence, illegitimacy, drug addiction, lack of family responsibility, and apathy toward educational opportunities." It is clear that Clinard prefers self-help programs that have impact on the disadvantaged and that are not designed to change the social system and the dominant people of power who generate and perpetuate disadvantaged circumstances [3, p. 311].

Demonstrations led by the Southern Christian Leadership Conference were part of a protest and self-help movement that was directed at the dominant people of power, rather than toward the disadvantaged as suggested by Clinard. Because there is little understanding of this kind of movement, Martin Luther King, Jr., also escaped the bibliography in Clinard's book about community development. It is interesting to note that the courageous community-development activities of King that were designed to change the established systems of oppression in America were recognized internationally but ignored in books about community development and community action authored by American social scientists at elite universities.

Another example of sociology written for members of the establishment is revealed in the limited perspective on community power that was published in a book on the sociology of education. The author, Wilbur B. Brookover, states that "every community has a power system. ... There are people or groups in every community who make important decisions and have the ability to enforce them. ... One cannot understand a community until he is able to locate the sources of power. ... Decisions affecting the entire community may be made under informal circumstances at a poker game, luncheon, or party. ... School people need to know the sources of power and need to have the support of the dominant power groups in the community if the school program is to function smoothly [2, pp. 378–379]. Yet, James Allen, Jr., former Commissioner of Education for the State of New York, credited the new initiatives taken by school boards throughout the country to achieve quality education for all to the pressure from below, from community subdominants. He testified that "Negroes in their demonstrations, in their peaceful demonstrations, have done more than any other segment of our society to push us to the point, where we have now gone" [1, p. 207].

If a balanced framework, gradual evolution, or a smoothly functioning program is the goal of individuals who say that they support social change, then protest activity by the disadvantaged is ignored as it has been by several social scientists studying community development and community action. The continuation of such omissions is bad social science that no longer should be tolerated if a comprehensive understanding of social organization and change is one of the goals of scientific research.

Actually subdominant people are a great source for social change in all institutions in any society. They make their contributions to change through the community-development movement, which is the primary way that change in behalf of the poor and oppressed is initiated.

Following the riots in Los Angeles, New York City, Detroit, and other great cities, George Gallup sent his pollsters into black and white communities to discover what could be done to prevent civil disorders in central city ghettos. White dominant people of power listed better law enforcement as the number one priority, while black subdominant people of power said the provision of more and better jobs was the best way to prevent riots. Despite the fact that most riots occur in black ghettos, the nation acted upon the white priority, ignored the voices of the disadvantaged or subdominant people, and began teaching the National Guard and the Army better techniques of riot control. Not only did the nation act upon the white priority, it summarily rejected the number one black priority, which was jobs.

George Gallup published his findings in August of 1967. By January of 1968, the president had made up his mind to ask the Office of Economic Opportunity to reserve only $35 million to pay for emergency operations for the approaching summer. Congress passed $75 million to finance summer programs in 1967. The *New York Times* called this reduction in funds for antipoverty programs a "squeeze on the poor." Indeed it was a squeeze; for in July of 1968, the Associated Press reported that "summer jobs for slum youngsters ... [in New York City] were cut from 43,000 [the previous year] to 25,000 for lack of funds to finance them."

Consider this sequence of actions and how the dominant people of power continue to ignore the priorities of subdominants. One year after the riots and one year after the people who engaged in the riots said that more and better jobs were ways of preventing further riots, the dominant people of power ignored or rejected their analysis. Jobs were decreased and police power was increased. What, then, was there for poor and oppressed people to do? They protested. The protest was a self-help move as subsequent actions proved.

Wednesday, 10 July 1968, one thousand five hundred youth demonstrated at city hall in New York City. They were demanding more summer jobs. The mayor was annoyed by the behavior of the demonstrators. He said it was disgraceful. The day following the demonstration, however, the

Associated Press reported that the mayor dug into the city's empty purse and came up with enough money to finance at least 10,000 more jobs for youngsters in poor families.

The city and federal governments did not act earlier upon the request of black and poor people for more and better jobs until a protest community-action movement was launched. Their request was published and made known in the Gallup poll following the riots. But the city and federal governments ignored or rejected their request. By not acting upon the priority of poor and black people, the city and federal governments were inviting demonstrations and protests that came like thunder and lightning at city hall during the following summer. The poor and the oppressed had to force their priorities upon the community that ignored the findings of the Gallup poll.

One conclusion that should be readily apparent from this case is that all people have power, subdominants as well as dominants; however, only dominants have the power to implement community programs that require the resources that they may control. But subdominants as well as dominants have veto power. Elsewhere in an analysis of community development and the public schools, I pointed out that the veto power of subdominants is not invoked often and that many, therefore, fail to realize that it exists. "Thus, school superintendents and other public officials are surprised when their plans run aground due to veto actions of subdominants." I further pointed out that "because it is unanticipated and comes from an unexpected source, the veto power of subdominants is considered to be disruptive..." [7, p. 224].

Community development is a process of getting people in the community to take action in their own behalf, based on goals of their own choosing. Political action is one important end result of community development. Each person benefits as a result of collective effort. He or she benefits in personal and concrete ways, such as obtaining more food, higher wages, better housing, or improved public services. The purpose of community development is to take action that will change the circumstances of individuals. Community development is organizing people into powerful groups for the purpose of getting the political machine to do that which it will not do unless pressured into acting. Community development is helping people to organize and make decisions about their own destiny. Community development is concerned with institutional change. In community development, the people choose their own representatives to negotiate major issues with the society at large. They are not selected by the establishment.

The dominant people of power have difficulty dealing with community development and the demands of subdominants. The dominant people are reluctant to share their power. They will not deal with subdominants on the terms of subdominants. Dominants want to act on their own list of priorities that may not be the priorities of the subdominant people. As long as dominant people of power continue to deal on their own terms with the subdominants—be they young people, poor people, or black and brown people—fuel will continue to be added to the protest movement. Community conflict will escalate.

Several social scientists—for example, Jay Schulman and Ward H. Goodenough—have concluded that conflict is inevitable in community development. Goodenough [in a personal communication] describes one goal of community development as a "search for self-respect." He goes on to say that "[community-] development efforts that acknowledge the legitimacy of this goal are more likely to be distressing to many influential persons in the dominant sector." In community development, Schulman has stated [in a personal communication] that "issues must be drawn that are specific ... [and that have] direct and immediate payoff to the poor." He further stated that "there must be a commitment to the use of conflict tactics and an eagerness to engage in direct confrontation with authority holders."

The community-development movement recognizes the existence of incompatible desires among the people in a pluralistic society. Conflict then is a legitimate process by which a community attempts to accommodate the many different desires of its members. The major issue is how to deal with the inevitable conflict in community development in a controlled non-violent way that enhances everyone—the dominants and the subdominants.

For a few years during the early seventies, I served as a member of the Regional Health Advisory Committee for Region II of the Department of Health, Education, and Welfare. We explored ways of helping regional, comprehensive health-planning agencies become more effective. I was chairman of a subcommittee that studied the representation of the poor and minority groups in health-planning agencies. We drafted a position paper that the entire committee endorsed and issued. The paper was entitled, "Why and How to Involve People of Disadvantaged Circumstances in Governing Boards of Comprehensive Health Planning Agencies," and it made the following points:

1.   That a free society remains free only when there is continuous participation of the governed in the instruments and institutions of government, including official and voluntary agencies;

2.   That a community should be involved in selecting its own representatives and that representatives should have sufficient knowledge of,
loyalty to, and links with a locality to adequately make known the needs, interests, and way of life of a constituency;

3.   That it is beneficial for a policymaking board to have a fine mix-
ture of members with local loyalties and members who represent special-
interest groups as well as unaffiliated members at large;

4.   That such a decision-making group that is truly representative
may experience tension, but that such tension usually is creative with
deliberations among representatives of different special-interest groups
serving as a self-correcting device for the organization;

5.   That representatives of disadvantaged populations ought to be
present in numbers sufficient to have an impact upon deliberations beyond
that of token participation and that such representation should be not less
than one-fifth of all board positions as the "critical mass" necessary for a
significant effect upon decision making;

6.   And finally, that policies and plans that promote the public interest are likely to be those policies and plans that are forged on the anvil of
controversy by competing interest groups and that it is more appropriate to
encounter controversy around the conference table where it can be dealt
with in a controlled way, where bargaining, trade-offs, and compromises
can be worked out.

In general, we tried to say that disadvantaged people who are members
of a board must be looked upon as partners who have an equal say about
what is and what ought to be, just as any other board member. We, of
course, shall not bring about this state of affairs until our governing boards
and bodies of all of our community organizations and agencies are
heterogeneous, consisting of representatives of the various economic, age,
ethnic, and racial populations in the community — we shall not set out to
deliberately bring about this kind of participation, unless we genuinely
believe in being orderly in a lawful way where laws and regulations that protect and punish derive from all the people and apply equally to all of the
people. We shall not create truly democratic and diversified decision-
making structures until older people, affluent people, and white people can
acknowledge that they do not always know what is best for the young, the
poor, and the blacks.

In a seminar on planning and evaluation at the Laboratory of Community Psychiatry of the Harvard Medical School a specialist in community
psychiatry said that the most rapid way to bring about change in an organi-

zation is to give it new clients. In responding to the demands of a different clientele, a system necessarily must change or cease to exist. The psychiatrist further suggested that an organization could contribute to orderly change by deliberately introducing within itself dissident interests to which the total system must respond.

The idea of deliberately bringing dissident elements into a system as a way of contributing to planned social change (as opposed to revolutionary action) is not new. Vilfredo Paredo, the Italian sociologist born in 1848, had something to say about this. Paredo believed that "leaders maintain themselves in power by ... bringing into the governing class ... individuals who might prove dangerous to the governing group. If such recruiting does not take place, in the absence of a free use of force, sooner or later there will be an uprising. ..." [Crawford 1948, p. 567].

All of this is to say that if black and brown people, poor people, and young people were invited to help make the rules of the game, maybe they would be more inclined to abide by these rules. I would warn, however, that their participation will tend to change the rules and the way in which the rules are enforced. Also, new participants will tend to evolve new games. This is as it should be in a democracy. As it is, the rules that currently govern our communities and their institutions are made by decision-making structures whose members are predominantly white, affluent, and adult. These are today's dominant people of power. Bertrand Russell has called the "love of power one of the strongest of human motives" [1962, p. 101]. A cardinal principle about power is this: People who have it are reluctant to share it. The dominant people of power must learn how to share their power with subdominants. Otherwise, there is no alternative but to force the social change required by revolutionary action that could evolve if subdominants were involved in the decision-making structures.

References

1. Allen, James E. 1967. "Testimony of Dr. James E. Allen, Jr., Commission of Education, State of New York." *Hearing before the United States Commission on Civil Rights in Rochester, New York, 16–17 September 1966.* Washington, DC: Government Printing Office.

2. Brookover, Wilber B. 1955. *A Sociology of Education.* New York: American Book.

3. Clinard, Marshall. 1966. *Slums and Community Development.* New York: Free Press.

4. Crawford, Rex. 1948. "Representative Italian Contributions to Sociology: Paredo, Louis, Vaccaro, Gino, and Sighele." In Harry Elmer Barnes, (ed.), *Introduction to the History of Sociology.* Chicago: University of Chicago Press.

    5.   Moynihan, Daniel Patrick. 1969. *Maximum Feasible Misunderstanding*. New York: The Free Press.
    6.   Russell, Bertrand. 1962. *Power*. New York: Barnes and Noble.
    7.   Willie, Charles V. 1968. "New Perspectives in School-Community Relations." *Journal of Negro Education* 37 (Summer).

Chapter 21

Theoretical Implications: Stability and Change

As time and space are connected in nature, so are social process and social structure in humanity. Both must be considered in understanding human adaptations. They are a manifestation of the principle of complementarity.

The concept of homeostasis was introduced by the Harvard physiologist Walter B. Cannon [1939]. It refers to the tendency for systems to maintain a steady state, constantly correcting for imbalance and disequilibrium. Several social scientists have used this concept as a major frame of reference for organizing and analyzing social data. But as noted earlier, the concept of homeostasis in social organization hardly ever fits reality [DuBois 1972: 249]. Living systems also are characterized by homeokinesis [DuBois 1972: 249]. That is, they must maintain a continuous rate of change or else decay. Thus, in all living systems there are tendencies toward both stability and change. The absence of homeostasis or of homeokinesis is a sign of pathology. Theoretically, stability and change coexist.

There is a tendency for some social scientists to denigrate stability or the status quo and to idolize change or reform; others denigrate change and idolize stability. Actually, aimless change is potentially as harmful to persons as order that is reactionary. Innovative approaches that help some individuals should be stabilized and retained in institutions for the purpose of helping all the people. Stable institutions are concerned not with perpetuating themselves but with discovering new and improved ways of serving humanity, since their ultimate reason for being is to sustain and support all individuals. Thus, stability and change are related; both are needed in human society. As stated by Myron Bloy, Jr., every society, sooner or later, faces the conflict between its traditional order and the forces within it pressing for fundamental change. "Ideally," said Bloy, "the conflict issues in a new social synthesis combining elements from both past and present" [Bloy 1965:15]. A social synthesis is the outcome of interaction between social structure and social process.

217

Each synthesis eventually stabilizes into a new social structure. A tendency of all social structures is to exclude experiences that interfere with fulfillment of the purpose for which they were organized. That which is excluded tries to be included; in this attempt, existing social structures and the ways they function are challenged by the excluded. Human institutions that resist such challenges contribute to social stability; human institutions that embrace such challenges contribute to social change. Under varying circumstances, it is beneficial to humanity for the institutions of a particular society to resist change and to embrace change. How the institution functions determines which is more advantageous. Human institutions that help people should be stabilized and those that harm people should be changed. Any institution that harms any human being in a particular society is a candidate for social change and eventually will be challenged by those whose interest it does not fulfill.

In terms of race, ethnicity, and socioeconomic status, the self-interest of the group that dominates the society is different from that of the group that is subdominant. All of this is to say that self-interest — an attribute quite different from selfishness — is the basic motive for human action. Human social organizations, including their stable and changing norms, cannot be understood apart from the self-interests of the individuals and groups within a society. Social scientists who urge some groups to adopt the norms of others without determining whether the self-interests of the varying groups differ perform a professional disservice to the groups, and the individuals within them, and to the total society they advise.

There is a tendency, for example, to advise the outgroup to act like the ingroup and the subdominant group to act like the dominant group. The black racial group in the United States that is subdominant in terms of numbers and power often is urged to pattern its resistance to being excluded from the opportunity system in this country after the resistance efforts of the Jewish ethnic groups. The advice fails to consider that most Jewish people in the United States are part of the dominating white race. The self-interests of dominant and subdominant groups seldom are the same.

The absence of similarity in some of the self-interests of dominant and subdominant groups or ingroups and outgroups is not cause for alarm. As mentioned earlier, a polymorphic population is better capable of dealing effectively with an environment than one that is homogeneous. Also, a diversified population with various groups that have different self-interests is a source of self-correction for pathology within a society. Social pathology exists when the institutions of a society harm rather than help the people. The purposes of social institutions are clarified and the effectiveness of their function enhanced in the process of challenge and response by the various groups within a society as they struggle to obtain fulfillment of their special needs.

The goal in human society is to mold expressions of the self-interests of all social groups—those of the various racial, ethnic, and socioeconomic populations—into socially creative rather than socially destructive patterns [Gilkey 1966:140]. This can be done if the self-interests of dominants as well as subdominants, and members of the ingroup as well as members of the outgroup, are recognized as valid. When this is done, social structures and social processes are created that facilitate expressions of minority and sub-dominant self-interests.

In the light of this analysis, one is better able to understand why Merton states that not infrequently the nonconforming minority represents the ultimate values of a society more effectively than the conforming majority [Merton 1968:421]. Also based on this analysis, one can better understand why the Moynihan thesis that the disadvantaged minority should adopt the principles of the advantaged majority is contraindicated [U.S. Labor Department 1965:29]. Such would eliminate the dissent of the minority that tends to be society's way of correcting itself.

Georg Simmel recognized conflict and collision between the individual and social claims [Walter 1959:149]. Also there is conflict between the claims of different social groups, especially dominant groups and subdominant groups. Simmel believed that if the individual lived only according to the norms of the total society without observing other standards, one would be an ethical abnormality [Walter 1959:146]. Human society that is ethical and fair accommodates the claims of dominants and of subdominants, and the norms of ingroups as well as those of outgroups. When these contrasting norms are arranged into a harmonic whole (as if in a salad bowl rather than a melting pot), Simmel said they cease to be obstacles to humanity; they strengthen society and lead to new creations [Walter 1959:143].

With reference to race and ethnicity, the pathological tendency has been for the ingroup to transform its own virtues into outgroup vices. As observed by Merton, "the moral virtues remain virtues only so long as they are jealously confined to the proper in-group." In other words, "the right activity by the wrong people becomes a thing of contempt, not of honor" [Merton 1949:187]. Not only is the different normative action of the outgroup denied as a valid contribution to social organization, the virtuous activity of the outgroup that conforms to the standards of the ingroup is transformed as vice. This places the outgroup in a double bind, damned if it behaves like the ingroup and damned if it does not [Merton 1949:184]. Appropriately, a society that generates such circumstances for its various racial and ethnic minority groups should be characterized as ethically abnormal or in a condition of social pathology.

Failure to recognize the validity of the contrasting norms of different racial and ethnic groups may destabilize not only the society but a'so the personalities of its human beings. Under these conditions, some members of the subdominant group develop feelings of self-hate and racial inferiority [Clark and Clark 1947:169–178], and some members of the dominant group develop feelings of self-superiority and racial supremacy, to justify the existing harmful social arrangements [Kardiner and Ovesey 1962:379; Ordway 1973:123–145].

Another condition of social pathology is the arrangement wherein all members of the dominant group and the ingroup are always one and the same. When this happens, the dominant ingroup's existence is threatened by any change and it tends to become increasingly exclusive as a way of retaining prestige and power [Merton 1949:187].

In general, dominant groups tend to favor stability and subdominant groups tend to favor change; ingroups attempt to maintain the status quo and outgroups seek to reform the social system. When an ingroup consists of individuals who identify with both dominant and subdominant sectors of the community power structure, its members attempt to stabilize and to change society. Such a condition is healthy and beneficial for all because each group's actions are tempered by multiple cross-cutting goals. Single-purpose groups that are concerned only with stability or with change are less accommodating to variations in the human condition and pluralistic human needs.

As pointed out earlier, the welfare of each individual within a society is the ultimate test of that society's effectiveness. However, a society seldom rearranges its institutions to accommodate the special needs of oppressed individuals until such individuals exercise their unique authority and ultimate power personally to cease cooperating in their own oppression. This power is available to all human beings in all societies and cannot be taken away by any other authority, although a person may decide not to use it out of fear of the consequences of such use.

Seldom do societies change because an individual has exercised his or her unique personal authority and ultimate power of veto action. Indeed, individual power tends to have a social impact only when others are influenced to become allies. Since the input of subdominants is of value in social organization for self-corrective and other reasons, at issue is the kind of social structure and social process that facilitates the exercise of power and authority by subdominants without denying power and authority to dominants. Robert Dahl writes about the merits of pluralistic distribution of power in human society because it rarely leaves any group powerless [Dahl 1967:189–190].

A pluralistic system consists of a series of decentralized decision-making structures. In such an arrangement different sets of leaders exist, some with different objectives from others. Social systems with decentralized governance structures tend to resolve conflicts more by negotiation and compromise than by unilateral decision. Variety and heterogeneity are accommodated better under these conditions. Moreover, if one set of leaders is unsympathetic to the needs of a minority, the members of such a group may turn to another set of leaders when the system is decentralized. In summary, decentralized governance structures reduce considerably the severity of conflict that a whole system with only a centralized governance structure would experience and keep many questions from becoming strictly either/or kinds of conflict in which the dominant majority group always wins and the subdominant minority group always loses [Dahl 1969:180–190]. Finally, according to Dahl, decentralized governance structures "help to provide a secure base to which opposition may retire when it has suffered defeat elsewhere, in order to sally forth and challenge their opponents [in the future]" [Dahl 1967:188]. Clearly, decentralized decision-making structures facilitate the participation of subdominants; centralization enhances the possibility that the goals of the dominating majority will prevail.

If change that is essential to the viability of social systems is desired, then the participation of subdominants should be facilitated. They are inclined toward change so that their self-interests are accommodated in an effectively functioning system. If stability that is essential to the viability of a social system is desired, then control by dominants should be facilitated. They are inclined toward stability as a way of guaranteeing the fulfillment of their self-interests.

The double-victory hypothesis of social organization asserts that the self-interests of dominants and of subdominants can be mutually accommodated. A solution that is mutually beneficial, as required by the double-victory hypothesis, is attainable if the goal is to maintain an effective system, but not necessarily the most efficient system. Local administrative units may be effective instruments of democracy, but one cannot speak with confidence about their efficiency [Dahl 1967:180].

A double-victory that contributes to stability and change in society is possible in a hierarchical but decentralized governance system with both centralized and decentralized decision-making structures.

The centralized structure should be loving (that is, it should make a proper estimation of the needs of varying classes of individuals), and guarantee equal opportunity so that none (dominant or subdominant) is denied access to the system and its resources in an arbitrary, capricious, or unethical way; it should not attempt to hold on to exclusive prerogatives in the face of others' fair claim [Willie 1978:77]. Centralized decision-making structures are concerned with principle and with the public good.

Decentralized decision-making structures are concerned with practice and individual benefits. These decentralized structures are person-centered and concerned with matters of equity, including the just and fair use of available resources among the various populations within a society.

Obviously, a human society that is both loving and just is a more viable social system; a human society concerned about principle and practice is a better system in which to live; a human society that guarantees equality of access to its institutions and equity in the use of resources promotes both stability and change. In summary, a combination governance structure that is both centralized and decentralized fosters stability without resisting the fair claims of any of the people, and "brings about reform more through adjustment and a gradual accumulation of incremental change than through sweeping programs of comprehensive and coordinated reconstruction" [Dahl 1967:190].

Moreover, in a loving and just system stability is maintained and change is fostered not by force but by negotiation [Dahl 1967:190] and by appealing to a common system of beliefs. Indeed, "[one should never] expect people to adopt behavior or carry out programs for which they have no underlying system of beliefs" [Leighton 1946:295]. Alexander Leighton states that a system of beliefs enables people "to express themselves, ... evolve ideas and feelings so they can live and work together, care for their families, protect themselves, [and] gain what they need" [Leighton 1946:294].

The coexistence of decentralized and centralized structures in a governance system guarantees that the self-interests of both subdominants and dominants are honored and accommodated in loving and just ways wherein principle and practice are united in a way that helps society and does not harm individuals. A system of hierarchical and diversified decision-making structures is possible only in a society that honestly attempts to implement the double-victory hypothesis, that believes the welfare of each individual is the ultimate criterion of institutional worthiness, and that strives to be loving, just, and effective, rather than efficient.

While, theoretically, decentralized decision-making structures increase opportunities for the participation of subdominant populations, there is not a linear association between the amount of decentralization and the extent of their participation. As stated by Charles DeCarlo in an article entitled "Perspectives on Technology," human society is more appropriately described as consisting of simultaneous rather than linear events [quoted in Bloy 1965:20]. Decentralized governance structures are beneficial to all only if they are simultaneously available and accessible to all so that a compromise may be negotiated that accommodates the self-interests of all. When local or decentralized structures are presided over by despotic leadership, or when there is not equal access to these structures, or when they are not representative of the varying racial, ethnic, and socioeconomic status groups in the community that are associated with ingroup and outgroup as well as dominant group and subdominant group interests, they may be less effective than centralized structures in protecting the rights, privileges, and prerogatives of subdominants.

During the middle part of the twentieth century, for example, the Supreme Court of the United States assigned the responsibility to decentralized structures of designing plans that implemented its order requiring unitary public school systems equally available to minority students and majority students. Ralph McGill believed it was a wise act for the Supreme Court to assign this responsibility to local federal judges because of their familiarity with local problems [McGill 1964:246]. What McGill did not consider when he approved of this policy is that the minorities whom school desegregation was supposed to benefit had been excluded from full participation in local educational and political structures to which local federal judges would turn for assistance in designing desegregation plans. Thus, most school desegregation plans were developed by political office-holders and lawyers who were members of the white ingroup and the dominant power group. Consequently, many of the plans so devised had the objective of preventing desegregation, according to McGill. He said that these local participants took the Supreme Court decision that delineated the rights of children and "dishonestly distorted it" [McGill 1964:246–249]. His judgment is that history will draw a harsh indictment of the local leaders who did this.

Decisions may be devolved upon decentralized decision-making structures to the benefit of all, and especially subdominants, only if such structures are, simultaneously, diversified. When the practice of diversification is not implemented along with the principle of decentralization, the outcome usually is harmful. In his study of Reconstruction, W. E. B. DuBois discovered this information that apparently was not taken into consideration by the U. S. Supreme Court. He found that schools for blacks began in many southern states at the initiative of the federal Freedmen's Bureau

[DuBois 1969:654], that "when the Confederates returned to domination, the public schools ... were greatly curtailed" [DuBois 1969:644], and that local control meant "racial particularism," "reaction," and "prejudice." In general, he found that "wherever there was retrogression, particularly in Negro schools, it can be traced to the increased power of the [local] district administrators." He concluded that this accounted for the "difficulties" and "failures" in most of the southern states [DuBois 1969:664–665]. Thus, familiarity with local situations and circumstances may be used to harm rather than help subdominants when these subdominants are not actively involved as negotiators in local decision-making structures. In the light of these findings, one may conclude with Dahl that "members of a minority who feel oppressed in their localities would ordinarily search for allies in the national political arena" [Dahl 1967:182]. Decentralization enhances subdominant participation only under the condition of simultaneous diversification.

In addition to the contribution that decentralization and diversification make both to stability and change, cross-cutting cleavages involving nominal and graduated population parameters also promote stability and change that are constructive. Peter Blau describes the two parameters: "a nominal parameter divides the population into sub-groups with distinct boundaries without an inherent rank order. A graduated parameter differentiates people in terms of a status rank order which is in principle continuous, so that the parameter does not draw boundaries between strata" [Blau 1977:31]. Race and ethnicity are examples of nominal parameters; socioeconomic status is an example of a graduated parameter. Blau states that there is an association between nominal and graduated parameters in human society. He believes that "the degree to which parameters intersect, or alternatively consolidate differences in social positions through their strong correlations, reflects the most important structural conditions in a society which have a crucial consequence for conflict and for social integration" [Blau 1977:32]. Blau concludes that "differentiation and integration are complementary concepts" and that they can be understood, in part, by analyzing "the degree to which differentiation occurs within or among society's substructures, [and] how these structural conditions affect the rates of association among groups and strata" [Blau 1977:32–34].

It is true that cleavages separating population parameters tend to generate conflict. However, conflict can be creative when it results from cross-cutting cleavages which tend to pull the society together; cleavages that do not cut across nominal and graduated population parameters tend to tear the society apart. Dahl described cross-cutting cleavages as those that do not overlap and reinforce each other. "If all the cleavages occur along the same line ... then the severity of conflict is likely to increase" [Axelrod 1970:144–164], to the point of becoming destructive. Thus, stability or change that results from the efforts of groups that have overlapping and reinforcing cleavages and not cross-cutting ones is likely to be helpful to some but harmful to others. But stability or change fostered by, for example, racial and ethnic groups whose members are affiliated with both dominant and subdominant populations is better capable of achieving a negotiated solution that is mutually beneficial to all.

When the cleavages are cross-cutting, racial and ethnic group members are found among dominants and subdominants in the community power structure. This is a healthy social situation. When all or most of the members of one racial or ethnic group are dominants and all or most of the members of another racial or ethnic group are subdominants, the social situation is unhealthy. William Wilson has called attention to the fact that a class structure within the black community has definitely taken shape. He attributes the integrationist ideology of black civil rights leaders to changes in the black occupational structure; and he warned of the possibility of a schism within the black community due to the economic differentiation of its members [Wilson 1978:124, 134]. Others, such as William Robert Miller, have arrived at an opposite conclusion. While Miller acknowledges economic differentiation within the black population, he states that the unity which Martin Luther King, Jr., achieved between the different social classes by making middle-class blacks the backbone of a crusade for human dignity "was perhaps his most remarkable unsung achievement" [Miller 1968:308].

The issue would appear to be not the presence of differentiation within a nominal parameter but how the different status groups function in human society. John Rawls states that those who have been favored may gain from their good fortune only on terms that improve the situation of others. This theory is based on the premise that the distribution of talents is a common asset in a society [Rawls 1971:101]. W. Arthur Lewis, the economist, also states that differentiation need not result in schism and disunity if there is full integration in which the citizens in one area have a right to participate equally in economic activity in any part of one's society. Moreover, he said that people will consent to differentiation if some of the wealth produced in the richer areas is used to improve facilities in the poor areas [Lewis 1966:69]. The implication of these statements is that dominants and subdominants complement each other, that in a healthy society dominants function for the benefit of subdominants even as subdominants help and assist dominants. The absence of mutual fulfillment of the different sectors of a graduated parameter, and the absence of cross-cutting cleavages between graduated parameters and nominal parameters, usually lead to catastrophic change or repressive stability within a society. Such was the experience in the United States before and during the Civil War.

Both stability and change can be either constructive or destructive. They are fostered by conflict, conciliation, and cooperation. These are the events that link social structures and social processes. They make a creative contribution to stability or change when there are cross-cutting cleavages between nominal and graduated parameters of the population so that all racial or ethnic groups have members who are both dominant and subdominant, and so that no individuals or groups are dominant in all situations or subdominant in all situations. The probability that a society will exhibit these characteristics is increased under the social conditions of (a) equality of access where each individual or group has the opportunity to fulfill self-interest or group-interest, (b) diversification in the participation of governance, (c) decentralization in decision-making, and (d) equity in the use of common resources. Clarification of the latter phrase is needed so that it is not misunderstood as a statement of ideology. By focusing on the use of common resources (rather than their distribution) one accepts the fact that they may be differentially distributed within the population because of variations in talents and other circumstances of the people. These differences, however, are not necessarily harmful; in fact, they are beneficial if used to help all. The social structures and social processes described and the constructive change or stability that they may engender are possible in a society where the welfare of each individual is the ultimate goal, and where effectiveness in the achievement of this goal rather than efficiency in the operation of the social system is the ultimate measure of success or the public good. Such a society is both loving and just.

References

Axelrod, Robert. 1970. *Conflict of Interest.* Chicago: Markham.

Blau, Peter M. 1977. "A Macrosocial Theory of Social Structure." *American Journal of Sociology* 83 (July).

Bloy, Myron B., Jr. 1965. *The Crisis of Cultural Change.* New York: Seabury Press.

Cannon, Walter B. 1939. *The Wisdom of the Body.* New York: Norton.

Clark K. B., and M. P. Clark. 1947. "Racial Identification and Preference in Negro Children." In Theodore M. Newcomb and Eugene L. Hartley (eds.), *Readings in Social Psychology.* New York: Holt, pp. 169–178.

Dahl, Robert A. 1967. *Pluralistic Democracy in the United States.* Chicago: Rand McNally.

DuBois, W. E. B. 1969. *Black Reconstruction in America.* New York: Atheneum. First published in 1935.

DuBos, René. 1972. *A God Within.* New York: Scribner's.

Gilkey, Langdon. 1966. *Shantung Compound.* New York: Harper & Row.

Kardiner, Abram, and Lionel Ovesey. 1962. *The Mark of Oppression.* Cleveland: Meridian Books.

Leighton, Alexander H. 1946. *The Governing of Men.* Princeton: Princeton University Press.

Lewis, W. Arthur. 1966. *Development Planning.* London: Allen and Unwin.

McGill, Ralph. 1964. *The South and the Southerner.* Boston: Little, Brown.   .

Merton, Robert K. 1949 and 1968 editions. *Social Theory and Social Structure.* New York: Free Press.

Miller, William Robert. 1968. *Martin Luther King, Jr.* New York: Avon.

Ordway, John A. 1973. "Some Emotional Consequences of Racism for Whites." In C. V. Willie, B. M. Kramer, and B. S. Brown (eds.), *Racism and Mental Health.* Pittsburgh: University of Pittsburgh Press.

Rawls, John. 1971. *A Theory of Justice.* Cambridge, MA: Harvard University Press.

U. S. Labor Department. 1965. *The Negro Family, A Case for National Action.* Washington, DC: Government Printing Office.

Walter, E. V. 1959. "Simmel's Sociology of Power: The Architecture of Politics." In Kurt H. Wolf (ed.), *Georg Simmel, 1858–1918.* Columbus, OH: Ohio State University Press.

Willie, Charles V. 1978. *The Sociology of Education.* Lexington, MA: Lexington Books of D. C. Heath.

Wilson, William Julius. 1978. *The Declining Significance of Race.* Chicago: University of Chicago Press.

Part IV

Macrosocial Studies

Social Movements and Leadership: Conflict, Conciliation, and Cooperation

Chapter 22

New Learnings for Sociology
from the Civil Rights Movement

The Civil Rights movement is now into its fourth stage, the implementation period that began in 1969 the year after Martin Luther King, Jr., died. Thus far the movement has spanned more than 50 years, from the 1930s through the present. The movement has been reasonably successful, although there is still much more to be achieved, as this analysis will reveal. Insufficient time has passed to fully assess its effectiveness. But indications are beginning to emerge.

Contrary to popular opinion, one conclusion that can be stated categorically on the basis of the analysis that will follow is that school desegregation — one of the goals of the Civil Rights movement — has significantly reduced disparity between majority and minority races in level of educational attainment.

The Civil Rights movement has passed through four stages and has achieved four great national victories. Stage I was the period of litigation from 1930 to 1954. Stage II was the period of demonstration from 1955 to 1964. Stage III was the period of legislation from 1964 to 1968. Stage IV is the period of implementation from 1969 to the present.

The four great victories of the Civil Rights movement occurred during the litigation and legislation stages. These victories were: (1) The Supreme Court decisions of *Brown* v. *Board of Education,* which legally sanctioned equal access to public education on a nonsegregative basis in 1954 and 1955; (2) the Civil Rights Act of 1964, which prohibited employment discrimination and authorized the federal government to terminate funds to school districts guilty of discrimination; (3) the Voting Rights Act of 1965, which suspended qualifying methods for voting that disfranchised racial minorities, and which required the federal government to monitor changes

Paper presented at the annual meeting of the American Sociological Association thematic session of Social Movements as Innovations: The Civil Rights Movement, Tuesday, August 25, 1981, Toronto, Canada.

in voting laws or procedures where discriminatory devices had been used in the past; and (4) the Fair Housing Act of 1968, which prohibited intentional discriminatory practices and practices that have a discriminatory effect in the sale and rental of housing [Larson and McDonald 1980].

There is insufficient space to discuss each of these victories, their varying effectiveness in implementation, and what we have learned from this that is of benefit to the field of sociology and to society. I shall confine this discussion, then, to an analysis of the stages of the Civil Rights movement, the impact of this movement's educational outcomes upon minority and majority populations, and an assessment of new learning we have derived for sociology from examination of this movement.

Discussed first is why the Civil Rights effort of this century is classified as a social movement.

Definition of Social Movement

I prefer Hans Toch's more general definition of social movement: "an effort by a large number of people to solve collectively a problem that they feel they have in common" [Toch 1965:5]. The important phrases in this definition are "large number of people," "solve collectively," and "a problem in common." These phrases clearly suggest that social movements are not the work of mindless mobs; they have purpose.

In a social movement, purpose and action emerge from the people, a large number of people. It, therefore, is not subject to control by a single individual, by any individual acting on his or her own authority or the authority of an organization or agency. A single individual may propose changes in what is identified as a common problem, in collective methods of solving that problem, and in the purpose or goal to be achieved. In a social movement, anyone has the authority to propose; but only the people as a collectivity have the power to dispose of such suggestions.

If one embraces this definition of social movement, efforts to secure constitutional rights in recent decades qualify. The Civil Rights effort has had changing leadership. It has been beyond the control of any individual, organization, or segment of the population. Current assertions that the Civil Rights movement was fostered by blacks with middle-class aspirations to feather their nests represent misunderstanding of the nature of social movements. The movements emerge from the people, a large number of people, and are sustained by them. Toch states that "social movements are usually [catalogued] under the general heading of collective behavior" [Toch 1965:5].

Misunderstanding of the Civil Rights movement frequently is a function of a narrow focus on the method of collective action that ignores the purpose. Method and purpose go hand in hand in social organization and always ought to be kept jointly in focus in social analysis.

Thus social movements — and particularly the Civil Rights movement — are not without goals. Neither was the Civil Rights movement designed by individuals or characterized by mob rule. It was a collective effort initiated by the people, and it remained that way despite efforts of the news media to personify the social movement and to individualize its collective leadership.

An analysis of the Civil Rights effort during the past fifty years provides sociology with a better understanding of the various stages of social movements, the interrelationships connecting these stages, and the implication of these stages for the theory of social structure and social process.

Stages of the Civil Rights Movement

Stage I: Litigation. According to law professor Norman Vierira, author of *Civil Rights in a Nutshell,* 1938 was the date when the legal attack on the separate-but-equal doctrine began [Vierira 1978: 64]. Specifically, he referred to the case of *Missouri ex rel Gains* v. *Canada,* 305 U.S. 337 (1938). In that decision, the U.S. Supreme Court invalidated a plan under which Missouri provided law school for whites only and financed the legal education of black citizens at out-of-state institutions.

> That decision [was] followed in 1950 by Sweatt v. Painter, 339 U.S. 629 (1950), and McLaurin v. Okla., 339 U.S. 637 (1950). Sweatt held that even an in-state "Negro law school" was constitutionally insufficient if it failed to provide an education equal in both tangible and intangible respects to that offered to whites. ... The obvious next step would be a frontal assault on the separate-but-equal doctrine in primary and secondary education [Vierira 1978: 64–65].

William Hastie dated the legal victory for the current Civil Rights movements two years earlier in 1936. He referred to the case of *Pearson* v. *Murray* in Maryland, 169 Md. 478, 182 Atl. 592 (1936). The National Association for the Advancement of Colored People (NAACP) lawyers believed that "any favorable decision in a state court would win speedier and less grudging local acceptance than a similar mandate issued by a federal court." In *Pearson,* the state courts gave "a clear and forthright opinion" that the "out-of-state scholarships [for black law-school students was] constitutionally inadequate as a substitute for the Maryland legal education provided for white citizens of that state" [Hastie 1973: 26].

Regarding the legal strategy, the NAACP lawyers believed that the U.S. Supreme Court was not ready in the early 1930s to repudiate the doctrine of separate but equal. Thus widespread litigation was undertaken to eliminate the disparities and inequality in financial provision for education of minority children in localities where black teachers, students, and parents were willing to "risk economic reprisals and even violence [for] bringing suit against state and local officers and institutions of education" [Hastie 1973: 25]. Note that the NAACP made its legal staff available but the local people had to make their own decision whether they were willing and able to endure a court case. The consequences for some were severe.

During argument for a case that challenged the unequal facilities for the races for interstate passengers on buses in 1946 (*Morgan* v. *Virginia,* 388 U.S. 373 [1946]), a Supreme Court justice "from the bench invited counsel to argue the constitutionality of the separate but equal doctrine. ... The invitation was declined." The lawyers "were carefully avoiding the presentation of this ultimate issue to the [Supreme] Court" until it had been raised in litigation in the lower court, according to William Hastie. The lawyers did not wish to raise the ultimate issue until "a record of the consequences of imposed racial segregation" had been made in lower courts so that the Supreme Court would have legal precedent grounded in agreed upon evidence for reversing the 1896 *Plessy* ruling. To ask the Court to repudiate its 1896 decision without further evidence on the record was too much of a risk to take, so the lawyers believed [Hastie 1973: 26].

Meanwhile, the NAACP legal department was preparing a solid foundation of precedent in the local cases it had won. These demonstrated various forms of inequality that were unconstitutional according to the 1896 decision. In addition to building a record, these local cases became "a focal point of public interest that created an opportunity to rally disappointed and discouraged [blacks] to fight" [Hastie 1973: 26–29].

Finally, the Brown decision came in 1954, *Brown* v. *Board of Education,* 347 U.S. 483 (1954). Having declared in the *Sweatt* case from Texas in 1950 that state-imposed segregated legal education for black citizens was a denial of equal protection of the laws guaranteed by the Constitution, the U.S. Supreme Court in that year, according to Hastie, had come "within one step of invalidating all required racial segregation in public education" [Hastie 1973: 29]. The *Brown* decision had to repudiate the separate but equal doctrine given the evidence on which the Court had ruled in the *Sweatt* and *McLaurin* cases.

The Solicitor General filed a brief for the United States in these two cases that stated that "racial segregation is itself a manifestation of inequality and discrimination, ... [and that] 'the separate but equal' theory ... is wrong" [quoted in Hastie 1973:30].

In the *Brown* decision in 1954, the legal stage was won. Hastie believed at that time that "the road ahead lay short and straight to the objective, an equalitarian legal order" [Hastie 1973:30]. But such was not to be. Litigation was only stage I of this social movement. It had lasted nearly twenty years.

Stage II: Demonstration. Anthony Lewis, in his book *Portrait of a Decade,* acknowledged that law was a powerful force working against racial discrimination between 1954 and 1964. He also learned during those years that "law alone is not enough." He said, "Americans characteristically think not only in legal but in moral terms." It was during this period that "the American conscience was finally touched" [Lewis 1965:10].

Stage II, the period of demonstration, came into full bloom with the Montgomery bus boycott in Alabama, which was precipitated by an event occurring on December 1, 1955 when Rosa Parks refused to move back on a crowded bus so that a white passenger could have her seat, and for that refusal was arrested [Reddick 1959:112]. The demonstrations continued from Alabama to Arkansas, to North Carolina, to Tennessee, to Georgia, to Mississippi, to Louisiana. In many instances, they were concerned with schools; in some instances they were not. Lewis described blacks at that time as following a "course of reason and restraint" [Lewis 1965:11]. Always the protests were nonviolent.

Of the Montgomery bus boycott, writer William Miller described how Martin Luther King, Jr., brought his church people along. He said King took "an ordinary congregation of middle-class Negroes, with all their smugness, prissiness, and status consciousness, and made them something more like a fellowship of committed Christians, the backbone of a dangerous and demanding crusade for human dignity ... perhaps his most remarkable unsung achievement" [Miller 1968:308].

In Little Rock, it was nine black children who tried to exercise their legal right to attend Central High School. They were turned away by a crowd and National Guardsmen [Lewis 1965:41]. On May 31, 1961 James Meredith, an honorably discharged staff sergeant, filed suit contending he had been denied admission to the University of Mississippi "solely on racial grounds" [Lewis 1965:185]. In Greensboro, North Carolina, college students demonstrated in 1960 when they were refused service at a lunch counter [Lewis 1965:72].

Demonstrations were necessary to force the nation to live up to the letter of the law. The Southern Manifesto indicated the states had no intention of abiding by the *Brown* decision. They had refused to honor the *Plessy* decision in 1896, which required that they provide equal if separate education decades earlier. They believed they could refuse to abide by the law again at the midpoint of the twentieth century. If the nation had been forced to proved equal facilities for the races whenever they were separate, segregation would have ended before the *Brown* decision simply because it would have been too expensive. Although whites who were in charge asserted that this is a nation of laws, they did not abide by *Plessy* and were in the process of ignoring *Brown* until blacks put a stop to such practices by their nonviolent demonstrations.

A common ideology of these demonstrations emerged. Mrs. Parks decided to cease cooperating in her own oppression and so did the little children in Little Rock, the former Air Force sergeant James Meredith in Mississippi, and the college students in Greensboro, North Carolina. Some paid with assaults on their bodies for such noncooperation. Others were spared.

As the demonstrations gained momentum, the people were ready to sacrifice everything. Finally, the demonstrations culminated in a March on Washington on August 28, 1963. More than 200,000 Americans, most of them black, demonstrated in Washington "for a full and speedy program of Civil Rights and equal job opportunities." A *New York Times* reporter, E. W. Kenworthy, called it "the greatest assembly for a redress of grievances that this capital has ever seen" [Lewis 1965:216].

Daniel Bell's appraisal of the protest indicated how inadequate was our sociological knowledge and understanding of this social movement, particularly its demonstration stage. Bell advised blacks to behave like whites and adopt the model of a bureaucracy for the selection of their leaders and the identification of grievances. He expressed consternation over the fact that "new leaders are quickly 'thrown up' as the movement spreads from civil rights to schools, to rent strikes, to claims for preference in jobs." He said new pressure tactics, "such as stall-ins or lay-downs have alarmed the older Negro leadership, as well as the white liberals."

Bell was particularly concerned that "almost every week ... [another] man or woman is acclaimed as a civil-rights leader" and that "experience, education and social standing are not necessary for this kind of leadership."

He was saddened by the fact that "carefully worked out programs for social change by the established organizations go unreported"[quoted in Lewis 1965:228–229].

Despite the consternation of some whites, stage II, which lasted a decade, was successful. Anthony Lewis of the *New York Times* said, "the issue in 1964 was more than race. It was the unity of the country" [Lewis 1965:228]. The demonstrations had pressed this understanding upon President Lyndon Johnson, who then used all of his political ingenuity to get the Congress to enact the Civil Rights Act of 1964, which ushered in stage III, the period of legislation.

Stage III: Legislation. On July 2, 1964 the President put his signature on the Civil Rights Act. The Civil Rights movement saw in the act not all that was desired, according to William Miller, but an important step [Miller 1968: 206]. The period of legislation that began in 1964 lasted four years. It ended in 1968, the year Martin Luther King, Jr., died. Stage III was a period for whites to respond. They did. In the short span of half a decade, the most authoritative legislative body in the United States passed the Civil Rights Act of 1964, the Voting Rights Act of 1965, and the Fair Housing Act of 1968.

That law is still a powerful institutional force in regulating human conduct is clearly revealed in an analysis of the access to educational opportunities that all blacks have experienced since 1969 to the present in stage IV, the implementation period of the Civil Rights movement. Stage IV also was a period that required positive actions by whites. So that perspective may be obtained on what has happened in recent years, gains at the close of the first decade in stage IV will be compared with educational opportunities available to blacks, other racial minorities, and whites toward the beginning of the movement in the 1940s.

Stage IV: Implementation. The positive facts about access to education in the United States that occurred for blacks and other minority races from the litigation stage to and through the implementation stage in the Civil Rights movement are enumerated [National Center, 1980:16].

During the period of litigation back in 1940 (as seen in Table 22.1), a decade and a half before *Brown*, this was the situation with reference to education. Of all blacks and other races over 25 years of age, only 7.7 percent had completed four or more years of high school, and as few as 1.3 percent had completed college; in 1940, half of the blacks and other minority races had completed less than 5.7 years of school. For whites of the same

Table 22.1.

Level of School Completed by Persons Age 25 and Over by Race, United States 1940–1979

| | Race (25 Years and Over) | | | | | | | |
| | Blacks and Other Races | | | | Whites | | | |
Date	Less than 5 Years of School	4 Years of High School or More	4 Years of College or More	Median School Year Completed	Less than 5 Years of School	4 Years of High School or More	4 Years of College or More	Median School Year Completed
1940	41.8	7.7	1.3	5.7	10.9	26.1	4.9	8.7
1950	31.4	13.4	2.2	6.9	8.7	35.5	6.4	9.7
1960	23.5	21.7	3.5	8.2	6.7	43.2	8.1	10.8
1970	14.7	36.1	6.1	10.1	4.2	57.4	11.6	12.2
1979	9.2	52.6	10.7	12.1	2.7	69.7	17.2	12.5

Prepared from data reported in National Center for Educational Statistics, *Digest of Educational Statistics 1980*, Washington, D.C.: U.S. Government Printing Office, 1980, p. 16. Note: Prior to 1950, data exclude Alaska and Hawaii. Data for 1979 are for the noninstitutional population.

age group in the same year, 26.1 percent had completed four or more years of high school, 4.9 percent had graduated from college; their median year of school completed was 8.7 years, which was 53 percent higher than the median for minorities.

In 1960, a half decade after *Brown* and during the demonstration stage, great racial differences persisted in access to education; for blacks and other minority adults, 21.7 percent had completed four or more years of high school and 3.5 percent, four or more years of college. The median for school years completed had risen in 20 years only 2.5 years to a level of 8.2 years for racial minority populations. Meanwhile, for whites during this period and for the same age group, 43.2 percent had completed four or more years of high school; 8.1 percent had completed college; and the median year of school completed moved forward another year to 10.8 years. Thus five to six years after *Brown*, whites continued to have access to more education than blacks and other minorities; but the difference as reflected in the median had been reduced for whites to just a third greater than that for the minorities.

By 1970, five years after the first comprehensive piece of federal antidiscrimination legislation of this century had been enacted, and as the nation moved into the stage of implementation, the proportion of racial minorities who completed four or more years of high school jumped to 36.1 percent; 6.1 percent completed four or more years of college; and the median for years of school completed moved nearly two years forward in less than a decade to 10.1 years. Among whites in 1970, 57.4 percent of the population had completed four or more years of high school (this is the first time that a majority of all whites over 25 were classified as high school graduates); 11.6 percent had completed college; the median years of school completed moved forward 1.4 years from a decade earlier to a high of 12.2 years. However, this median was only about one-fifth greater than the median for racial minorities.

Finally in 1979, a decade into the stage of implementation, a majority of all blacks and other minorities 25 years of age and over (52.6 percent) were high school graduates (this is the first time that blacks achieved the level of a majority of adults who were graduates of secondary school); 10.7 percent had finished college; and the median year of school completed had risen to 12.1 years. Whites over 25 years of age also continued to make progress in 1979, with 69.7 percent completing high school and 17.2 percent completing college, resulting in a median for years of school completed of 12.5 years. At the end of the first decade of implementation, the median education for whites was only 3 percent ahead of blacks and other minority races.

In summary, for blacks and other minority races, about half of the adult population over 25 years of age had less than an elementary school education in 1940 during the stage of litigation. By 1979 at the end of the first decade in the stage of implementation, the median had risen more than 100 percent in slightly more than a third of a century to a point where more than half were high school graduates.

These facts lead to the conclusion that the Civil Rights movement so far as access to education is concerned helped blacks and other racial minorities, did not hinder educational progress among whites, but reduced the disparity between the races in median years of school completed from a large difference of 53 percent during the litigation stage of the Civil Rights movement to a small difference of 3 percent during the implementation stage. The nation is headed toward parity and equality in educational opportunity but has not yet achieved it in that only half of the blacks are high school graduates compared to two-thirds of all whites, and only 1 out of every 10 blacks is a college graduate compared to slightly more than 2 out of every 10 whites over 25 years of age.

The Civil Rights movement has significantly moved ahead the process of equal access to education. (Resistance to the movement is growing, however. This could be an analysis of another paper.) These data clearly indicate that social scientists and others who claim that the Civil Rights movement has been of limited effect and that the alleged limited benefits have been experienced only by middle-class blacks are wrong. They also indicate that social scientists and others are wrong who claim that Civil Rights laws and regulations have completely eliminated a semicaste or dual educational system.

New Learnings for Sociology

What have we learned from the analysis that is beneficial to sociology? In terms of social process, we see principles of asymmetry and discontinuity at work in the nonviolent demonstrations of the Civil Rights movement, particularly those led or inspired by Martin Luther King, Jr., who insisted that one should meet physical force with soul force. This way one "stirs the conscience of the opponent so that reconciliation becomes a reality" [quoted in Hoskin 1968:94]. During the decade of the demonstrations Anthony Lewis said, "American conscience was finally touched" [Lewis 1965:10]; thus, the asymmetrical process of opposing evil in a manner that is different from the way that evil is manifested worked. After a decade of nonviolent demonstrations, the United States Congress passed the Civil Rights Act, the Voting Rights Act, and the Fair Housing Act.

The principle of discontinuity is manifested in the shift in strategy by blacks from controlled conflict in the courts during the litigation stage of the movement to civil disobedience and spontaneous demonstrations in the streets during the demonstration stage. The strategy of discontinuity—of orderly action followed by disorderly action—was necessary as it became clear that the dominant people of power, as stated in the Southern Manifesto, had no intention of abiding by the Supreme Court order to desegregate the public schools in an orderly way. If orderly implementation of the school desegregation court decision had occurred soon after 1954, a discontinuous strategy of demonstration would not have been necessary. Beyond evidence contained in the Southern Manifesto that every legal means would be used to resist rather than implement the law, Marian Wright Edelman reported that 99 out of every 100 black children were still in segregated schools a decade after they lawfully won their class-action court case that was supposed to grant them desegregative relief [Edelman 1973:33]. It was the discontinuous strategy of demonstration based on a foundation of favorable court decisions emerging from a legitimating orderly effort of litigation that eventually brought about change.

As stated earlier, at the end of the decade of demonstrations, in 1964, the unity of the nation was at stake. Back in 1928 Justice Brandeis had warned that "in a government of laws existence of the government will be imperiled if it fails to observe the law scrupulously" [quoted in Lewis 1965: 250]. There was clear and present evidence that the government had no intention of enforcing the school desegregation law. What, then, were blacks to do who had rightfully won in an orderly way access to all schools to which they were still denied? They had no alternative but to use a disorderly approach.

The decade of demonstrations could have been avoided if whites who controlled the government had used a continuous strategy of lawfully implementing school desegregation as a public policy that had been lawfully prescribed by the court. Of school desegregation law enforcement, the government's attitude was negative. Kenneth B. Clark tells us that "the negatives of one determine the negatives of the other" [Clark 1974:15].

Dominants and Subdominants. This leads to the question: Whose responsibility is it to break the cycle of negative adaptations that stimulate each other? To answer this question, one must determine who is dominant and who is subdominant in the set of social relations. In *Plessy* v. *Ferguson,*

163 U.S. 537 (1896), the court attempted to deal with the issue of racially equal treatment by ignoring who was dominant and subdominant. Law professor Vierira said, "the Court ... chose to interpret segregation as a mutual separation of the races which branded neither group inferior, so long as equal facilities were provided for each. ... Unfortunately, the majority's rationale overlooked the fact that segregation was imposed by whites, who were politically and economically dominant" [Vierira 1978:64].

The issue of who is dominant and who is subdominant is a power issue. Power is the capacity to influence or force others to act in a prescribed way. In the light of this definition, the Civil Rights movement revealed that both black populations and white populations have power. They both have the power to veto conventional behavior as blacks did during boycotts, the sit-ins, freedom rides, and other demonstrations. For example, the federal government and the District of Columbia government stopped transacting business August 28, 1963, although it was not an official holiday. It was the date of the March on Washington. With more than a quarter of a million people descending on that city from all over the nation, the government could not continue with business as usual. The March on Washington is one of several illustrations of veto-power-in-action by blacks.

Veto power over custom and convention does not distinguish blacks from whites. Whites also have the capacity to disrupt social organization, and to do it better than blacks because of their larger numbers. However, they seldom do. What distinguishes whites from blacks, therefore, is their capacity to implement innovations that require new or additional community resources. Whites, who control community resources allocated by local governmental authorities, had the power and authority to implement court orders and public laws. This capacity is why whites are labeled as dominants. Whites refused to implement school desegregation through school boards and city councils, which they controlled. One can refuse to implement a new requirement only if one has the power and authority to implement it. The power to implement is the major capacity that distinguishes whites from blacks. The decade of demonstration never would have occurred if whites, the dominants, who controlled school boards, had acted in an orderly and timely way to implement the 1954 U.S. Supreme Court decision.

It is important to determine who is dominant and who is subdominant because these two categories have different responsibilities in power relationships. Subdominants cannot do for dominants what dominants must do for themselves. And dominants cannot do for subdominants what subdominants must do for themselves.

If subdominants feel betrayed and oppressed because they had followed the orderly requirements of the social system, used the courts, and won their case, but still were not granted relief from racial discrimination, they have no alternative but to cease cooperating in their own oppression. This Rosa Parks did in Alabama; this the nine children did in Little Rock; this the college students did in North Carolina; this James Meredith did in Mississippi. Any oppressed people will continue to be oppressed until they decide to cease cooperating in their own oppression. This is a responsibility that subdominants must undertake for themselves. It is not an action that dominants, including liberal dominants, can assume on behalf of subdominants.

The decision to cease cooperating in one's own oppression is a responsibility of subdominants and theirs alone because they are the people who will suffer even more through retribution if their bid for freedom is unsuccessful. Those who would not suffer have not the right to offer others as a sacrifice.

The predisposition toward self-sacrifice is a prerequisite for self-liberation. The NAACP recognized this principle during the 1930s and 1940s, made its legal staff available, but insisted that the decision must be a local decision by subdominants who were willing to risk reprisals.

The decision that is uniquely that of dominants, that cannot be assumed by others for them, is their decision to make the system inclusive and available to all so that all may benefit together from existing resources. John Rawls discussed this issue in his book, *A Theory of Justice*. He stated that no one deserves a more favorable starting place in society. Yet these distinctions do not have to be eliminated to be fair. According to Rawls, "the basic structure can be arranged so that these contingencies work for the good of the least fortunate." Thus, no one should gain or lose because of one's arbitrary place in the distribution of assets "without giving or receiving compensating advantages in return. ... In other words, those who have been favored ... may gain from their good fortune only on terms that improve the situation of those who have lost out" [Rawls 1971:101–104].

The decision to do what Rawls has suggested is that of dominants, and theirs alone, because to make a formerly exclusive system inclusive is to sacrifice one's privileges and prerogatives. In this situation, the principle is applicable also that no one has the right to sacrifice another. Subdominants do not have the right to sacrifice dominants.

If subdominants do not make the decision that is only theirs to make, things will continue as they are. There will be business as usual as members of the subdominant group grow increasingly bitter, resentful, disspirited, and eventually revolutionary.

But if the dominants do not make the decision that is their own — that is, make the system inclusive and share resources with others, after subdominants have indicated that they want to be counted in, eventually there will be an uprising. Paredo observed many years ago that "leaders [read, dominants] maintain themselves in power by bringing into the governing class ... individuals who might prove dangerous to the governing group. ... If such recruiting does not take place, in the absence of a free use of force, sooner or later there will be an uprising" [quoted in Crawford 1948:567].

During the Civil Rights movement, after the dominants decided not to implement the 1954 Supreme Court decision, include subdominants and dominants in desegregated schools and share educational resources with them, there was an uprising just as Paredo predicted there would be. And the uprising did not begin to subside until new antidiscrimination public laws were enacted during the 1960s and increasingly enforced during the 1970s.

Mention of new public laws that are more or less inclusive, their enforcement, and the impact these have had on diminishing the level of disruption due to demonstrations by subdominants bring me to the final point that I would like to emphasize.

Double Victory. The Civil Rights movement gave us a new perspective on the outcome of power negotiations. Usually, the parties to a power struggle either win or lose. But the Civil Rights movement during the 1960s introduced the concept of a double victory. The Civil Rights Act of 1964 is such an example. The educational statistics already mentioned demonstrate how this and other public laws benefited and made the educational system more accessible to blacks and other subdominant populations.

What few people realize is that the 1964 Civil Rights Act also benefited whites. The Bakke case is a classic example. The University of California Medical School at Davis set aside 16 seats for minorities. "As a practical matter ... the larger the proportion of seats held for minorities, the greater the exclusion of nonminorities" [Sindler 1978:103]. A Supreme Court justice whose swing vote made a majority said, "the University's special admissions program violated Title VI of the Civil Rights Act of 1964 by excluding Bakke from the medical school because of his race," which is white; Bakke was not able to compete for the 16 reserved seats for minorities, but minorities theoretically were eligible to compete for all seats including those that were also available for whites. Each morning that Allan Bakke arises and goes forth to develop his medical career he should whisper a prayer of thanks for the efforts of blacks in the United States, who brought sufficient pressure upon the government for the enactment of a public law in 1964 that protected his right to have access to a medical education. This is but one of many examples that the Civil Rights movement has been a double victory for the majority as well as minorities.

In the Civil Rights movement we see litigation and legislation as social processes of controlled conflict between dominant and subdominant interest groups. In this process, both groups negotiate a solution that mutually fulfills their disparate interest both to sustain and to change the social system. The negotiated solution that is mutually fulfilling is the only viable solution according to situational analysis. The miracle in social organization is that groups with necessarily disparate interests can share common institutions and achieve a mutually beneficial solution. This is what Martin Luther King, Jr., called the double victory — a concept that deserves a place in the lexicon of political sociology.

Self-Correction in Social Organization. Analysis of the Civil Rights movement has demonstrated the different responsibilities and obligations of dominant and subdominant groups as complementary. One without the other is incomplete. The antinomy of the two is eternal. Their continuous negotiation is the means of both developing and self-correcting social organization. There is nothing intrinsically good or bad about dominant and subdominant power positions. Both are needed and necessary. Situational analysis reveals that the subdominants usually are aware of this but dominants usually are not. Daniel Moynihan a decade and a half ago said that "it is clearly a disadvantage for a minority group to be operating on one principle, while the majority of the population, and the one with the most advantages to begin with, is operating on another" [Moynihan 1965:29]. By not recognizing the complementary function of dominant and subdominant groups in sustaining and changing society, members of the dominant group often project on subdominants their own attitudes and values and then discount those that differ from their own as being of little if any benefit. This orientation eliminates the source of self-correction in social organization. The ideal type construction implied in Moynihan's comment is of value in ordering our observations of society. But analysis of the Civil Rights movement causes us to recognize two ideal types — one for dominants and another for subdominants. Neither should be classified as a deviant process.

Continuity and Discontinuity. In terms of social process, analysis of the Civil Rights movement further contributes to sociological knowledge by

244   MACROSOCIAL STUDIES

recognizing both continuities and discontinuities as of value. For example, the litigation stage not implemented in good faith was then followed by a demonstration stage that was discontinuous with the orderly process of litigation. Likewise, the orderly legislative process was discontinuous with the previous stage of demonstrations but was necessary as a way of calling off the disruption. Having learned that disruptive discontinuity is an outcome of the absence of positive continuity, we see that the social process in our society during the Civil Rights movement returned to a stage of continuity with the orderly legislative process being followed by an orderly implementation process when dominants did what they were supposed to do. We cannot overemphasize as an important finding in political sociology that dominants have only themselves to blame for disruptions in the social order when lawful requirements are not orderly implemented. A negative discontinuity on the part of dominants tends to generate a negative discontinuity by subdominants [Clark 1974:15]. In the absence of good faith implementation, subdominants do have the power of veto. Veto action is implemented by way of activities that are discontinuous with the conventional and orderly way of doing things.

Situation analysis understands discontinuity to be as significant as continuity in social organization. Through the process of continuity the system is sustained; through the process of discontinuity the system is changed. Both are of value.

Symmetry and Asymmetry. Finally, in terms of social process, analysis of the Civil Rights movement has helped sociologists to understand better the function of symmetrical and asymmetrical relationships, and the significance of both. A relationship that is symmetrical is something of value if it is positive. A positive symmetrical relationship is one characterized by a double victory in which the self-interests both of dominants and of subdominants are mutually fulfilled. But a negative symmetry, according to Kenneth B. Clark, is based on "the uncritical assumption that individual human beings are expendable in the interest of some higher cause, that a higher morality justifies transitional immorality. ... An illustration is human beings concerned about the insensitivity and violence of others who resort to insensitive violence to bring about a more moral system" [Clark 1974:14–15]. Clark states that this approach will not work: "the negatives of one determine the negatives of the other; unreversed, they will increase geometrically" [Clark 1974:14–15].

It was the nonviolent orientation of the demonstration stage of the Civil Rights movement that taught us the value of asymmetrical relationships.

The sociological principle is this: "there must be an *asymmetry* between the form in which evil manifests itself and the form of our opposition to evil" [quoted in Miller 1968:310]. This, of course, is what King meant when he advocated opposing physical force with soul force.

Summary

In summary, the Civil Rights movement of the twentieth century has taught us many new principles in sociology. Most of all it has taught us to emphasize situation sociology, which identifies dominant and subdominant populations as complementary and interdependent with disparate self-interests and different role responsibilities, that nevertheless can be harmonized into a double victory that is mutually beneficial. Moreover, the Civil Rights movement has taught us to analyze asymmetrical as well as symmetrical relationships, and discontinuities as well as continuities, since neither process is deviant. In connection with new understanding about social process, the Civil Rights movement has also taught us that ideal typologies characterize both dominants and subdominants in the social structure and that it is inappropriate to project the characteristics of one group upon the other, since each category has obligations and responsibilities in the society that are uniquely its own. For social scientists who have taken the time to reflect, the Civil Rights movement has been beneficial both personally and professionally. I would hazard the guess that some variant of litigation, demonstration, legislation, and implementation is likely to characterize other major social movements in the future, although the sequence of stages may differ, largely because dominants are reluctant to share their power.

References

Clark, Kenneth B. 1974. *Pathos of Power.* New York: Harper & Row.

Crawford, Rex. 1948. "Representative Italian Contributions to Sociology: Paredo, Louis, Vaccaro, Gino, and Sighele." In Harry Elmer Barnes, (ed.), *Introduction to the History of Sociology,"* Chicago: University of Chicago Press.

Edelman, Marian Wright. 1973. "Southern School Desegregation, 1954-1973: A Judicial-Political Overview." *The Annals* 407 (May): 32-42.

Hall, Raymond L. 1978. *Black Separatism.* Hanover, NH: University Press of New England.

Hastie, William H. 1973. "Toward an Equalitarian Regal Order, 1930-1950." *The Annals* 407 (May): 18-31.

Hawley, Willis D. 1981. "Increasing the Effectiveness of School Desegregation — Lessons from the Research." In Adam Yarmolinsky, Lance Liebman, and Corinne S. Schelling (eds.), *Race and Schooling in the City,* Cambridge, MA: Harvard University Press, pp. 115–162.

Hoskin, Lotte. 1974. *"I Have A Dream."* New York: Grosset and Dunlop.

Larson, E. Richard, and Laughlin McDonald. 1980. *The Rights of Racial Minorities.* New York: Avon.

Lewis, Anthony. 1965. *Portrait of a Decade.* New York: Bantam.

Martindale, Don. 1981. *The Nature and Types of Sociological Theory.* Boston: Houghton Mifflin.

Miller, William Robert. 1968. *Martin Luther King, Jr.* New York: Avon

Moynihan, Daniel Patrick. 1965. *The Negro Family: The Case for National Action.* Washington, DC: Government Printing Office.

National Center for Education Statistics. 1980. *Digest of Education Statistics 1980.* Washington, DC: Government Printing Office.

Rawls, John. 1971. *A Theory of Justice.* Cambridge, MA: Harvard University Press.

Reddick, L. D. 1959. *Crusader Without Violence.* New York: Harper & Row.

Sindler, Allan P. 1978. *Bakke, DeFunis, and Minority Admissions.* New York: Longman.

Toch, Hans. 1965. *The Social Psychology of Social Movements.* Indianapolis: Bobbs-Merrill.

U. S. Bureau of the Census. 1980. *Statistical Abstract of the United States.* Washington, DC: Government Printing Office.

Vierira, Norman. *Civil Rights in a Nutshell.* St. Paul: West.

Whitehead, Alfred North. 1957. *The Concept of Nature.* Ann Arbor: University of Michigan Press.

Willie, Charles V. 1969. *Church Action in the World.* New York: Morehouse-Barlow.

_____. 1977. *Black/Brown/White Relations.* New Brunswick: NJ Transaction.

Chapter 23

Marginality and Social Change

This is a period when all around us we hear the call for unity as a way of building an effective power base to foster or withstand social change. Our hypothesis in this chapter is that unity is not enough, that marginality is an essential component in a healthy human society. Moreover, we assert that effective social systems endure the tension between the need for unity and the requirement for marginality. We know a great deal about unity and stability but not so much about marginality and social change.

The marginal man, according to Stonequist, "is poised in psychological uncertainty between two (or more) social worlds" [Stonequist 1937: 6–8]. In general, Stonequist discussed marginality as a negative effect.

Relatively the More Civilized

Only in the last chapter of his book did Stonequist recognize in a limited way any positive contribution of marginality in human society. In a very brief discussion, he pointed out that "the marginal man is the key-personality in the contacts of cultures. It is in his mind that the cultures come together, conflict, and eventually work out some kind of mutual adjustment and interpenetration." Stonequist concluded that "the life histories of marginal men offer the most significant material for the analysis of the cultural process as it springs from the contact of social groups" [Stonequist 1937:222].

Robert Park, who was Stonequist's teacher, saw the marginal person not so much as a supersensitive and uncertain individual. Rather he considered the marginal person to be "the individual with the wider horizon, the keener intelligence, the more detached and rational viewpoint." In fact

Reprinted from Charles V. Willie, *Oreo — A Perspective on Race and Marginal Men and Women,* Wakefield, Massachusetts: Parameter Press, 1975, pp. 40–49.

he said, "The marginal man is always relatively the more civilized human being." According to Park, the marginal person — the more civilized human being — "occupies the position which has been historically that of the Jew in the Diaspora" [Park 1937:xviii] and, I might add, that of blacks and other racial minorities in America. Of course, it may be difficult for persons who have not controlled their ethnocentrism to call Jews, blacks, and other minorities more civilized. But that is what Robert Park said of Jews. I believe that he shared a significant insight in that statement and that he indicated an understanding of the function of marginality.

Harvey Cox, in his book *The Secular City,* made a comment similar to that of Park. He said, "[the Jews], when they were wandering and homeless ... seem to have been closest to fulfilling their calling" [Cox 1965:55]. Cox probably achieved this insight because his analysis of urban society focused more upon freedom and social process than upon control and social structure. In fact he indicates in the subtitle that his book is a celebration of the liberties of the secular city and is an invitation to its discipline. Most sociological studies begin first with an analysis of patterns of discipline or social control and eventually may get around to analyzing alternative expressions of freedom and social change. But many sociological studies never get this far.

In the 1960s during the height of the civil rights revolution, Commissioner James Allen of the Department of Education in New York State was asked what, in his opinion, had made the greatest contribution to change in the educational system in that state. He seriously considered the question for a while and then responded that blacks in their demonstrations, in their peaceful demonstrations, had probably done more than any other group to bring about educational change, and he urged them to continue their efforts. Apparently the peaceful demonstrations benefited all parts of society. Please note that Commissioner Allen did not refer to the powerful Board of Regents in New York State as the primary initiator of educational change. It seems that Allen was trying to tell us something about the role of marginal people in social change.

It is interesting to note that the blacks who have been recommended for receipt of the Nobel Prize for Peace have been residents of the United States and the Union of South Africa, two countries in which they are subdominant or marginal people in terms of political power. Apparently their experiences as marginals have contributed to their leadership capacity to seek peace.

If Blacks Would Act Like Whites

A proper understanding of the function of marginality in human society would have prevented Daniel Patrick Moynihan from prescribing that blacks be made over in the image of whites in his 1965 report on the black family. Specifically, Moynihan said that retardation of the progress of blacks as a group is due to the fact that their alleged matriarchal family structure is *"so out of line* with the rest of American society" [U.S. Department of Labor 1965:29] (italics added). The implication is clear that, if blacks would act like whites in their family life, they might be treated like whites. According to this formulation, blacks are responsible for their own oppression, especially those blacks in female-headed, one-parent families. Arthur Jensen in 1969 made a similar case with reference to intelligence. He stated that "The remedy deemed logical for children who would do poorly in school is to boost their IQ's up to where they can perform *like the majority ...*" [Jensen 1969:3] (italics added). Again the implication is clear: If blacks would think like whites, they might be treated like whites. Neither Moynihan nor Jensen remotely considered that what blacks do and think may be what they ought to do and think in terms of their existential condition and that what they do and think might ultimately be beneficial for whites too. One can understand this principle if one can understand the function of marginality in social life.

For example, the employment of black women outside the home as workers in the national labor force was a pioneering marginal activity over the years which eventually resulted in an increasing number of white women being employed outside the home. Had blacks been made over in the image of whites as prescribed by some social scientists, white women would not have been able to observe the creative effects of work for pay as they were able to do by observing the work experience of black women. Back in 1940 only 25% of the mature white women 35 to 44 years of age were in the labor force compared with 45% of the black women. Today more than half of the mature white women and black women are in the labor force [U.S. Bureau of Census 1972:1–372]. Thus the gap between the proportion of women in the labor force in the two racial populations is narrowing.

Joe Feagin has reported that, as far back as 1900, about 4 out of every 10 black women were members of the labor force, a proportion far greater than that for whites [Feagin 1970:23]. The opportunity to work has been a creative experience for black women over the years, possibly related to "rising family aspirations for a higher standard of living" [Feagin 1970:24]. White working women probably are unaware of the fact that they may be modeling their behavior after blacks.

The enlarged proportion of black women in the labor force compared with whites repeatedly has been referred to as an overrepresentation of black women. The phrase "overrepresentation" can be used only if the labor force participation rate for white women is looked upon as the norm for all women. It is interesting to note that seldom are white women said to be underrepresented in the labor force compared with blacks. This statement is seldom made because most social analysts do not hold up the behavior of blacks or other minorities as an archetype or model for whites or the majority. Yet, if it is appropriate to say that black women have been overrepresented in the labor force, it is appropriate to say that white women have been underrepresented. Most social analysts are inclined to make the first statement because they have not adequately recognized that their attitudes are ethnocentric, that they use happenings within their own group as a criterion of what ought to be. They still believe that the way of life of the majority should be the model for the minority. This attitude has been clearly spelled out by Moynihan and Jensen.

When the majority has an ethnocentric view of social organization, it fails to recognize the unique and significant contributions of marginal people whatever their age, sex, race, or social class may be; moreover, we fail to recognize that the adaptations of the subdominant, minority, or marginal group may be beneficial for all, including the majority and the minority.

The Rebel and Society

As black women demonstrated to white women the benefits of employment in the labor force, marginal people in general have led the way and pointed to a new day. We are not alone in making this observation. I like the way René Dubos has stated the case for marginality. He calls the rebel "the standard-bearer of the visionaries who gradually increase man's ethical stature." Also he believes that "as long as there are rebels in our midst, there is reason to hope that our societies can be saved" [Dubos 1968:5–6]. For those who have given their primary allegiance to the study of social structure, social control, and *homeostasis,* the Dubos statement may appear to be sentimentalism. But for those who recognize the need to study social process as well as social structure, or *homeokinesis* as well as *homeostasis,* this statement points in the direction of that which has been neglected in our sociological research.

Homeostasis and Homeokinesis

As those who are familiar with physiology well know, the concept *homeostasis* — a theoretical formulation of the tendency for organic systems to maintain a steady state, constantly correcting for imbalance and disequilibrium — was introduced by the Harvard physiologist Walter B. Canon [1939]. It was readily adopted by social scientists such as Talcott Parsons and others and became a major frame of reference for organizing our thoughts about social organization as well as organic systems.

Homeostasis, a basic concept which aids us to organize our thoughts about living systems, was not challenged until the recent writings of the Rockefeller University microbiologist René Dubos. Categorically, he has stated, "Living systems are characterized not by homeostasis, but by homeokinesis" [Dubos 1972:249]. With reference to physiology, Dubos states, "Homeostatic processes that appear to be successful because they exert protective or reparative function at the time they occur commonly elicit malfunction at a later date." For example, "The production of scar tissue is a homeostatic response because it heals wounds and helps in checking the spread of infection. But in the liver or the kidney, scar tissue means cirrhosis or glomerular nephritis; in rheumatoid arthritis, it may freeze the joints; and in the lung it may choke the breathing process." Dubos concluded, "When the end results of homeostasis are evaluated over a long period of time, it becomes obvious that the wisdom of the body is often a short-sighted wisdom" [Dubos 1972:248]. Dubos then went on to state why homeostasis — the tendency for living systems to maintain a steady state — is not an appropriate concept for the purpose of analyzing social systems. "Man differs from the rest of the animal kingdom," said Dubos, "not by his biological endowments but by the use he has made of them, usually in a conscious way." He called our attention to the fact that "man" is reflective and interpretive: "man" thinks and reflects about what he sees, and he interprets it, trying to find meaning in what he encounters. Dubos was critical of social scientists who have adopted the homeostatic attitude toward "man". He stated that this causes such scientists to be "insensitive to the potentialities for social change." In fact he states, "The concept of homeostasis in sociology and economics, like the concept of climax in ecology, is a postulate which hardly ever fits reality" [Dubos 1972:248–249]. Indeed living systems must maintain a continuous rate of change, or homeokinesis; otherwise they atrophy, decay, or disintegrate.

As we see it, homeokinesis is not so much a concept in opposition to homeostasis as it is complementary to it. In social groups, we have both the tendency to maintain our traditions and customs and another tendency to transcend, change, and reach out beyond our present circumstances, what Dubos calls homeokinesis.

Transcendence

A problem in contemporary as well as historical social science is the absence of a sense of transcendence — the ability to go beyond one's boundaries or limitations. Transcendence is what marginal people tend to bring to social organization. For example, in sociology the idea of the self is usually discussed as if each person tends to act in accordance with his or her understanding of the way others expect. This is part of the truth. This idea of the self focuses upon control, conformity, social expectation, and homeostasis. But people are not entirely passive agents who are acted upon by external forces.

Human beings are concerned with aesthetics too, with the beautiful. According to Lionel Trilling, it was Hegel who gave art an importance that it had never before had in moral philosophy. Hegel saw art as "the activity of man in which spirit expresses itself not only as utility, not only according to law, but as grace, as transcendence, as manner and style" [Trilling 1955:xii]. To gain a proper understanding of the self and human society, we must consider the urge for freedom and change in people as well as the need for control and stability, the desire to try new things as well as to conform to the old, the tendency to homeokinesis as well as homeostasis.

Moses and Martin Luther King, Jr.

Two classic social movements illustrate the function of marginal people as contributors to social change through the impact of their movements upon the total society. The ancient and contemporary freedom movements among Jews and blacks are quite similar and so are Moses and Martin Luther King, Jr., the people who led them. We present a brief analysis of these men as living examples of marginality and the kind of leadership that flows therefrom.

When blacks have exhibited capacities so as to effectively compete with whites in America, they have been roundly put down by whites, and also they are dubbed as oreos by blacks. We would suppose that more people have read the autobiography of Malcolm X than the life story of Martin

Luther King, Jr. Both, of course, were great men. But Martin Luther King, Jr., was university educated and comparatively well to do. Malcolm X was street educated and poor. Malcolm X could be idolized but looked down upon by middle-class persons who, therefore, found him to be a more acceptable folk hero. Martin Luther King, Jr., was misunderstood by both white liberals and black militants [Miller 1968:294]. Even liberal social scientists and radical students have been quick to call educated blacks "white Negroes" and intelligent women "masculine."

The leaders of social movements need not necessarily possess the characteristics of the people whom they lead. Take Moses, for example. Moses was a marginal man all right. He had experiences very much unlike the enslaved Jewish people whom he led to freedom. Yet Moses was a magnificent leader whom the people followed for forty years.

Martin Luther King, Jr., "was born without fanfare in comfortable, ... conventional circumstances" [Bennett 1964:5]. King's mother and father attended college. His father was the pastor of a leading Baptist church in Atlanta, Georgia. King earned academic degrees from Morehouse College, Crozer Theological Seminary, and Boston University. His family was definitely middle class. Yet Martin lost his life in Memphis where he came to participate in a demonstration with garbage workers. He too was a marginal man and a magnificent leader much unlike the poor people who followed him.

There were other similarities between these two men. Both had detractors among their own people who questioned their integrity and authenticity before and after their death. Sigmund Freud, the Jewish psychoanalyst, claimed that Moses actually was an Egyptian who tried to force his own monotheistic brand of religion upon Jewish people [Freud 1939:3–65]. John A. Williams, the black writer, claimed that Martin was a middle-class snob [Williams 1970:151–154] who tried to force his own philosophy of nonviolent resistance upon black people [Williams 1970:57].

Both were leaders who demanded no dominion for themselves [Buber 1958:87]. Because of the immense power which Moses and Martin possessed despite the absence of any formal authority and because of their great humility, the two men often were puzzlements to their own people, as well as to others. From time to time they were murmured against, but the people continued to follow them. Moses and Martin had to contend with high governmental authorities who tried to restrict their movements, but they negotiated successfully in behalf of the enslaved and the poor.

Martin Buber has stated that one who is to be the liberator "has to be introduced into the stronghold of the alien." Freedom movements are "a kind of liberation which cannot be brought about by anyone who grew up as a slave, nor yet by anyone who is not connected with the slaves; but only by one of the latter who has been brought up in the midst of the aliens and has received an education equipping him with all their wisdom and powers ..." [Buber 1958:35]. Moses was a liberator of slaves who was reared in the household of aristocrats. Martin was a liberator of the poor who was educated in the schools of the well-to-do. They did not grow up as slaves or as poor people but nevertheless were connected with them. They truly were marginal men who found identity in the synthesis of groups so that each person in the groups (and each group) could learn from the other and be more than what either was alone.

This concept of the marginal person as synthesizer recognizes that members of the out-group do not have to behave as if they were members of the in-group and that members of the minority do not have to think and act like members of the majority to be effective participants in society.

In conclusion, may we return to the Parkian idea that marginals are always a little more civilized than the rest of us. Is there anyone for marginality? Or are we all too busy unifying our separate tribes?

References

Bennett, Lerone. 1964. *What Manner of Man?* Chicago: Johnson.

Buber, Martin. 1958. *Moses.* New York: Harper & Row.

Dubos, René. 1968. *So Human an Animal.* New York: Scribner's.

_____. 1972. *A God Within.* New York: Scribner's.

Cox, Harvey. 1965. *The Secular City.* New York: Mac millan.

Feagin, Joe R. 1967. "Black Women in the American Work Force." In Charles V. Willie (ed.), *The Family Life of Black People.* Columbus, OH: Merrill.

Freud, Sigmund. 1939. *Moses and Monotheism.* New York: Random House.

Jensen, Arthur R. 1969. "How Much Can We Boost IQ and Scholastic Achievement?" In *Environment, Heredity, and Intelligence.* Cambridge, MA: Harvard Educational Review, Reprint Series No. 2.

Merton, Robert K. 1949. *Social Theory and Social Structure.* New York: Free Press.

Miller, William Robert. 1969. *Martin Luther King, Jr.* New York: Avon.

Park, Robert. 1937. Introduction to Everett V. Stonequist, *The Marginal Man.* New York: Scribner's.

Stonequist, Everett V. 1937. *The Marginal Man.* New York: Scribner's.

Trilling, Lionel. 1955. *The Opposing Self.* New York: Viking.

William, John A. 1970. *The King God Didn't Save.* New York: Coward-McCann.

U.S. Department of Labor. 1965. *The Negro Family.* Washington, DC: Government Printing Office.

U.S. Bureau of the Census. 1972. *Census of Population: 1970. General Social and Economic Characteristics.* Final Report PC1–C1. Washington, DC: Government Printing Office.

Chapter 24

Theoretical Implications:
Conflict, Conciliation, and Cooperation

Social scientists have produced a large and refined body of literature on social conflict but have studied in only a limited way social cooperation. Also little attention has been given to negotiation or conciliation, which are located between conflict and cooperation. Finally, few social scientists have analyzed systematically ways of monitoring conflict and cooperation to ensure that they are helpful rather than harmful.

The perspective of this analysis is that conflict in intergroup relations may be either helpful or harmful, and that cooperation in intergroup relations may be either helpful or harmful, depending on the goals of groups, their social circumstances, and the nature of their interaction. Thus, conflict is not intrinsically bad; and cooperation is not intrinsically good.

The principle of complementarity asserts that individuals and institutions are necessary in social organization, that dominant and subdominant groups are essential, and that social structure and social process are functionally related. These necessary, essential, and interrelated phenomena are different from each other, and therefore are in conflict. At the same time, each phenomenon or category is discrete, incomplete, in need of other categories to achieve wholeness, and therefore must cooperate. Thus both conflict and cooperation can enhance as well as harm society and its various groups.

This is an important perspective for the sociological study of race, ethnicity, and socioeconomic status because of the popular view that racial and ethnic conflict is bad and that cooperation among such groups is good. Whether conflict or cooperation is bad and whether they are good depends upon the goals and interests of the various groups, the extent to which they are fulfilled, the access of group members to opportunities in the society, and the presence or absence of equity in the use of common resources. This means that social conflict and social cooperation cannot be understood apart from their social context. Specific social stiuations, therefore, should

255

be studied to determine the conditions under which they are beneficial or harmful.

Alexander Leighton studied the coercive relocation of thousands of American citizens of Japanese ancestry from their homes in the Pacific coastal region to camps in the interior of the United States during World War II. He discovered these facts about conflict and cooperation. Adaptation to stressful circumstances through aggressive actions that resulted in conflict had alternative consequences: They got results by causing authorities to alter their ways of doing things to relieve the frustration that often is associated with aggression; they resulted in increased repression out of fear on the part of some camp administrators who felt vulnerable and threatened [Leighton 1946:265-267]. Likewise, cooperative actions generated alternative consequences, some unanticipated: citizens of Japanese ancestry who cooperated with the relocation authorities were freed from some of the circumstances that disturbed them if their compliant behavior found favor with camp administrators; but others discovered that cooperative behavior served to perpetuate the adverse influences, particularly those resulting from the ill-advised proposals of camp administrators [Leighton 1946:264].

My studies of black students in predominantly white colleges revealed that most adapted according to the requirements of the situation: black football players achieved their goal of the hiring of a black assistant coach by withdrawing and boycotting spring practice; black members of the Student Afro-American Society obtained an increase in their appropriation after an aggressive presentation before the Student Assembly that ended in conflict; black elected presidents of undergraduate and graduate student bodies cooperated with the student establishment and were therefore designated as articulators of the student point of view and negotiators in behalf of student interest. Withdrawal, conflict, and cooperation were three different forms of adaptation by black students who attended these predominantly white schools. Each adaptation was efficacious in terms of the circumstances [Willie 1977:214-217]. These illustrations further indicate the absence of any intrinsic value associated with any form of adaptation.

The social context within which one functions and one's goals are basic determinants of adaptations that are likely to be most effective. The social context consists of dominant and subdominant populations. Their differing goals, actions, and reactions greatly influence outcomes. Neither dominants nor subdominants are fully in control in any situation of intergroup relations. This is why an examination of the context is important.

When the American colonies (the subdominants) decided to cease cooperating in their own oppression and pressed their claims for participation and representation in the British governance structure as a contentious issue, the outcome may not have resulted in total separation from Great Britain (the dominant) if Britain had cooperated with the colonies by accommodating some of their interests rather than contesting their fair claims. When she visited the United States during its bicentennial celebration, the Queen of England explained the American Revolution as a consequence not of the action of the colonies but of the inept reaction of the British Empire. She said Great Britain lacked the statesmanship to know the right time and the manner of yielding what is impossible to keep [quoted in Willie 1978:77].

History reveals that despite the vast expanse of its empire, Great Britain was not fully in control of the political situation when the colonies decided to rebel. The colonies believed that cooperation between them and the British Empire was contraindicated slightly more than 200 years ago. Conflict was more efficacious for the subdominants then, in terms of their self-interest. However, cooperation may have been a wiser response for the dominant, if it wanted to retain the empire. All of this suggests that one's social location has a great deal to do with the form of adaptation that is considered to be appropriate.

Intergroup relations and school desegregation present circumstances not unlike those that existed between the colonies and the British Empire. A study of 10 educational systems under court orders to desegregate their schools concluded that the disruptions, protests, and school boycotts that did occur probably would have been fewer if school boards had supported desegregation from the outset [Willie and Greenblatt 1981:338]. Moreover, the study found that lawsuits for systemwide school desegregation usually were escalations of simple requests from racial and ethnic minorities for minimal improvements or changes in the use of common educational resources. Often these simple requests were ignored or rejected by local school authorities. The rejection was a perilous error. Most local school authorities had not learned from the British experience how a dominant should respond to the fair claims of subdominants. School boards' intransigence over particular issues of equity pressed by racial and ethnic groups sometimes resulted in systemwide school desegregation ordered by a federal or state court. Cooperation by school authorities with subdominant minorities in the fulfillment of some of their goals and interests might have resulted in different outcomes.

This discussion has introduced the asymmetrical principle pertaining to group relationships that is clearly revealed in a macrosocial analysis. When there is contention between dominants and subdominants, for example, and one group mirrors the response of the other, the similarity in reaction is not likely to lead to a resolution of the conflict but to an increase in self-preservation anxiety. An illustration of this principle and its outcome of mutually heightened self-preservation anxiety is the aggressive and conflictive response of the dominating British Empire to the aggressive initiatives of the subdominant American colonies and the aggressive and conflictive response of school boards after the 1954 *Brown* decision of the U.S. Supreme Court, which outlawed segregation in education to the aggressive initiatives of subdominant minorities. Self-preservation anxiety in dominants as well as in subdominants leads to suspicion, scapegoating — including attacks on people who have little or nothing to do with the causes of stress — and ultimately to confused or violent actions wholly inappropriate to the circumstances [Leighton 1946:266–273]. To reduce self-preservation anxiety and to create the conditions for a negotiated solution to conflict, one party must make an asymmetrical response to the actions of the other.

The idea that there must be an *asymmetry* between the form in which evil manifests itself and the form of the opposition to evil had a profound effect upon Martin Luther King, Jr., who cautioned against humiliating the enemy even when one is able to do it. He said the goal must be to win the enemy's friendship and understanding, not to hate and harm the enemy. Psychologically, hate damages the victim as well as the person who hates. King said, "hate destroys a ... sense of values and ... objectivity" [King 1964:43–44]. However, the asymmetrical approach, wherein one responds to violence with nonviolence (or to physical force with soul force), gives the responding person and population self-respect, strength, and courage, and also "stirs the conscience of the opponent so that reconciliation becomes a reality" [King 1964:170].

These statements about nonviolence and asymmetrical responses are not merely assertions. They are learnings that King derived from reflecting on his experience in the Montgomery bus boycott and other nonviolent demonstrations, and thus should be considered seriously as social science evidence. There, he saw the asymmetrical response that blacks gave to the custom of racially segregated seating on city buses was effective. He noted that blacks in that city believed "it was ultimately more honorable to walk the streets in dignity than to ride the buses in humiliation." He called this asymmetrical response to legally enforced segregation "a massive act of noncooperation" that manifested the determination of blacks to be free [King 1964:169]. Generically, the asymmetrical response in conflict situations facilitates clarification of distorted, selective, and restricted views of reality [Nye 1973:1–26]. The symmetrical response locks in hate and its debilitating effects on the human personality and on human relationships, and its distortions of the reality of humanity. Becoming increasingly aware of the antihuman assumptions inherent in our frequently used symmetrical responses, King observed that "[our] existential situation is estranged from [our] essential nature" [King 1964:167].

The essential ingredients of effective human relationships are trust, confidence, and respect. Robert Merton has observed a complex of interactions in dominant and subdominant relationships. At the root of those that are effective "is the confidence or trust that each has in the other" [Merton 1976:79]. In his book *The Will to Believe and Other Essays in Popular Philosophy,* William James said that "a social organism of any sort whatever, large or small, is what it is because each member proceeds to his own duty with a trust that the other members will simultaneously" [quoted in Leighton 1946:140]. By way of these two scientists of humanity the idea of trust has been introduced as an essential component in human relations, and the principle of simultaneity has been referred to again.

Trust or confidence is a social phenomenon that has value independently of the competence of the interacting individuals or groups. Merton said that "for the ultrarationalists among us, it comes hard to recognize that in organizational life, the prime ingredient of reciprocal confidence is not competence" [Merton 1976:79]. Langdon Gilkey, the theologian, goes even further than Merton and states, based on his everyday experience in a prison camp, that "rational behavior in communal action is primarily moral and not an intellectual achievement, possible only to a person who is morally capable of self-sacrifice" [Gilkey 1966:93]. It is by way of self-sacrifice, or restraint on the fulfillment of individual or group self-interest, that trust and confidence are engendered.

According to Merton, there is an "obligation for generosity of behavior by those enjoying rank and power" [Merton 1976:80]. Also, there is an obligation for magnanimity of behavior by those who experience subdominant status. Moreover, there is an obligation for one group to teach individuals in the opposite group the value of its way of adapting. Generous people do not respond in kind but do more than is required of them. Magnanimous people do not respond in kind but take less than that to which they are entitled. The asymmetrical response, then, is an indication of the presence of generosity and magnanimity in the social system. These are the responses of individuals who are committed not to winning or losing but to one another. Such commitment instills confidence between dominants and subdominants [Merton 1976:80], rather than self-preservation anxiety. This analysis enables us to better understand King's advice that one should seek not to defeat or humiliate the enemy. That is, one should not seek or give an enemy his or her "just due."

Despite what has been said, history reveals a tendency for humanity to become estranged from its transcendent nature. When this happens, human beings tend to treat each other as if they were only things. Few groups relinquish power because to do so is just and reasonable [Gilkey 1966:90]. Under condition of the exponential accumulation of power, one form of power must be checked by another form if tyranny is to be avoided [Gilkey 1966:90]. This is where the principle of asymmetry is applicable. To overcome evil in a way that leads to reconciliation, there must be asymmetry in the way that evil is expressed and the way in which it is checked. With sufficient strength one can meet physical force with physical force, overcome it, and suppress opposition and insubordination. This approach is the antihuman approach, which also suppresses the possibility of reconciliation. Where there is not reconciliation, ultimately none is safe and secure — neither dominants nor subdominants. Human safety and security is guaranteed only by way of commitment to one another. Thus, any method or technique of winning that does not "stir the conscience of the opponent" [King 1964:170] and "contribute to an understanding with the enemy and release ... goodwill" [King 1964:44] so that "reconciliation becomes a reality" [King 1964:170] is contraindicated. Reconciliation, trust, and confidence are components of human reality. It differs from the reality that mirrors the structure of nature. Harmful and helpful interaction between different racial, ethnic, and socioeconomic groups demonstrated these facts.

Finally, the macrosocial studies point toward a way of monitoring human social systems so that they can be rescued from their antihuman tendencies. A hierarchy of coordinated decision-making structures is the best way of guaranteeing equal access to the opportunities in a society and equity in their use, especially for racial, ethnic, and socioeconomic groups.

Conflicting interests are inevitable in any society. Mediating structures are needed to deal with impasses when they occur. Third party intervention is necessary in complex social arrangements. If no mediating structure is available, such should be developed before there is a crisis so that it may attain the legitimacy to act when needed.

When no legitimate third party is available and conflict emerges and reaches an impasse between dominant and subdominant groups or other contending parties, a mediating structure has to be invented. Such an invention tends to proceed down the hazardous trial-and-error course of helping the adversaries find a basis of reconciliation, with little prior experience.

When there is no organization within a particular system capable of mediating, the third-party good offices of an organization in another institution may be required. Mediating is more clumsy when different institutional systems are involved. It is better that the third party be a unit of the particular institution in which adversarial individuals or groups are based. Such mediators are more familiar with the details of the social context and are less likely to be unfair to either party through inadvertent error. Whether inside or outside a particular institution, third party intervention should be planned for and encouraged in complex social systems that are characterized by pluralistic populations and groups.

Louis Kriesberg tells us that "power differences very significantly determine the outcome of conflicts", that extreme power differences almost invite domination and repression as an outcome, that winners have been known to engage in retribution and punishment that go beyond the initial aims of their victory, and finally that compromise and new norms reflecting the self-interests of both sides are more likely outcomes of conflict when power differences are less great [Kriesberg 1982:240]. Institutionalized third parties tend to equalize adversaries' strength, help the parties exchange more information about each other, help them better understand each other's assertions and demands, help them explore areas of mutual benefit and avoid situations of joint damage, and plan for restoration of the offended party to the status one would have occupied before harmed [Kriesberg 1982:223-240].

Because self-interest is the basic motive of human action, it is difficult to resolve conflicts in ways that achieve the above indicated goals in decentralized local structures where different racial and ethnic populations are unequal in size and where populations of specific groups are disproportionately distributed between dominant and subdominant sectors. It is particularly difficult to achieve and implement a just solution not only because difference in size of contending groups is a component in outcome, but also because retribution is a possibility when the winner is unchecked by other power sources. Under these conditions, racial minorities have found legislative enactments, court decisions, and executive orders at state and federal levels very helpful in redressing their local grievances [Blackwell 1975; Burgess 1969:259]. These are the products of political institutions that have been legitimated as third parties by the society at large; they are available and can be called upon to intervene when parties at the local level reach an impasse. That third party intervention from afar has been necessary and essential in guaranteeing equal access to opportunities and equity in the use of resources demonstrates the complexity of conciliating differences among racial, ethnic, and socioeconomic groups in the United States. While decentralized decision-making structures increase subdominant participation, the simultaneous existence of third party intervention agencies at a higher level is required to effectively monitor the local scene and to ensure that it operates in loving and just ways.

References

Blackwell, James E. 1975. *The Black Community*. New York: Dodd, Mead.

Burgess, M. Elaine. 1969. "Race Relations and Social Change." In Melvin M. Tumin (ed.), *Comparative Perspectives on Race Relations*. Boston: Little, Brown.

Gilkey, Langdon. 1966. *Shantung Compound*. New York: Harper & Row.

King, Martin Luther, Jr. 1964. *Strength to Love*. New York: Pocket Books First published in 1963.

Kriesberg, Louis. 1982. *Social Conflict*. Englewood Cliffs, NJ: Prentice-Hall.

Leighton, Alexander. 1946. *The Governing of Men*. Princeton: Princeton University Press.

Merton, Robert K. 1976. *Sociological Ambivalence and Other Essays*. New York: Free Press.

Nye, Robert D. 1973. *Conflict Among Humans*. New York: Springer.

Willie, Charles V. 1977. *Black/Brown/White Relations*. New Brunswick, NJ: Transaction.

_____. 1978. *The Sociology of Urban Education*. Lexington, MA: Lexington Books of D. C. Heath.

_____. and Susan L. Greenblatt. 1981. *Community Politics and Educational Change*. New York: Longman.

Part V

Summary and Conclusion

Chapter 25

Social Theory for a Science of Humanity

One purpose of this review and analysis of a quarter of a century of my research into race, ethnicity, socioeconomic status and their interrelationship was to discover information that might enhance our social science knowledge of humanity. On the basis of this study, I have identified 12 theoretical principles that have to do with social organization and social research.

Humanity

My first theoretical principle asserts that *humanity is a complex phenomenon with finite limitations in time and space and infinite possibilities in the structure and process of social organization.* Humanity has limitations because time and space are irrevocable, irreplaceable, and interconnected. While nature is the essential foundation of humanity, freedom, choice, and purpose are necessary for human existence. Without these, human beings would be mere things covarying in time and space devoid of the capacity to modify their patterns of interaction. Thus, freedom, choice, and purpose are identified as uniquely human characteristics. Their presence is the reason for describing humanity as transcending nature while remaining a part of it.

It is appropriate, therefore, for social scientists to study *what* people do and *how* they act. But a social science that is a science of humanity must also discover *why* people act. A science of humanity should discover why people use their freedom in similar and varying ways, why people make similar and alternative choices, and why people embrace similar and different purposes.

A social science that fails to analyze why people act the way they do is incomplete. It is incomplete when it studies only the natural aspects of humanity, analyzing covariations among individuals as if they were things and not thinking and feeling people who are free to choose and to act with purpose.

264

Self and Society

Self-interest is the basic motive of human action. This is a second theoretical principle based on the review and analysis of my previous studies. Self-interest is not at all the same as selfishness. Self-interest is manifested in the actions of human beings who are free to be a part of social organization or to separate from others, who choose to withdraw from others, to cooperate or to conflict with them, and who engage or disengage others for the purpose of helping, harming, or ignoring them. All human activities, including those of self-sacrifice, are for the purpose of fulfilling oneself.

Human actions, including those that are self-fulfilling, are never predetermined and beyond the possibility of modification. In addition to the absence of predestination, no person ever is fully in control of any social situation. One initiates action to which others may or may not respond. The acting person cannot compel others to respond in a prescribed way. For this reason, my third theoretical principle is this: *human social organization is beyond the control of any specific human being.* Thus, human society is described as presenting infinite possibilities, some of which may differ from any that ever existed, since none can fully control it.

Just as human social organization is beyond the control of anyone, a person cannot be fully controlled by society. Thus my fourth theoretical principle recognizes the integrity of the individual and of the society. *Self and society exist in a dualistic relationship with each dependent on the other but neither fully controlled by the other.* Social scientists appropriately study norms, which are customary ways of behaving in a society. Norms serve as references for individuals. People tend to conform individual behavior to customary ways of doing things. However, social custom is a product of individual habit that becomes a common way of behaving among an increasing number of people within a society. The customs or norms of society originate from individual habit that is adopted by a number of people as a way of fulfilling their self-interests. In addition to studying social norms, a science of humanity also should observe and understand human self-interest to determine why norms originate, stabilize, and change.

Presumably, social norms change as human self-interests change. A science of humanity should study patterns of normative behavior in society and the dispersion of individual behavior around such norms. Studies of dispersion may provide evidence of emerging new norms and the residual practices of disintegrating old norms. A current defect in social science analysis is the practice of giving more attention to social norms or measures of central tendencies and less attention to coefficients of variation. The latter are indicators of the range of dispersion of behavior that is necessary to fulfill a variety of self-interests. Also study of the dispersion of behavior around social norms helps us to understand why norms are more stable or less stable. Stable norms fulfill a range of self-interests; unstable norms do not. A science of humanity that acknowledges the integrity of self and of society and their interdependence recognizes the value of norms in social organization as a tendency toward stability and the value of individual behavior dispersed around norms as a tendency toward change. Of course, change and stability are essential in social organization. Thus, how and why there is deviation from a norm should be studied as well as how and why there is conformity to it.

Because self and society are interdependent, one cannot be fulfilled without assistance from the other. Any attempt to fulfill either the self or society by activities of one that harm the other should be classified as pathological. This thesis leads into my fifth theoretical principle that *the preeminent goal of humanity is to enhance both self and society.* Social activity that is not designed to achieve the double victory of mutual enhancement is against humanity. A common goal of mutual enhancement is possible when individual human beings and the groups with which they affiliate recognize their inability to achieve fulfillment for their own interests and needs unassisted.

Social Structure

Acknowledging the requirement for complementarity, I set forth my sixth theoretical principle that *effective human social structures are diversified in a dualistic way, consisting of groups that are dominant and sub-dominant in social power.* Dominants generally are responsible for developing universal principles for social organization such as those pertaining to equality of access to the resources of human society. Subdominants generally are responsible for developing particular procedures for social organization, such as those pertaining to equity in the use of resources of human society. Equality of access and equity in use are interrelated phenomena in social organization. Together, they enhance society.

A diversified social structure of both dominants and subdominants is something of value because it guarantees full consideration of a range of social concerns. Also, the interaction of individuals of these two power status categories is a way of ensuring that social organization will deal with both universal and particular issues. Social structures are effective if they sustain individuals and maintain society. They are more capable of performing this two-fold function when they are diversified, consisting of individuals with dominant and subdominant power interests. Any attempt to limit all of the participating people within a particular group of a social structure to individuals who have interests, needs, and purposes similar to one's own is contraindicated and should be classified as pathological.

Although dominant and subdominant status positions are needed in human social structures, neither one nor the other is more or less valuable. There is no need, therefore, to strive for dominant status; it has functional but no intrinsic value. Human talent is so distributed within the human population of a society that probably no one is able to perform the roles and responsibilities of dominant status positions in all groups of a social structure or in all social structures.

The most appropriate arrangement in human social organization is for individuals to be dominant in some social structures and subdominant in others. When the members of a particular population are distributed among both dominant and subdominant power categories, these individuals readily understand the necessity of powerful and less powerful people working together for the benefit of the whole group. A distribution pattern such as described is one of cross-cutting cleavages. But when the members of one population are found exclusively in the category of dominant power interests and the members of other populations are clustered exclusively in the category of subdominant power interests (and vice versa), a condition of pathology exists in which there is heightened tension about self-preservation, mistrust, estrangement, and misunderstanding. Such a distribution pattern is one of reinforced cleavages. Cross-cutting cleavages strengthen society; reinforced cleavages weaken it.

To facilitate the circulation of individuals of specific populations between dominant and subdominant status positions in different social structures of a society, the dominants are obliged to teach their opposites the behavior appropriate to the dominant position. Dominants in one social structure who are generous and who habitually give more than their fair share may acquaint subdominants of that structure with this practice. The subdominants may find the practice efficacious and applicable to other social structures in which they may be dominants. Also, subdominants in one social structure should teach their opposites the beneficial effects of magnanimity, of receiving less than that to which one is entitled, so that the dominants in that structure will know how to act in another structure where their status position may be different. Thus, my seventh theoretical principle is that *dominant and subdominant status positions are abstractions of social structures and may be occupied by a variety of different individuals; an individual who is dominant in one social structure may be subdominant in another; the same individual may occupy different status positions within the same structure in different periods of time.*

Contemporary social scientists tend to merge the concrete and the abstract so that individuals within specific populations are identified with specific power status categories as if the arrangements were fixed and not subject to modification. In the United States, for example, membership in specific racial and ethnic groups and location in specific status sectors are discussed as if predetermined. The confounding of concrete and abstract aspects of social organization so that no differentiation is made between them is an error in social science analysis that should be corrected.

Social Process

If self-interest is the basic motive for human action, and if interaction between dominant and subdominant power positions is essential in a well-functioning society, both cooperation and conflict are inevitable processes of social interaction.

Cooperation is inevitable because all individuals are interdependent; none is self-sufficient. One person must do for another what the other cannot do for oneself. And so it goes with everyone. This is my eighth theoretical principle. One who does not cooperate in fulfilling the interests of others cannot expect others to cooperate in the fulfillment of one's own interest. Moreover, none is invincible; cooperation with others is the ultimate means by which one's safety and security are guaranteed. Cooperation, then, is a self-interest activity.

My ninth theoretical principle has to do with conflict. *Conflict is inevitable because of the dualistic organization of society's populations into groups or categories with different power interests that necessarily function in different ways to fulfill different purposes.* Although purposes and self-interests may differ, dominants and subdominants have one goal that is held in common. It is the enhancement of the total society. Always, however, there is tension in achievinig this goal. There is tension, for example, in ways of achieving equality of access (a primary responsibility of dominants) and in ways of achieving equity of use (a primary responsibility of subdominants). Both are necessary in the enhancement of the total society.

In humanity, there is simultaneity in the existence of social processes rather than linearity. This is my tenth theoretical principle. Processes of conflict and cooperation coexist. Symmetrical patterns of social interaction between dominants and subdominants, for example, may be followed by asymmetrical patterns. Simultaneity refers to the dualism that is a requirement of social processes in human social organization. Simultaneity is the essential reality of human social processes as complementarity is the essential reality of human social structures. Because of these realities, synthesis of human experience is possible.

Synthesis of human experience is the ultimate outcome of simultaneous social processes and complementary social structures. This is my eleventh theoretical principle. Synthesis unites the thesis and the antithesis, the old and the new, what has been and what could be into what is. What is may be better or worse than what-was or what-will be. Through synthesis, the infinite possibilities of humanity are manifested for good or evil. The idea of simultaneity is against the idea of progress for it recognizes that humanity can experience the worse at the same time, before, or after humanity experiences the best. Synthesis, therefore, is a human outcome of social processes and social structures that advocates both stability and change and embraces both the past and the future. Synthesis, a human product of complementarity and simultaneity, differs from the products of nature that emerge from structures that function according to the reality of unity and from processes that function according to the reality of linearity.

Scientists of humanity who neglect to ask why questions, fail to understand the significance of complementary structures and simultaneous processes. They prefer to discover how components fit together in a unitary system and covary in a pattern that is linear. Those who do this overlook what is uniquely human in human populations.

The Social Context

Simultaneity and complementarity are contextual realities that together provide humanity with options for correcting harmful actions. A social process always cooperative and without conflict may result from a defective social structure — one that is mostly homogeneous and insufficiently diversified with people representing dominant and subdominant interests. A social process always conflictive and without cooperation again may result from a defective social structure. Although fully diversified, such a structure may be one that does not recognize differences as valid and legitimate events and experiences to which the total society should adapt and, therefore, rejects the idea of a double victory. All of this suggests that *there is interaction between social structure and social process so that one cannot be fully understood without examining the other.* Together, they are the social context. This is my twelfth and final theoretical principle.

Index

271